P9-CJM-944

Writing London Volume 2

Also by Julian Wolfreys

Books:
Occasional Deconstructions
*Critical Keywords in Literary and Cultural Theory**
*Victorian Hauntings: Spectrality, Gothic, the Uncanny and Literature**
Readings: Acts of Close Reading in Literary Theory
*Deconstruction · Derrida**
*Writing London: the Trace of the Urban Text from Blake to Dickens**
*The Rhetoric of Affirmative Resistance. Dissonant Identities from Carroll to Derrida**
*Being English: Narratives, Idioms, and Performances of National Identity from
    Coleridge to Trollope*

Co-authored books:
Key Concepts in Literary Theory, with Ruth Robbins and Kenneth Womack
Peter Ackroyd: the Ludic and Labyrinthine Text, with Jeremy Gibson*
Als ob ich tot wäre, with Jacques Derrida and Ruth Robbins*

Edited and co-edited collections:
J. Hillis Miller: a Reader
The Beetle, Richard Marsh
Thinking Difference: Critics in Conversation
Glossalalia
The Edinburgh Encyclopaedia of Modern Criticism and Theory
Introducing Criticism at the 21st Century
Introducing Literary Theories: a Guide and Glossary
*The Mayor of Casterbridge: Contemporary Critical Essays**
Victorian Gothic: Literary and Cultural Manifestations in the Nineteenth Century, with
    Ruth Robbins*
Literary Theories: a Reader and Guide
The French Connections of Jacques Derrida, with John Brannigan and Ruth Robbins*
The Derrida Reader: Writing Performances
Re: Joyce: Text, Culture, Politics, with John Brannigan and Geoff Ward*
Victorian Identities: Social and Cultural Formations in Nineteenth-Century Literature,
    with Ruth Robbins*
Applying: To Derrida, with John Brannigan and Ruth Robbins*
Literary Theories: a Case Study in Critical Performance, with William Baker*

* Also published by Palgrave Macmillan / Macmillan Press

writing London

Volume 2: materiality, memory, spectrality

Julian Wolfreys

First published 2004 by
PALGRAVE MACMILLAN
Houndmills, Basingstoke, Hampshire RG21 6XS and
175 Fifth Avenue, New York, N.Y. 10010
Companies and representatives throughout the world

PALGRAVE MACMILLAN is the global academic imprint of the Palgrave Macmillan division of St. Martin's Press, LLC and of Palgrave Macmillan Ltd. Macmillan® is a registered trademark in the United States, United Kingdom and other countries. Palgrave is a registered trademark in the European Union and other countries.

ISBN 0–333–91429–5

This book is printed on paper suitable for recycling and made from fully managed and sustained forest sources.

A catalogue record for this book is available from the British Library.

A catalogue record for this book is available from the Library of Congress.

10   9   8   7   6   5   4   3   2   1
13 12 11 10 09 08 07 06 05 04

Printed and bound in Great Britain by
Antony Rowe Ltd, Chippenham and Eastbourne

Contents

Acknowledgements

I would like to thank the following:

Charmian Hearne for having commissioned this project in the first place; Emily Rosser at Palgrave Macmillan for having faith in my ability to complete it and infinite patience during countless delays; John Leavey, the Department of English, and the College of Liberal Arts and Sciences at the University of Florida for support and funding at crucial stages in the research for this book; Rebecca Brown, whose indefatigable skills in copy-editing and proof reading ('I have a feel for the semi-colon which is exquisite'), and critical observations on the minutiae of arguments have been invaluable; all of the students in my graduate seminars on the twentieth-century British novel in 2001 and 2003, who engaged in the contours of reading, which became in some strange fashion the present volume; the organizers of the MRG and EGO conferences at the University of Florida, who invited me to give papers at those conferences, which were to become the chapters on Iain Sinclair and Maureen Duffy; I also wish to thank the following, all of whom have offered something, in some measure, great or small: Peter Ackroyd, Hélène Cixous, Pamela Gilbert, Afshin Hafizi, Jim Kincaid, Nicole LaRose, J. Hillis Miller, Nick Royle, Fred Young.

Parts of Chapter 4, on Peter Ackroyd, appeared in a very different form in Jeremy Gibson and Julian Wolfreys, *Peter Ackroyd: the Ludic and Labyrinthine Text* (Macmillan, 2000). A shorter version of Chapter 6, 'A coincidence of disparate incidents: London undone or, seven artists in search of the city', appeared as 'Undoing London or, Urban Haunts: the Fracturing of Representation in the 1990s' in Pamela K. Gilbert, ed., *Imagined Londons* (State University of New York Press, 2002: 193–218), and has been substantially revised and altered in the present version. The author would like to thank the editors and publishers of this work for permission to republish in the present form.

JULIAN WOLFREYS

Abbreviations

The following abbreviations are used for frequently cited works, which are given parenthetically throughout. Bibliographical details of all other works appear in the notes following first use, and subsequently as parenthetical citation.

D	Ackroyd, Peter. *Dickens* (1990) London: Minerva, 1991.
HDD	Ackroyd, Peter. *The House of Doctor Dee*. London: Hamish Hamilton, 1993.
DLLG	Ackroyd, Peter. *Dan Leno and the Limehouse Golem*. London: Sinclair-Stevenson, 1994.
B	Ackroyd, Peter. *Blake*. London: Sinclair-Stevenson, 1995.
LTM	Ackroyd, Peter. *The Life of Thomas More*. London: Chatto & Windus, 1998.
L:B	Ackroyd, Peter. *London: The Biography*. London: Chatto & Windus, 2000.
TC	Ackroyd, Peter. *The Collection: Journalism, Reviews, Essays, Short Stories, Lectures*. Ed. and introd. Thomas Wright. London: Chatto & Windus, 2001.
LC	Atkins, Marc, and Iain Sinclair. *Liquid City*. London: Reaktion Books, 1999.
AP	Benjamin, Walter. *The Arcades Project* (1982). Trans. Howard Eiland and Kevin McLaughlin. Cambridge, MA: Belknap Press, 2002.
ASCM	Besant, Walter. *All Sorts and Conditions of Men* (1882). Introd. Helen Small. Oxford: Oxford University Press, 1997.
DH	Bowen, Elizabeth. *The Death of the Heart* (1938). London: Penguin, 1962.
HD	Bowen, Elizabeth. *The Heat of the Day* (1948). Harmondsworth: Penguin, 1962.
CS	Bowen, Elizabeth. *The Collected Stories of Elizabeth Bowen* (1980). Introd. Angus Wilson. Harmondsworth: Penguin, 1983.
SF	Conan Doyle, Arthur. *The Sign of Four* (1890). Introd. Peter Ackroyd. London: Penguin, 2001.
W	Duffy, Maureen. *Wounds*. New York: Alfred A. Knopf, 1969.

C Duffy, Maureen. *Capital* (1975). Introd. Paul Bailey. London: Harvill Panther, 2001.

L Duffy, Maureen. *Londoners: an Elegy* (1983). London: Methuen, 1985.

FE Fisher, Allen. 'The Mathematics of Rimbaud'; 'Six Poems from *Brixton Fractals*'. In Allen Fisher, Bill Griffiths and Brian Catling, *Future Exiles: 3 London Poets*. London: Paladin, 1992.

SL Ford, Ford Madox. *The Soul of London* (1905). Ed. Alan G. Hill. London: Everyman, 1995.

L James, Henry. 'London' (1888). In *London Stories and Other Writings*, ed. and introd. David Kynaston. Padstow: Tabb House, 1989.

RR Lichtenstein, Rachel, and Iain Sinclair. *Rodinsky's Room*. London: Granta, 1999.

JSP Litvinoff, Emanuel. *Journey through a Small Planet* (1972). London: Robin Clark, 1993.

TI Machen, Arthur. *The Three Impostors* (1895). Ed. and introd. David Trotter. London: Everyman, 1995.

ML Moorcock, Michael. *Mother London* (1998). London: Scribner, 2000.

R Petit, Chris. *Robinson* (1993). London: Granta, 2001.

RD Sinclair, Iain. *Radon Daughters*. London: Random House, 1994.

LHSB Sinclair, Iain. *Lud Heat and Suicide Bridge*. Introd. Michael Moorcock. Maps Dave McKean. London: Vintage, 1995.

LOT Sinclair, Iain. *Lights Out for the Territory: 9 Excursions in the Secret History of London*. London: Granta, 1997.

SCA Sinclair, Iain, and Dave McKean. *Slow Chocolate Autopsy*. London: Phoenix House, 1997.

SM Sinclair, Iain. *Sorry Meniscus: Excursions to the Millennium Dome*. London: Profile Books, 1999.

D Sinclair, Iain. *Downriver (Or, the Vessels of Wrath): a Narrative in Twelve Tales* (1991). London: Granta, 2001.

LO Sinclair, Iain. *London Orbital*. London: Granta, 2002.

JH Stevenson, Robert Louis. *The Strange Case of Dr Jekyll and Mr Hyde* (1886). In *The Strange Case of Doctor Jekyll and Mr Hyde and Other Tales of Terror*, ed. Robert Mighall. London: Penguin, 2002.

PDG Wilde, Oscar. *The Picture of Dorian Gray* (1891). Ed. and introd. Peter Ackroyd. London: Penguin, 1988.

The London cycle goes forward.
Constructions loom in astral fogs. Clearly,
eras return.

Aidan Andrew Dun, *Vale Royal*

This exaggerated London oppresses the imagination and tears
the heart.

Heinrich Heine, *Englischen Fragmenten*

You can only be happy in London if you begin to consider your-
self a Londoner.

Peter Ackroyd, *London*

Introduction: London disfigured

This is London really young, really pagan, really idyllic . . . really holding its population by the spell . . . of contagious humanity and of infinite human contacts.

Ford Madox Ford

We have had, as we advanced, to multiply our irreducible data and to complicate more and more the simple hypothesis from which we started. But have we gained anything by it? Though the matter which we have been led to posit is indispensable in order to account for the marvellous sensations among themselves, we still know nothing of it, since we must refuse to it all the qualities perceived, all the sensations of which it has only to explain the correspondence. It is not then, it cannot be, anything of what we know, anything of what we imagine. It remains a mysterious entity.

Henri Bergson

The city's topography is a palimpsest within which all the most magnificent or monstrous cities of the world can be discerned . . . [But] who can fathom the depths of London?

Peter Ackroyd

I

Who indeed can fathom the depths of London? Any such attempt could well be dangerous, and if I sound like the Surgeon General or a government health warning – or perhaps that sign above the doors on the London Underground – at least I have the comfort of knowing I am not

3

alone in my eccentric wariness. Thomas de Quincey understood something about the injurious aspects of London, which many subsequent writers have not, when he wrote, 'in these three functions of sleep, diet, exercise, is contained the whole economy of health: and all three are woefully deranged by a London life'. There is an echo of De Quincey's sentiment in an internalized, psychologizing comment by Iain Sinclair. In *London Orbital*, Sinclair writes that 'the person who undertakes research into the city's history, minutiae and odd particulars, will become unbalanced' (*LO* 171). Finally, as if in affirmation of both De Quincey and Sinclair, the body and psyche of the London subject are both comically and seriously rewritten by the city in Geoff Nicholson's *Bleeding London*, when Judy Tanaka tells her therapist: ' "I display signs of both renewal and decay. Strange sensations commute across my skin. There is vice and crime and migration. My veins throb as though with the passage of underground trains. My digestive tract is sometimes clogged. There are security alerts. There's congestion, bottlenecks. Some of me is common, some of me is restricted. I have flats and high-rises. It doesn't need a genius to see what's going on. Greater London, *c'est moi*".'[1]

I for one do not intend therefore to try to fathom the depths of the city, not in any concrete manner, and certainly not in this introduction. As will be seen, both in the introduction and throughout *Writing London – Volume 2*, the very idea of thinking or writing London is inimical to any ontological project or indeed any project the purpose of which is definition. The city resists ontology, and thus affirms its alterity, its multiplicities, its excesses, its heterogeneities. To echo *Writing London*,[2] London is not a place; it cannot be placed. Its 'first cause' a waterway (*SL* 27), London takes place; it is a fluid city, a city of singular, endless flows (both spatial and temporal), which can only be seen – if at all – if one sees indirectly, from the corner of one's eye or, 'to either side of what is seen' as Aidan Andrew Dun has it.[3] Seeing London is, it might be said, a matter of being open to the gift of vision, of receiving a vision incommensurable with and in excess of the merely visual.

As a city always on the move and only apprehended from the corner of one's eye, London is unavailable to any generalization, summarization, or finite identification. One cannot fathom London because there is neither beginning nor end. One can never get to the bottom of an abyss, particularly when the abyss *is* meaning or identity, an identity we might say without identification. The very idea of getting to a bottom, to the end of something, is of course absurd, although the assumption behind introductions is that nothing could be less absurd:

if we can introduce can we not, after all, conclude? The notion that an introduction is made possible is articulated in the theological postulation that 'in my beginning is my end'; yet, the singularity of London defies any such teleological imperative. For it is such that it can only be apprehended when it is understood that London 'becomes by its immensity a place upon which there is no beginning' (*SL* 10), while, to recall the words of Friedrich Engels already discussed in *Writing London*, the city is also a place 'where a man may wander for hours together without reaching the beginning of an end' and is therefore a 'strange thing'.[4] Thus, this is only the merest pretence at an introduction, an imposture. For this introduction will not have summarized the present project. Neither will it provide an overview of the arguments of the particular chapters, although I will have recourse here to allude however fleetingly to specific aspects of the chapters as each speaks to the attempt to bear witness faithfully on the part of the writers in question to London, and so respond to the materiality of the city through the materiality of language and the interanimation between the two materialities.

II

Through my focus on the materiality of London and the impossibility of offering any determinate meaning for – or image of – that city, a subsidiary, yet no less significant interest will trace itself, concerning the way in which the city as singularity shows how 'the materiality of language functions as cultural intervention' through 'its havoc-wreaking effect on the inherited institutions of interpretation'.[5] In turn, and through this insistence on the traces of materiality, memory, and spectrality that inform any act of writing the city, it is to be understood that writing London 'is conceived of actively as one name for a site in which legacies are relayed, constellations of "textual" events reconfigured, hermeneutic regimes reimprinted or, alternately, where epistemo-linguistic ruptures occur in which reinscriptions become possible'.[6] Here writing should be understood as also a reading, but a reading in ruins, a reading always in the wake of signs that have already departed, always coming after those signs belatedly and yet always in pursuit of them, and which can never therefore, because of the temporal disorder that is herein implied, come to a close. Moreover, what may come to be witnessed here, albeit in passing in this focus on the question of materiality and its non-synonymous quasi-cognates, memory and spectrality, is that if, in the words of Tom Cohen, 'there is a "materiality" to which reading [and writing are] directed, a moment in the experience of memory and sign systems that moves us from a mimetic to a performative model of the text as virtual or historial event', then responding faithfully to the various material contours of the act of writing London may serve as one small illustrative intervention in 'a broader translation of textual legacies' and the 'identity of "literature" as an institution' ('A' 285).

The understanding of materiality on which Cohen and I draw is obviously taken from Walter Benjamin, as it is expressed particularly in 'Theses on the Philosophy of History', from which I borrow in this introduction, and the *Arcades Project*, to which I have recourse throughout *Writing London – Volume 2*. As Samuel Weber acknowledges, any reading of the city after Walter Benjamin's response to Paris in the *Arcades Project* must necessarily admit to 'the *allegorical cast* of apparently material reality'. Weber proceeds, '[n]ever does Benjamin appeal to a "materiality" of objects that would not simultaneously involve a signifying structure'.[7] Clearly, following Benjamin, materiality does not function merely in one register, but engages in processes of translation, and therefore an immaterial, if not spectral, transference between differing materialities. Furthermore, Benjamin's comprehension of the historicity of city images – 'only in a particular time do they become readable' ('SST' 19) – points to a haunting force that banishes the illusion or presumption of a universal transhistoricality, hence the necessary recourse in critical interventions to the allegorical and, with that, the spectral in unfolding the poetics of the city. 'Such allegorical exposure', Weber asserts, 'takes responsibility for the unknowable that sits at the heart of all efforts to decipher and decode, interpret and communicate. To take responsibility, in other words for something that cannot be controlled, but that nevertheless calls insistently for response . . .' ('SST' 17). I am seeking to be open to that which I cannot predict, that which I cannot control or determine, certainly that which I have no way of programming. This is the responsibility of reading, a responsibility which anticipates the arrival of the impossible (that which Weber is calling the unknowable), and yet which must admit that it can only prepare itself for being unprepared, for no arrival or return can ever be known except as an after-effect, a moment of ruinous, disjointing apparitional memory. It is this *allegorical* exposure (to give the experience merely one possible name amongst many), this being-open and opening onto the articulation of the other from within material reality that is witnessed *in* and *by* Bowen, Duffy, Ackroyd, and Sinclair. Each recognizes in his or her own manner the responsibility that London imposes on them, a responsibility also entailing a recognition of the undecidability and, with that, the limits of narrative apprehension. London calls to each writer 'insistently for response'. London is 'always just beyond the horizon', as Ford Madox Ford puts it, but nonetheless, 'all the time London is calling' (*SL* 73).

III

If the city calls, and calls unceasingly, it does so in more than one voice simultaneously. More accurately, one should not speak of voices but instead of so many acts of writing generated simultaneously. Understood thus, it clearly demands different modes of response, other modes of representation than those privileging single or continuous voices or identities. As we have already indicated, the city is a machine, albeit a spectral one; in this, it is both an apparatus for the projection of ghosts and a singular instance of phantom-technicity. This is announced by Manfredo Tafuri, in terms that resonate with Benjaminian concepts of historicity and materiality. Tafuri suggests that the city be understood as 'an ensemble of channels of communication'. In that it is this, it 'becomes a sort of machine emitting incessant messages'.[8] At the same time, the city is also understandable as what Ignasi de Solà-Morales has remarked as a 'limitless multiplicity of positions from which it is possible . . . to erect provisional constructions'.[9]

One such 'construction' is envisioned as the act of writing the city. This is envisaged as one possible site for translation, for putting in place a transformative textual practice that bears upon historical, cultural, ideological, and political practice in literary studies and what we call the humanities. The starting point for engaging in this transformation has to come with a rethinking of the spectral, analogical relation between the so-called real and particular textual networks such as those which play between the sign and the material. Two crucial affirmations must be made, without the articulation of which we cannot proceed. First affirmation: the city must be read as the singular effect of so many 'silhouettes that are both imprecise and singularized, faint outlines of voices, patterns of comportment, sketches of affects',[10] which, each time encountered, offers the opening to response of the imminence of a singularity that touches us even as we come into contact with it. There is no identity without its being written, and writing takes place only through fleeting marks, barely there without amounting to the whole picture. Second affirmation: recognizing the repetitious singularity of the touch, by which we also come to glimpse the endless circulation and repetition of the instant of nothing other than the iterable, we must make a double affirmation: on the one hand, here, in the constant encounter with this instant, insistent 'nothing' is the inscription of the spectral; on the other hand, that 'there is no pure and simple "one," no "one" in which "properly existing existence" . . . is, from the start, purely and simply immersed' (*BSP* 7).

With these affirmations in mind, it is possible to read urban derangement as acknowledged above differently. Rather than seeing the effects of London in a deleterious light, there is the potential here to acknowledge an act of writing on the body as the gift of the city, whereby the assumption of discrete, finite undifferentiated ontologies of being and identity come to be deconstructed through the spectral motions of inscription. Though immaterial, such phantoms and the traces they impose have an indelible, material effect. If corporeal and psychic derangement and unbalancing are amongst the somatic, psychosomatic, and sensory responses to the city, then we have disclosed within us the possibility for reconsidering how we read the process of being translated by the city; so that, as beings, our being-in-the-city serves as a singular map, a decentred guide that gives access in singular fashion to any future writing of the city. This access starts from the recognition that what unbalances us are the multiple signs of a possession, of a haunting, through which we can come to apprehend the city. In coming to a realization of the experience of the haunting effects of London, we have what Walter Benjamin would describe as an experience of the auratic, whereby we have intimations of 'the phantasmagorias of space and time' (*AP* 12).

For this reason (and for many others which will come to be seen), it has to be said that London is now more than ever a ghost town. A mnemotechnic, its name is to be taken less as a signifier indicating some brute inarticulable reality or collection of material objects, than as a performative mark, a momentary gathering point, and a nexus of mnemonic and spectral effects 'reduced within and by signifying networks already replete with mnemonic imperatives, hermeneutic assignations, tropes' ('A' 280). Considered from this perspective, writing London is always a response to what takes place in and through that name, and so is 'bound to inscription, memory, temporality, and political intervention' ('A' 281). As such, London names and is read as naming a materiality that 'would seek to be located not in the world's objects but in *mnemonic* constellations and representational regimes' ('A' 281). The city is then a phantom site, a 'spectral machine'[11] apprehended only through its revenant traces, the marks of memory belonging to no one person and yet, democratically, to anyone who knows that he or she is a Londoner and who is open to the to-and-fro oscillations of involuntary and impersonal memory. The city is understood and received, if at all, only through the precarious materiality of countless past moments, phenomena, and impressions, all of which come and go, disrupting the present through a disquieting anamnesis channelled by the novelist, the film maker, the artist, the poet. What London is, or might be, remains undecidable, offering 'to the mind's eye singularly little of a picture' (*SL* 7). Accepting this means that, even in apprehending the city indirectly, one is always exiled, one is always estranged from within this identity; one is always haunted in and by the very act of seeking to gauge the poetics of London, where 'London' names the measure, the taking place of a poetics irreducible to any mere form.

London thus only reveals or gives itself, *if* it does this at all, through acts of self-disclosure and inscription in the very appearance of resisting its own revelation. In its most apparently familiar appearances, there remains nonetheless the invisible, the undecidable, self-disclosure arriving, to paraphrase Heidegger, as that very aspect which conceals itself.[12] This is to be witnessed in process in fleeting instances, mere flashes of sensory memory, in Emanuel Litvinoff's autobiographical novel, *Journey through a Small Planet*. Sound and smell are particularly registered: there is the 'sour smell of London' (*JSP* 28), the 'evil-smelling strangeness' (*JSP* 29); 'everything', we read in a description of Smithfield Market, 'was penetrated by the stench of neighbouring offal yards' (*JSP* 144). The sound of rain is recalled as having different material properties; it resounds with 'an oily suck of viscous liquids . . . in gutters as if London was bleeding into the sewers' (*JSP* 96), while, on another occasion, 'rain sizzled on the naphtha flares and gusts of wind flapped the tarpaulin covering the [market] stalls' (*JSP* 52). What is produced through such performative marks is not an image of the city, so much as a serial effect belonging to what can be described as a singular '*signature-system*'[13] that both inscribes and is inscribed by the city. Through a 'mnemonics of *inscription*' ('PT' 115), an intervention in mimetic representation takes place, as the city is concealed by the very traces that remark it. Thus, the act of writing London engages in that intervention termed by Walter Benjamin (and which, through the work of Tom Cohen I explore at the beginning of this section) 'materialistic historiography'.[14]

Only arriving as the spatial and temporal articulation of that which announces its inaccessibility to mimesis, direct vision, and representation *as such*, London admits to the unveiling of the complex historicity and materiality of the textual network. In effecting this revelation, the poetics and technicity of the city intervenes in, thereby drawing attention to, the limits and crises of mimetically and ontologically grounded models of historicism that seek to muster, in Benjamin's words, a 'mass of data to fill the homogeneous, empty time' ('TPH' 262). This phrase, 'homogeneous, empty time' is used again by Benjamin to indicate a universal, undifferentiated temporal linearity, as well as a narrative teleology marked by a simple temporal motion indicated in the phrase 'Once upon a time', of which Benjamin is dismissive ('TPH' 262). The city as mnemotechnic – along with the response in writing that is open to mapping the work of the mnemotechnic – confounds narrative generated by any concept of simple, successive historical progression, homogeneity, or periodic compartmentalization. At the same time, reading the complexity of the city's traces should remind us that 'nothing that has ever happened should be regarded as lost for history' ('TPH' 254). In line with Benjamin's conception of materialistic historiography, texts such as those encountered in *Writing London – Volume 2*, allow that the 'past become[s] citable in all its moments' ('TPH' 254). Accepting this, we understand that the past is never over, nor is it ever simply a matter of historical facts observed, gathered, or objectively viewed from some discrete location in a present which remains somehow uncontaminated or overdetermined by the traces of the past. Rather, what we call the 'past' is a phantasmic network of traces ever present, if invisibly so, and capable of sudden apparition.

IV

Therefore, while it may be valid to speak, from particular philosophical perspectives, of the ontology of space or place, the condition of London, when read in all its materiality and historicity, and when reading for its remainders and traces, clearly cannot – indeed *must not* – be assigned an ontology. London is that to which no fixed place can be assigned. Displaced from within the very idea of itself, it cannot be determined or delimited. Neither does London present itself directly (to insist on this once more), nor can London be presented directly in any textual manifestation, as I aver implicitly above through reference to Heidegger's conception of *poiesis* (as a making) of the dwelling of being. The being of the city is always a becoming, a process, a performative projection from within and overflowing the contours of any perceivable identity or particular identity; or, as Ford Madox Ford has it, 'London is illimitable' (*SL* 15); it is so 'little of a town, [so] much of an abstraction' (*SL* 7).

Ford's *The Soul of London*, first published in 1905, offers the reader a fascinating moment of intervention – and in some senses, the signs of an irreversible rupture – in the poetics of urban representation, hence its brief significance here. One could equally begin with other novels, essays, or poems, but it is perhaps the very fact of *The Soul of London's* relative obscurity when considered alongside such canonical modernist texts as *The Waste Land* or *Mrs Dalloway* that we should pause to acknowledge Ford's text. Recognition is due in part perhaps to the fact that in the reading of relative obscurity there emerges the sense that *The Soul of London* has not been received, hardly read at all in any significant sense. Yet, as Alan Hill, editor of the Everyman edition asserts,[15] this small book, first begun in 1903, points towards many of the experiments in Modernist poetics which were soon to follow, particularly in those texts seeking to convey an urban sensibility in a mode of response appropriate to the onslaught of the senses that a megalopolis such as London imposed. As Hill remarks, Ford's interest was in registering 'impressions', rather than recording 'facts'.[16] It is in this shift from a more straightforwardly mimetic mode to one more implicitly if not explicitly phenomenological, that the transformation of registers gets underway. While it is arguable that particular writers at the end of the nineteenth century, such as Conan Doyle or Oscar Wilde, sought to convey impressions of the city, particularly through such overworked tropes as fog, disease, and the labyrinth, their texts, I would contend, are nonetheless only quasi-impressionistic. Their urban representations are still grounded, if not in facts, then in the deliberate misreading and misperception of facts for ideological and cultural purposes, as well as in modes of representation reliant on already familiar metaphors and the coercively rationalizing force of mimesis.[17] (See the discussion of fin-de-siècle novels in the first chapter.)

The Soul of London thus marks a significant departure from its immediate predecessors, recognizing in the act of writing London that there is, at least with regard to literary representation, 'a loss of adequation of sign to meaning' as Paul de Man puts it in discussing 'the loss of the symbolic in the failure to represent'.[18] However, Ford appears to have overcome, at least in part, the implicit negativity in such failure, with its attendant lapse into a language which states that it cannot say what it sees, that it can only bear witness to that which cannot be represented and admit its inadequacy. For a start, there is that title, with its suggestion of an immaterial, animating force to the city, a force that, if not seen or available to representation, can still leave its mark upon perception. Implied is not so much an identity as a force, one that is approachable, if at all, only through indirection, approximation, and a seriality of endless substitutions – of analogy and often stark comparison. London is 'immense without being immediately impressive'; it 'attracts unceasingly . . . the best of all earthly things . . . without being susceptible of any perceptible improvement' (*SL* 13). The rhyme in this sentence is interesting. Ford is not saying that the city is not subject to or capable of influence, reaction, or some measure of transformation, but that whatever *translation* might take place, it is not available to any then available recording or visible representation by the senses or intellect. There is in this the inference of a radical materiality to London, a materiality, in the words of Arkady Plotnitsky, 'that is unavailable to any formalization, representation, phenomenalization, and so forth, and hence to any vision'. That which London *is* (and it is not some *thing*, or *as such*) 'may only form an (irreducibly invisible) part of a formal vision'.[19] It is the work of writing London to figure that formal vision, to produce a materiality of the letter that expresses and irreversibly performs the materiality of the city and its material effects, while maintaining that which is irreducibly invisible in all its spectral force. It is there and yet not there, and this is caught in Ford's language because 'the way of saying' (*AI* 89) assumes a material significance all its own. Thus Ford can write that the Londoner is the one who can comprehend that while 'all the time London is calling', it is 'always just beyond the horizon' (*SL* 72). Up close, the city has an 'indecipherable face . . . without order . . . with very little of discoverable purpose', and a 'want of logic' (*SL* 69).

There is a very curious moment here, which should give us pause. This moment has to do with a gesture towards anthropomorphization that is immediately withdrawn. We receive a sketch or outline, a moment of inscription, nothing more than a faint adumbration. A face is apprehended but cannot be read; this is a face and yet no face, the face is effaced, retreating in the very instant of its presentation. This is so much the case that the effect, when perceived at all, is one of 'the incongruous' (*SL* 38). Any classical organization on the part of the viewer or writer is unavailable, 'classification impossible' because of 'its utter lack of unity' (*SL* 36, 13). Toying with representation, Ford admits that transformation or what Paul de Man calls 'substitutive exchange' (*AI* 127) does not function when responding to the city. For similar reasons, while England is small, London is illimitable, as has already been remarked. Ford chooses 'illimitable' as the last in a disconcerting quasi-mathematical series, the formula beginning with 'small' (England), proceeding to 'infinitesimal' (the world), before defining the condition of the city in terms of its illimitability. What we glimpse in *The Soul of London* is the foregrounding of imagination or perception's agency. I thus take *The Soul of London* as my point of departure in this introduction because of its own faithfulness to both the condition of the city and the act of writing that city. For it is a text that 'defies summary', it sets scenes for 'characters who never actually appear', while also offering, in its response to the call of London, a 'journey of discovery into the nature of modern city life and our ways of coming to terms with it'.[20] *The Soul of London* thus offers itself as an emblematic marker, figuring at once an irreversible movement away from modalities of representation in the nineteenth century and an inauguration of other languages of the city.

V

What can the brief example of Ford Madox Ford indicate for us? If there is to be received and subsequently delineated a (multiple and always heterogeneous, often heterodox) poetics of the city, however cautiously or provisionally, then London cannot merely be understood through simply formal, aesthetic, or phenomenological modes that insist on a more or less controllable series of equally more or less familiar, stereotyped, or even clichéd representations. There is a performative materiality of the letter to Ford's text: it does not show the city so much as it unfolds a constellated image produced from and producing London's traces. It situates itself in its sketches, outlines, and affects as an appropriate response to the multiplicity without order or number of London's countless traces that articulate the city not 'as it really is', not in imitation of the material object in the real world, but through the mnemonic archiving of rapidly gathered vivid impressions as they flash upon the mind's eye, leaving their trace on memory's retina.

I should pause to point out that that materiality of the text being addressed here is understood through two models: as that which is inflected through a Benjaminian materialistic historiography, already announced, but also in the light of Paul de Man's engagement with materiality. Of the Kantian sublime, de Man remarks, 'the radical formalism that animates aesthetic judgement . . . is what is called materialism' (*AI* 128), and so establishes a phantom passage between aesthetics and materiality, between the formal and the historical. In the light of this connection, writing London as here imagined is one such articulation of a radical formalism which is also a materiality, albeit a materiality without matter as I remark above. Given this understanding, representations of London must be taken to be irreducible to the limiting literary stagings of a few hoary tropes, metaphors, or figures still in thrall to the suggestion of some more or less direct representability, whether in the name of mimetic or historical fidelity; indeed, it is this very irreducibility and the concomitant experience of singularity that is explored in the chapters that follow.

As I have already remarked, the singularity, that 'singular-plural', that goes by the name 'London' cannot be exemplified, even as it gives itself, unveiling itself in a performative gesture of disclosure that is also a concealment, a seriality of traces of that which has always already retreated. The city is without a single example that would serve metonymically in suggesting a general principle or paradigm. Yet this singularity of the city, which is also the singularity of a structure of traces provisionally definable as 'the *without example*' – to borrow a phrase of Derrida's[21] – does not work only by negation or the impossibility of representation. Rather, the singularity of the *without-example* that I am identifying in the proper name 'London' (and all that comes to echo within and be received through that proper-improper name) is readable as the play of heterogeneous traits, whereby one comes to understand that what takes place in this play is a 'site of intelligibility – the ground of representation [though not representation as such] – that is not exhausted by the given'.[22] Rather the given or what gives place, in taking place, in allowing the possibility of that which arrives as that taking-place we call a reading, exceeds and refuses the teleology of representation by which it has its very chance. Such traits therefore articulate, even as they disorganize, a structure that plays representationally on the very kinds of paradigm which, in taking place, is left in ruins, and which can never be reassembled as such. Becoming ruined, translation is underway irreversibly.

Salman Rushdie offers an example of this when he writes of London: 'this is a city that has cleansed itself in flame, purged itself by burning down to the ground'.[23] Yet, if London is a city of flame, consumed repeatedly in fire as Peter Ackroyd comments in *London: the Biography*, it is therefore phoenix-like, translating itself and rising as other from its ashes to produce itself anew. The implied image of the phoenix allegorizes the temporal irreversibility of time, as well as figuring the motif of a network of traces irreconcilable as a permanent or stable ontology, while the iterability of eternal return is remarked.[24] In its suggestion of redemption, Rushdie's allegorical image also intimates London as a

sacred site. However, London, which in Rushdie's account is a somewhat hellish place much like Shelley's in *Peter Bell*, is a 'treacherous
city', in its constant state of transformation and translation becoming
'transformed into Jahannum, Gehenna, Muspellheim' (*SV* 262). Endless
becoming is figured through the city's multiple voices, the 'dawn
chorus', the 'chattering of road-drills, chirrup of burglar alarms,
trumpeting of wheeled creatures, clashing at corners, the deep whirr
of a large olive-green garbage eater, screaming radio-voices . . . [the]
roar of the great wakening juggernauts . . . From beneath the earth
came tremors denoting the passage of huge subterranean worms that
devoured and regurgitated human beings' (*SV* 262). The perception of
the city is one composed of a series of interruptive, eruptive reinscriptions sketched as a cacophony of machinic traces. A constellated image
is produced through the dialectic of nature and technicity. Urban temporality is marked, the day begun, by technological articulation. The
modern city is produced through an aural landscape that cannot be
resolved into homogeneous representation. There is no ontology of the
city here, only the struggle between a complex, a *signature-system*, of
competing identities, the outcome of which is undecidable. The sonic
chaos, analogous to some medieval infernal vision, is resistant to any
architectonic ordering, and the hellish aspect of modernity is all the
more enforced in the tension between the discourses of animal and
machine sound, erasing in the process the human except in that last
image of vomit.

The motif of the natural competes with that of technicity: words
such as *roar, scream, chatter, chirrup*, and *trumpet* mark and disturb any
absolutely machinic identity, while conversely, signs of the machine
city resist naturalization. While there is an intimation of the jungle as
the primal allegorical figure for the modernity of the city, this metaphor
will not work, quite. It fails in its representation and so draws attention
to itself as merely one more inscribed figure for the city because of the
persistence of the technological. However, the metaphor is undeniably
calling for our attention because it is such a cliché in the expression of
the identity of cities. Rushdie's representation of London is so obviously
a *literary* passage, the technicity and materiality of language putting language to work in so inhuman a fashion. There is a temporal evolution
in the passage which remains disquieting, disruptive from within the
logic of representation because difference is maintained throughout; it
is never suppressed in the movement of the passage according to some
assumption of seeing the city whole. Rushdie knows this is impossible,
and this may perhaps explain the sense of ambivalence haunting the

presentation of London in *The Satanic Verses*. Thus in this particular image – an image without image[25] – the city is received, it is returned to the reader, as a discontinuous series of material surges and interruptions; the graphic trace of vocalization, alliteration, assonance, the frequency of punctuating plosive – all project, even as they are projections of the city. The experience of London is the experience of the 'disintegration of experience', to cite Sara Danius;[26] and here is the experience of urban modernity, a modernity figured indirectly through the allegorization of sound. In this, there is the admission of the impossibility of any immediate access to or representation of the city through graphic, technical mediation, as the materiality of the letter affirms the city even as it denies comforting comprehension.

VI

At the risk, if not of protesting too much, then at least of seeming to be overly repetitious – (though this, I would insist is a necessary gesture preliminary to any onward motion) – what should already be clear by now is that it is a fundamental misperception on the part of the reader to suppose that one can perceive the city in terms of potential representation, or mimetic strategies of reproduction leading to representation. Such misperception (and quite possibly non-reading) announces a critical relapse into a logocentrism that the city, as multiple material resonance, memory, and spectral confluence confounds. The strategies that motivate mis-reading and logocentric or mimetic orientation and analysis, when viewed from the position of a singularity always retreating from, and always in excess of, the example, are revealed therefore as being somehow inadequate. They are somehow encrypted by the genetic trace (if you will) of their own ruination, which is available to reading only when one attends to the inscription of the city 'as affect, as force and as production rather than replication' (*ER* 124). The paradigm of mimetic representation is undone in the city text by what Derrida calls 'l'impossible comme *ce qui arrive*',[27] the impossible as that which arrives – and which never ceases to arrive, it has to be added; or to recall that earlier commentary on the ineluctable iterability of nothing, such impossible arrivals can be otherwise expressed as apparitioning.[28] In this phrase – the impossible as that which arrives – there is a perception of a motion or resurgence of that which takes place spectrally in the manifestation or revenance of the event as an *après coup* that is recognized, if it is recognized at all, in the instant of the disordering of subjectivity, presence, the present, a disruption that is both temporal and spatial, as both Derrida's comment and the belated arrival of recognition, figured in French, establishes.

In any poetics of urban representation, however, there is always and insistently that which is barely readable because the text is encrypted in particular ways. The impossible as that which arrives is hieratic in both its highly formalized or stylized appearance and its brevity of duration. There are those images or figures of the city that are scarcely to be caught; London is rendered through the most meagre of tropes, emerging in a kind of arrhythmic staccato punctuation, little more than scratches on the page, yet burdened, and burdening the reader, with everything in excess of any imaginable totality. It is as if London hovers in or, perhaps more precisely, on the surface of writing, being only discernible and describable as the material marking and yet never wholly of it, and serving some other encrypted communicative function. What that function might be is inaccessible. For, in order that such material fragments might communicate, the reader must have the proper access code, without which understanding is thwarted. Of course, there is not simply one encryption code. Within each text, the brevity of representation will vary and, at the same time, so too will the degree to which the passage resists or accommodates comprehension and reception. What such texts have in common, however, is a twofold articulation: on the one hand, there is the assumption of familiarity. If you know the London of these texts, you do not require representation. The merest analogy or aphorism, the starkest sign, all the more material for being so denuded of contextualizing mimesis, will suffice, a Londoner's equivalent of Proust's madeleine. On the other hand, immanent within such figurations of the urban, is the equal assumption that, not knowing the city, no amount of representational detail or carefully contrived description will offer any connection with London. Take, for example, the following line from a poem by Bernard Kops: 'Hackney! Sunday! Rain! You know the sort of day'.[29] There is a semiotic force reliant on cultural memory, where all the responsibility of apprehension is placed on the second-person pronoun. In the first three words, Kops reduces the North London location to the equivalent of a linguist's phonemes. Even then, their operation is only guaranteed in juxtaposition with one another, as is implied in the remainder of the line. That performative statement is both an affirmative and, simultaneously, a resistant speech act. Being told we know the kind of day to which the relationship of location, day, and weather testify we are put in the position of responding either yes or no. If the former, then the words function as we put them to work; if the latter, nothing the reader can do will engage the textual machinery. Either we know London, either we 'see' or 'feel' it, or we don't. There is no way around this aporetic encounter.

As the example from Kops establishes, any demands on reading and writing the city with any fidelity call for topographical, cultural, or symbolic recognition of particular dimensions in London's articulation and figural mapping. (It is this very principle on which Neil Gaiman relies in *Neverwhere*, in which characters from a parallel world underneath the streets of London have the names of stations on the London Underground.[30]) Indeed, without elevating the singularity of London to the status of an exemplary paradigm for the reading of all cities in this theoretical reflection (which is, in any case, always already ruined by a certain mnemotechnic revenance as I imply above), one particular aspect of reading the city comes sharply into focus. What London makes plain is that the reading and writing of any city finds itself transformed irrevocably by a motion that does not await consciousness but takes place ahead of any perceptual construction. One can only respond after the event of the emergence of the trace, but one has to apprehend the trace in order for its resonance to be recognized. The city undoes temporal assurance and subjective certainty; in relation to London, I am unbalanced, deranged. But even if I do know the city, my only genuine response can be one in which there is no attempted mastery or reduction of the heterogeneous, of the dissimilar; there can be no quieting of difference in the name of whichever manifestation of London I might hold to be more faithful, more accurate. Doubtless, some other trace can always arrive. This trait can always return, can always interrupt, and does so furthermore at every corner, down every passageway; and, of course, with every turn of the page.

VII

It is the possibility for crisis, the chance of intervention, in the stakes of representation of London that is discernible repeatedly in the novels I consider in this volume. In each, there are the signs of an eruptive and interruptive, irrevocable and irreversible disclosure or revelation. In each singular instance, narrative is irreversibly translated from within by the city in ways which manifest other signifying systems belonging to London, which surface from other historical moments, returning to bring about material effects, transformations, and deformations. A 'splintering in the unity' of representation founded in 'the human'[31] (which unity is witnessed as the desire of the human subject's gaze in fin-de-siècle texts) takes place through the eruption of the trace. By this we come to comprehend that, in any place, as the condition of any location and what takes place in such locations in the city, it is 'possible to say simultaneously that there are available but not totally determined symbols and that they are linked to the expression of concrete situations' (*TT* 168). More than this, the revenance of such symbols and traces and their irreversible power effectively exceeds expression in the unfolding of a performative event. This, in turn, does not simply produce a transformation of the apprehension of the city, but also of the various narratives' subjects. What we as readers witness is a rupture from within conventional representation, as the sign of its others, which the idea of the city makes possible, and which, as Bernard Steigler argues, 'must be understood as the emergence of a new organization of memory' (*TT* 169), which is machinic rather than human.

The problem of the city is not a new one, as Jean-Luc Nancy makes eloquently clear. What our focus on the singularity of London brings into sharp relief is a problem in, and for, philosophy, a crisis at the heart of thinking that is as old as philosophical discourse itself. Philosophy, writes Nancy, 'as the articulation of *logos*, is the subject of the city, where the city is the space of this articulation. Likewise, the city, as gathering of the *logikoi*, is the subject of philosophy, where philosophy is the production of the common *logos*.' The movement of Nancy's thought is provocatively fascinating in its chain of associations. Articulation, signification, spacing, and the differential structuring at the heart of conceptualization: all are here the principal coordinates of the urban map. It should be noticed that the materiality of the city is not merely represented *by* discourse; its material spacing *is* that articulation. A performative gesture, it is the embodied and embedded 'gathering', a gathering which is both the spacing and displacing that makes possible the community of discourse and the discourse of the community under the heading of, and as the performative technicity of *logos*. Thus the question is not one of the object and its representation but of a translation between one materiality and another wherein which translation is revealed in one form as that which is always already immanent within the other, not as its opposite, precursor, or reflection, but as the other within form or identity. Nancy continues:

> *Logos* itself, then, contains the essence or meaning of this reciprocity: it is the common foundation of community, where community, in turn, is the foundation of Being . . . The city [however] is not primarily 'community,' any more than it is primarily 'public space.' The city is at least as much the bringing to light of being-in-common *as*

the dis-position (dispersed and disparity) of the community represented as founded in interiority or transcendence. It is 'community'
without common origin. That being the case . . . the city . . . is [phi-
losophy's] problem. Or else, it is its subject or space in the mode of
being its problem, its aporia. Philosophy, for its part, can appeal to
the origin only on the condition of the dis-position of *logos* (that is,
of the origin as justified and set into discourse): *logos* is the spacing
at the very place of the origin. Consequently, philosophy is the
problem of the city. (*BSP* 22–3)

That Nancy here speaks of an articulated foundation as the 'bringing to
light' which is also that dispersal and difference which go by the name
'community' suggests to what extent, with regard to the city, we must
consider the appearance or unveiling of the city in terms of 'process'
and 'becoming', rather than product or ontological being. It also suggests that the question of the city – the question which is also the
predicament, both of writing the city and that which the city inscribes
– is a double question: of *poiesis* (meaning to make) and *tekhne* (a discovering, or a making-appear). The two figures just named are not separate; each accommodates the other, speaks to, and within the other, in
an act of intimate hospitality that does not speak of mastery or assim-
ilation on either side. 'As production (*poiesis*)', Bernard Steigler writes,
'technics is a "way of revealing". Like *poiesis*, it brings into being what
is not' (*TT* 9). *Writing London*, the very idea or possibility of inscription
announces this double figure: on the one hand, it names the act of
writing about the city, writing the city, in response to what the city dictates, even as it calls for and demands the response of inscription; on
the other hand, this doubling, differential trope *writing London* presents
us with the figure of the city writing – a topography of countless
palimpsests inscribing itself on itself, and on those open to the reception of the city's mnemotechnic inscription.

   That the city both institutes the double question and offers a reori-
entation which is also an opening on to responses to the question is
indicative, I think, of the way in which the city troubles philosophy. It
does so, we notice, by troubling the grounds of ontology through the
work of difference at the heart of, and as the very possibility for, the
very notion of origin or instituting identity. Indeed, city names community without common origin, as Nancy puts it. Far from being an
ontological name, 'community' names that which is improper, an articulation of an irreducible structuration of structure, that which is a figure
of catachresis perhaps, but certainly a bastard, monstrous, and hetero-

geneous figure, played out by the very spacing that makes the notion of the identity possible. It might be suggested even that 'community', 'city', and most pointedly *London*: all three thought not merely as architecture or topography but an endless gathering and constant transformation are not so much stable figures as they are disfigurations of the ontological, and of the ontological by which we mis-read such figures. Hence, what appears to amount to the condition of a dictum or aphorism in Nancy's remarks: philosophy is the problem of the city.

VIII

Derrida has remarked that 'traces of writing, language, experience . . . carry anamnesis beyond the mere reconstruction of a given heritage, beyond an available past'.[32] Thought of through such material agency the city is understood as *becoming* constantly; it arrives repeatedly and in different ways through the countless relationships of its subjects to its past, to its dead, to the traces of memory that maintain themselves and reiterate themselves, even while those traces are themselves transformed through temporal transmission, so that each 'memory' becomes a palimpsest of its earlier manifestation, while also being a translation. To paraphrase John Brannigan on the condition of the nation, we therefore experience 'London' 'as a form of haunting, as the continual presence of a relationship with the absent and the dead'. In admitting this, we find ourselves back almost at the beginning of this imposture of an introduction, with the acknowledgement of the mnemotechnicity of London, and of the city as ghost town; for writing London in both its senses is a 'form of social and cultural figuration which serves to activate the traces of past memory and experience, of connection to otherness and absence'.[33] The city arrives ceaselessly, hauntingly as this formless form; through a poetics, which is also a technics, it returns with a demand for awakening and activation, thereby opening to the good reader the act of writing London as both response and responsibility. To recall once more an argument from the first volume of *Writing London*: any London writer only writes *after* Blake and Dickens; the present volume itself writes *after* them; it writes in the wake of their legacy which, like London itself, is always ahead, always just beyond the horizon. *After* Blake and Dickens – and I insist on the temporal disorder which *after* installs – any act of writing the city must respond by assuming the responsibility for intervention in the stakes of representation, while assuming the crisis always implied in the return of memory, in any mnemonic inscription. For any true, any faithful act of writing London must – and indeed already does – intervene in the crisis of representation, in the contest over representational modes and regimes, however condemned to failure and betrayal such a writing might be. In doing so, writing London is charged with the performative affirmation of a materialistic historiography – distinct from any merely materialist or historicist account – in and by which there arrive the spectres of the city, whose return leaves both on *and* in us an irreversible and indelible imprint, the ghostly imprimatur of London. Without this, there would be no experience of the city; becoming aware of this, we should respond by echoing the words of Dracula, to Jonathan Harker:

– tell me of London and of the house you have procured for me.

I. Stages

1

Staging the city: London at the fin de siècle and the crisis of representation

> Victorian London was not only haunted by the ruins of its past, it was also possessed by dystopic visions of its future . . . a strong and stable modern metropolis . . . was . . . an impossible goal, for the future itself was already adulterated with spectres of collapse and loss.
>
> Lynda Nead

> A yellow pall of fog had suddenly descended on London . . .
>
> Marie Belloc Lowndes

> How might one free oneself from the cowardliness pressing upon social convictions of the present, subjugated as they are to reactive, mimetic, and regressive posturings?
>
> Avital Ronell

I

A moment of whimsy, for which I hope I'll be forgiven: my second epigraph is taken from *The Lodger*, first published in 1913.[1] There are two readings at least in this line, two *inventions* to be observed. Nothing new is created, but something is found, hence *invention*. What is found is within, *and yet* other than the obvious reading; as such, it is necessary that we read this if we are to see through the fog. *First reading*: the descent of the fog provides an atmospheric and mood-inducing setting. In anticipation of horror, of that which should not be witnessed, the curtain descends on the stage of the city. At the same time, however, the city is 'staged' in this gesture. Written two decades at least after the

25

canonical fin de siècle texts of Wilde, Stevenson, Conan Doyle, and others, *The Lodger* has recourse to *invention*, to unearthing the correct register, the appropriate discourse, for a fictionalized account of the Ripper murders. The image with which this line toys is clearly a potent one: *The Lodger* might be said to travel back, back into time, even as, it may be suggested, this novel – published when Modernism was well underway if not in full swing – appears to be haunted by the ghosts of both older texts and older Londons; which phantoms can be glimpsed all the more plainly, albeit paradoxically, because of that yellow pall of fog. *The Lodger* plays on what Iain Sinclair calls, with reference to *Dracula*, 'doctored memory, describing the past in the excited prose of a contemporary observer' (*LO* 404). There is an act of conjuration here, a kind of magic to borrow from J. Hillis Miller's definition of the work of literature as the opening up of a virtual reality.[2]

The magic involves also a process of communion, and in this invention takes place; *The Lodger* does not merely time travel or open itself to a past London, it *invents* that London, a city of 'mists and miasmas, busy streets and quiet courtyards' (Sinclair *LO* 404); the novel finds the city within itself, as other than itself, and, in so doing opens also the performative within the constative, in such a fashion that the former exceeds the latter. *Second reading*: this has already been arriving for some time in this paragraph, becoming imperceptibly more visible with each passing remark. The line from *The Lodger* is available as a performative summary of fin de siècle fiction, a summary on that fiction's power to obscure the city, to consume it, and to distort both its heterogeneous realities and the literary reception of those realities. In much fiction of the late nineteenth century (we might read) London having disappeared from view, shrouded as it was in a threatening, disquieting, and disorientating miasma: a prose seeing nothing in seeing the same everywhere, and seeing everywhere in the city as the same, as a series of endless manifestations of fear and horror.

II

Writing London: the Trace of the Urban Text from Blake to Dickens examined the various manifestations of the poetics and rhetoric of London by writers in the first sixty–seventy years of the nineteenth century, tracing a trajectory from the apocalyptic and encrypted to the ineffable and undecidable. This trajectory was complicated and compromised from the start. Encryption and ineffability, apocalypse and undecidability are not poles connected by the historical line pursued through the chapters of *Writing London*. Instead, they are intertwined figures returning repeatedly throughout the period in question.

The present volume takes up particular threads from *Writing London*, seeking to explore how writers of the last seventy or so years seek to inscribe the city's images and resonances beyond the modes of perception and techniques of articulation that are considered in the earlier study. If, as I argue in that book, after Dickens many texts referring to or representing London draw on a limited range of repeatable images and tropes of urban identification, how (in what ways) does the language of city writing re-imagine or affirm itself anew, or otherwise come to be given radically different forms of expression or articulation? I have already given a brief intimation of certain possibilities through reference to Ford Madox Ford in the introduction. But before such questions are imaginable, it might be asked: is it even possible, after Blake and Dickens, to produce different discourses in differing registers of or on London? What, if anything, can be said after Dickens (to use this formula once more), if *all that can be said* is that the condition of the city is ineffable, any writing having to respond by bearing witness to the fact that one can say nothing except to address this ineffability?[3] While there are exceptional and singular texts such as *Archimago* (1864) and Ford's *The Soul of London*, it remains the case that transformative acts of writing that irrevocably change the perception and reception of London's landscape remain few and far between, many still caught in the language of the latter quarter of the nineteenth century. Thus, between *Writing London* and *Writing London – Volume 2*, between, for argument's sake, *Our Mutual Friend* and the earliest short stories of Elizabeth Bowen, there is a gap to be addressed. Clearly, the popularity of the fin de siècle text's images of London is undeniable. Joseph Conrad's *The Secret Agent* is published in 1907, Lowndes' *The Lodger* in 1913; even T. S. Eliot – *even* Eliot – invokes urban mystery in *The Waste Land* in 1922, as a brown fog descends on London Bridge, transforming London into an 'Unreal City', through the appearance of the trace of the Baudelairean spectre.[4] And, more than a century after, the Ripper myth persists, not least in the Hughes Brothers' film version of Alan Moore and Eddie Campbell's *From Hell*,[5] the success of which attests to the persistence of the fin de siècle's most obvious and enduring tropes, images, and motifs. It is to such figures, their violent force and equally violent muting of other possible representations of the city to which this chapter turns. Without wishing to be whimsical again, it is as if that which haunts us from the fin de siècle has never gone away; it is as if each and every manifestation of the revenant merely serves to announce that it is always there.

Here, then, in the force of the trope, its insistent return, and its phantasmic hold over the imagination, is the predicament, perhaps more accurately the crisis, which I take to be at the heart of writing the city in urban fictions of the fin de siècle. This hold appears from one perspective and in certain lights to produce a violent hiatus in the writing subject who, in thrall to such force can see nothing other than variations of the same image repeatedly. It is a crisis of representation for which I argued in the introduction to *Writing London*. In that volume, my charge was largely polemic; revisiting this argument here as a means by which to move on, it is doubtless necessary that I substantiate such claims, or at the very least complicate them through this examination of certain late Victorian tropes and motifs of urban figuration. In one sense, the explanation for the preponderance and persistence of the penumbral, the chimerical, the crepuscular and threatening within the limited range of urban representations is all too obvious, at least with regard to the city. The network of images has been given ample, convincing analysis by Richard Maxwell, who summarizes his own arguments concerning novels of urban mysteries, as he defines them. The metropolis, Maxwell remarks, is for the novel, an 'artifact whose inhabitants cannot seem to grasp what it is they have made'.[6] In order to understand the mystery of the city, Maxwell argues (through discussion of Dickens and Hugo), allegorical figures are employed (*MPL* 292). Allegory might appear a strangely anachronistic mode in the modern city until, following Walter Benjamin, we recall that the 'roots of modernism and modernity can be traced to the Christian Middle Ages and to classical antiquity'.[7] It is precisely in the modernity of the nineteenth century that the traces of medievalism and the modern conjoin in a struggle resulting in the dialectical image, an image that is itself allegorical for Benjamin. Indeed, the modern is the 'time of hell' for Benjamin (*AP* 544). Urban modernity is always this underworld, this eternal nightmare, because everything everywhere is always the same, and always new; and 'to determine the totality of traits by which the "modern" is defined would be to represent hell' (*AP* 544). The 'allegorical significance of the descent' (*PH* 206) into the urban underworld is, argues David Pike, the 'framing motif' of the *Arcades Project*, providing a 'narrative framework' that 'informs every register of' Benjamin's project in his efforts to express the 'present day experience of the city' (*PH* 205). How may we perceive this, at least initially, in novels of the late nineteenth century? In much fin de siècle fiction the narratives of which take place in London, the descent into hell involves the traversal of the city from west to east, or from north, across the river, to the south. The determination of the modern in such narratives involves a constant repetition of a rather limited number of traits, with a number of variations on the hellish theme, in order that the descent be achieved all the more rapidly; and the passage to hell always involves a transition from familiar, well-lighted scenes to the squalor of dark streets and obscure back passages, in areas of the city where travel in fiction hardly, if ever, takes place.

In this chapter then (and with the allegorical condition of urban modernity in mind), I seek to unpack in an exploratory fashion dominant, recurring fictional figures of the urban, as these map an underworld that is not merely one aspect of London. Rather, for the writers in question, it can be said that hell *is* London. In sketching the contours of hellish urban modernity, I am not offering readings of particular novels but am instead working with a few passages chosen from particular writers of the last two decades of the nineteenth century. I focus solely and closely on the passages in question in order to stress what is shared in common in their representations of London, whether their writing is considered sensationalist or naturalist, whether it is driven by social concern, the market demands of genre fiction, or interests in aesthetic experiment. I do so in order to situate a departure point for the present volume, also recalling that gap between *Writing London* and the present volume, and speaking to that impasse first addressed in the earlier book. While there are many novelists from whom to choose – and, it could be argued, I have ignored two of the most prominent writers, George Gissing and H. G. Wells – I have limited myself to a number of passages from a few writers, as exemplary of what I term acts of urban mis-reading and non-reception. Mis-reading takes place because the city is not read on its own terms. Instead, particular traces of the city are gathered in acts of writing that function primarily through ontology and mimesis as twin modalities of delimiting expression, while at the same time allegorizing everything as a London that is everywhere alike.

III

There can be no question that ontological and ontic structures rely for the success of their effects on mimetic and imitative abilities on the part of the thinker. The operation of such structures and their untroubled reception implies a more or less unproblematized ability to eradicate or ignore that which is apparently surplus or irrelevant to the delineation of any manifestation of being or identity, or which is otherwise at odds with that identity considered as an undifferentiated totality. At work in this scheme also is the assumption of an adequate imitative depiction of real existence (so-called), along with the implication that the fidelity of the copy to the real bears in its apparent faithfulness a direct relationship to reality. Any discussion therefore of the 'nature', 'identity', or 'being' of a phenomenon such as a city in ontico-ontological terms requires the possibility that definition take place according to such representational, discursive, or epistemological adequation; also implied in this discussion is the appearance through such adequate means of full, simple presence or identity. The adequate in this understanding is that point reached in representational verisimilitude where the ideologies of representation and ontology are mystified, and where the 'truth' of an image becomes accepted, the ontological question coming to rest. As we have remarked with regard to the representation of the city, such adequation is reliant on the illusion of an unremitting homogeneity: the self-same everywhere, and everywhere the signs of the same in an allegorical harmony of elements in the service of the representation of that totality which is also modernity (to recall Benjamin). Speaking of the specific example of London at the fin de siècle, modernity *qua* hell must be implied as the totality of the city.

This is achieved in the texts in question not simply through the representational proximity or conflation of spatial elements; it occurs also through the enfolding of different temporal instances within the same image, even as they produce it. What is modern for the writers discussed in this chapter is the appearance within the new of the signs of primal, atavistic monstrosity as that which renews at every turn the modern city. The translation of the atavistic and primal into the perception of modernity reveals the ideological prejudices as well as the historicity of the ontological inquiry's formulation in the present example of late Victorian London. The politics of the ontological apropos of the modern city are unveiled at the close of the nineteenth century through the insistent image of a city allegedly in crisis. The presuppositions of fin de siècle texts are clearly in place, yet something does not quite function, and a fissure between representation and the ideology of ontology and representation opens. Tropes, figures, images, and motifs take over from within representation, their endless recurrence a sign of representation's failure to articulate the city; hence that sense of crisis, which, in being unable to cast a reflective eye on the act of representation, is displaced in turn onto the condition of the city itself, as being merely

the reception *of* London, and the answer to the ontological interroga-
tion: 'what is London?' Yet, paradoxically it is exactly in recourse to the
primal, the monstrous, in short to all those allegorical elements
employed to totalize the city, that writers of the fin de siècle expose the
limits of writing London when explored ontologically.

Likewise, mimesis, considered as the possibility of representation
whereby the empirical world is imitated faithfully, functions through
an implicit suppression of difference, and of the heterogeneous, if not
also of the other. This is not to say that a mimetic representation *does*
effect the exclusion of alterity or of difference, or that difference or the
other are not at work in the representation. Indeed, it is in the reading
of mimesis that the repressed often returns with surprising results. Some
of the most interesting, albeit violent readings of explicitly mimetic
texts are those which inadvertently or deliberately expose the work of
difference and the traces of the other within any supposed representational totality considered as a homogeneous whole. However, the problematic paradox of the mimetic act in art is that, all too often, the reader
is expected to assume, from a single scene or image, that the representation being read *is or points to* everything, that the apparent
completeness of representation is, at the same time, a complete and
homogeneous, self-sufficient figuration of the real. We are taught to read
any mimetic image, not only as self-sufficient and all-inclusive (which
gesture supposedly brings reading to a halt), but as a metonymy or
synecdoche for everything else, by which understanding we therefore
judge the writer or artist as successful or skilled. No single scene, no
single image of the city, to address the specific example with which I
am presently concerned, can make us *see* the city as such or as it is. Yet
the function of mimetic verisimilitude in late nineteenth-century
novels (and many others also) is precisely this: to make the reader *see*
in a certain fashion.

Mimesis therefore functions on behalf of particular ideological interests that extend beyond the borders of genre. In this way, many novels
of the fin de siècle are complicit in a crisis of representation (as already
averred), even as they are tyrannized by it. Caught in a hermeneutic
fever, acts of writing the city produce a miasma of representation that
is inaccurately read as inherent in the community of signifieds, not
the processes of signification. Not only can they not figure the city in
its truly inaccessible, ineffable totality, but, in limiting violently its condition to a totality of closed semblance and equivalence through the
constant reiteration of a few key images pertaining to horror, abjection,
the marginal and the monstrous, they also fail to receive the city; so

there is generated and imposed a certain symptomatic non-reception on the reader. In this, mimesis assumes a psychoanalytic purpose, one which the word already acknowledges, yet which is hardly ever admitted, if at all, in discussions of aesthetic or representational matters. In a psychoanalytic and medical register, mimesis is the psychosomatic, symptomatic occurrence or manifestation of conditions in an otherwise healthy body. Thus, in the novels of the fin de siècle, the mimetic symptoms of misrecognizing the city occur everywhere. Trying to understand, trying to accommodate adequately everything that one sees in London without acknowledging fully the impossibility of so doing is potentially injurious to the subject, as is the assumption that only one mode of representation or one discourse is adequate to the process. With a power that attempts to arrest reading through recourse to the mysticism of allegorical totalitarian transcendence, mimetic ideology in the fin de siècle operates through a brutal suppression of difference in the attempted suspension of historical and material transformation through the projection of an ontology of London as *the only ontology of the city*.

IV

The mimetic and allegorical representation of London in the late nineteenth century, as 'Babylon', as 'Sodom and Gomorrah', or as a purgatorial labyrinth inclining towards an abyssal inferno, is symptomatic, then, not so much of the city itself but of a somewhat pathological reception, which is, as I describe it above, a non-reception. We can, however, locate other instances of late Victorian representations of the city, which, while refraining from the more obviously allegorical, nonetheless register crisis. It is instructive to observe one such example, in order to suggest how pervasive is the restrictedness of urban representation in the effort to address – or indeed, fail to address – what cannot be grasped. Though not usually a novelist associated with the fin de siècle, Wilkie Collins is a writer of urban mysteries, to employ Richard Maxwell's phrase. As a mystery writer, Collins might be considered a transitional figure in the act of writing London, and thus he offers a provisional point from which to depart in this consideration of the problematic that persists in writing the city towards the end of the century. As will be observed, the transition in representation, a transition that remarks the historicity of urban description, takes place in a language caught between the assumption of control over the subject of representation and the failure of control. 'Confronted with a discourse [the heterogeneity that is London] that it cannot transform into an object' the language of representation 'forfeits control',[8] retreating into a restricted, telegraphic discourse. In doing so, it discloses its own anxiety through its adumbrated manifestations of *'displacement* and *condensation* limited by considerations of *representability'* (*JJ* 22). In this commentary on narratorial commentary, Colin MacCabe draws a telling connection between the processes of the psyche on the one hand and mimesis on the other.

Such manifestations are witnessed in the following example, taken from Wilkie Collins' *'I Say No'* (1885). Collins initially appears to identify difference as a constituent factor in the constitution of the city's identity, in this example in specifically economic terms, and in a manner that refuses to separate economic groups into local areas but which, instead, acknowledges the city as a place of difference's endless flow and interanimation:

> The metropolis of Great Britain is, in certain respects, like no other metropolis on the face of the earth. In the population that throngs the streets, the extremes of wealth and the extremes of poverty meet, as they meet nowhere else. In the streets themselves, the glory and the shame of architecture – the mansion and the hovel – are neighbours in situation, as they are neighbours nowhere else. London, in its social aspect, is the city of contrasts.[9]

Contrast and comparison are repeatedly brought together in this short passage, while, as a counterpoint to the repetition, there is another reiterated rhetorical gesture – that of negation, which serves in this instance to effect an apparently paradoxical intensity of focus on the intimacy of social extremity. That such effects are not stable and do not remain separable is emphasized shortly after, through the motion of a cab ride:

> the cab passed – by merely crossing a road – from a spacious and beautiful Park, with its surrounding houses topped by statues and cupolas, to a row of cottages, hard by a stinking ditch miscalled a canal. The city of contrasts: north and south, east and west, the city of social contrasts. (*I* 51)

The passage concludes with that echo and therefore with a reiteration *and* amplification, the one being, in this case, a form of the other. This doubling echolalia is of the words and effect ending the paragraph already cited, which opens Book Two, Chapter 12, of *'I Say No'* – 'In

London'. The insistence on contrast is redoubled, intensified, in the labouring of the phrase beginning and ending the final sentence. In this fashion, Collins constructs an inescapable recirculation – and an economy also, if you will – given further emphasis in the implication of all-encompassing topographical coordinates. Compass point encrypts the social and economic range being telegraphed, while the condition of the city is implied as an experiential totality. The passage is performative, for the movement of the cab journey is traced in the progression of the sentence itself. Moreover, there is a traversal that is also indicative of the architectonics of social inequality *and* proximity. This is structured by the motion of an implied gaze, from high to low, both socially and in terms of elevation, from the architectural detail of the rooftops, to the anonymous 'sameness' of housing for the poor, and beyond, into the abject, but equally constructed image of the canal. Indeed, we can also suggest, in the play of contrasts and, so to speak, the passage of, across the passage, the comparison between park and canal, as urban architectural reconfigurations, reinventions, of 'the natural'.

In a sense, Collins' brief representations are wholly familiar, recognizable, and, today, even clichéd perhaps. We see this in the figure of circulation. As its motion is economic, it is also corporeal; the city is organic, a mappable body, its lifeblood being both its economic vitality but also its destructive poison, circulation being already contaminated, the flow ending in the 'stinking' canal. Following the discussion of the obvious shared features of fin de siècle texts, above, Collins' brevity might be understood as being partially, if not wholly, consonant with the symbolic structures of urban textual generation pertaining to urban social degeneration that are read in the texts already considered. However, in this singular instance the apparent lack of development might lead the reader to overlook the ways in which the two extracts work. What seems necessary to read here is that brevity, rapidity, velocity even, is possible for Collins in the latter years of the nineteenth century because by this time particular images of London have become so familiar; urban imagery has become so exhausted, and repeated because so obviously 'true' from certain perspectives and within particular ideological formations, that any act of representation has become caught up in the repetition of dominant tropes. In one way, this offers the urban writer a kind of freedom: playing on, *with*, accepted tropes, images, commonplaces, the writer is freed to focus on narrative as though this could be divorced from setting or context. On the other hand, and as a result of what I am here describing provisionally as 'freedom', the writer's text is informed by an urban myopia, if not blindness. Relying on the stereotypes of representation, the city is no longer seen clearly, if at all. Or, to put this another way, what is 'seen' is nothing other than the limits of a certain kind of representation, of a certain way of looking at London. Thus, there is a double bind to be read here: mastery and entrapment. A modality of representation is mastered, and so too, concomitantly, is the subject of representation, in this case the city. At the same time, it is the act of writing the city which becomes entrapped, not in opposition to any sense of mastery but, rather, as that which emerges from within the illusion of control over representation, hence the perception of crisis.

However, what is also fascinating in Collins' descriptions is the absence of cause and effect, the direct attribution of conditions to location; there is not readable any psychologistic or anthropomorphic relativism, as is evident in other texts, to be considered momentarily. London, in Collins' writing, *just is* this concatenation and proximity of the economic, regional and the architectural extreme. The passages describe a bare materiality of existence in a materiality of language from within the limitations of mimetic representation by which particular manifestations of urban analytic prose had become caught at the close of the Victorian era. It is noticeable, as a sign of the performative materiality of Collins' language, that adjectival colouration and the aesthetic ideology on which this draws is restricted, limited to the park and canal, to the figures of an appropriated nature. Collins renders the city as immediately as is possible without the reader encountering the event of the city itself, so that material extremity is materially re-enacted in the adumbrated severity of discursive telegraphing. Through the bare use of comparison, Collins invokes the overflow of one region onto another, so that no location ever remains separable or self-contained in its identity. In this, all London is reduced to the monotonous monstrosity of the self-same, the endless reflection of modernity, the ineluctable temporality of hell. Thus, '*I Say No*' intimates the appalling horror of the city, and in doing so through the merest of sketched and suggestive figures, reveals that the symptoms announcing such monstrosity are not simply allegorical of course, even though they are phantasmic, symptomatic, as the play on the notion of circulation makes apparent. They are also traces of an otherwise indiscernible materiality and historicity. However, that the symptoms *are* so pervasive is understood if we recognize the endless transmission and amplification in many other novels of the period. And the signs are everywhere, across very different texts, such as Oscar Wilde's *The Picture of Dorian Gray*,

Conan Doyle's *The Sign of Four*, or Walter Besant's *All Sorts and Conditions of Men*.

V

Indeed, we need not even compare different writers but merely allude to two novels by Arthur Morrison, *A Child of the Jago* and *The Hole in the Wall*. Despite the fact that the former is a quasi-documentary revelation of the appalling living conditions of the working-class poor in the East End of London, owing much to naturalism, and the latter a criminal adventure set in London's docklands, both draw for their mimetic figuration of the city on similar tropes, images, and atmospheric effects. This, I would argue, should not be construed as an indication of Morrison's 'limited' abilities as a writer. Instead, it is indicative, once again, of the symptomatic overdetermination of the urban writer, as well as being a sign of both the text's cultural and historial interpellation and the crisis of representation that arises in the face of the otherwise ineffable nature of London. Response lags behind the material force of phenomenal imposition, and the act of writing the city is revealed to us as inadequate. It is not that the city is truly unspeakable; it is rather the case that discourse, within the bounds of mimetic and ontological adequacy, is being forced historically to confront the experience of the aporetic. Catachresis and analogy are the appropriate terms in which to apprehend the city, not metaphor or mimesis. Writing the city is no longer a question – if it ever was – of presentation but appresentation and, moreover, an appresentative act that is performative, which gives us to receive the city as other, in its own terms, as a gift that shapes and haunts our responses. Writing the city is, or rather becomes, in particular, singular examples in the twentieth century and beyond, a double act: of endless reading as response to that which arrives, and of writing otherwise, through what I would like to call *apophatic poiesis*: an act of making which causes the arrival of an impression through the indirectness of the figural. Which is merely to say writing in a manner open to the reception of all traces, rather than attempting to imitate or copy selectively, according to the acceptance of a limited and necessarily distorted number of unquestioned simulacra and phantasms.

Chief amongst such phantasmic projections of London at the fin de siècle considered ontologically is that of the city as monstrous, devouring entity (as already implied), and there are countless, obvious examples of such imaginary mapping of the city. Occasionally anthropomorphized, certainly organic, London, or particular parts of London, chiefly the East End, the docklands area, other working-class districts and those populated by immigrants (which are often the same areas as those of extreme poverty), are depicted as the source of anxiety, contagion, monstrosity once again, and thus in constant need apparently of surveillance and policing. From these concerns, it is easy to understand how 'literature is considered to be inextricably entangled with the health of the polis',[10] even if, in this entanglement, the medium of representation displays symptoms that are more problematic than those of the location it claims to represent, that is if the symptoms are more psychosomatic than material. Certainly, this can be read across publications of the late Victorian period, whether the textual imperative is one of voyeurism and vicarious thrill-seeking literary tourism, or, more immediately politically, a liberal or conservative impulse to unveil the squalor and degradation that is at once so intimately close to the centre of the Capital (and hence the centre of the Empire), and yet so remote for some as to appear a foreign land.

Walter Besant's *All Sorts and Conditions of Men* (1882) provides us immediately with disorientating coordinates of the foreign within London. In this novel, Besant describes the East End of London as 'that region of London which is less known to Englishmen than if it were situated in the wildest parts of Colorado, or among the pine forests of British Columbia . . .' (*ASCM* 28). Immediately, the reader is confronted with a landscape which, though within the nation's capital, could hardly be less familiar. The East End, remarks Besant, is 'an utterly unknown town', an 'immense, neglected, forgotten great city'. So occluded is this part of London that its own inhabitants do not comprehend either the condition of their city or their own abject marginalization, for they are those 'who have never yet perceived their abandoned condition' (*ASCM* 28–9). A remarkable line, it brings to a climax the articulation of a relationship between space and subjectivity. Almost completely abject, London's east, a city in its own right in the author's imagination, is figured through an accretive series of negatives, lacks, and absences – 'They have no institutions of their own to speak of, no public buildings of any importance, no municipality, no gentry, no carriages, no soldiers, no picture-galleries, no theatres, no opera – they have nothing' (*ASCM* 28). The East End, this other London, 'has little or no history' according to Besant (*ASCM* 29). Specifically, what is missing in the East End is a network of textual reflection on the materiality of place. There is no architecture, no culture, no social hierarchy, nor any of the other material manifestations of ideological and hegemonic structure which serve simultaneously to make visible one particular London, and to figure exclusively the communal identity or ontology of a certain middle- and ruling-class Londoners to themselves, taken as a group.

More than this, though, even the graveyards of the East End are filled with 'citizens as obscure as those who breathe the upper airs above them' (*ASCM* 29). The anonymous living and the dead people Besant's urban landscape. A shadowy double, an other of London, it appears – and this is perhaps not too much an exaggeration – as a chimera in the writer's imagination, composed from the fleeting traces of chimeras. The East End is a place overflowing with shadows and lives to which no names can be appended; hence, its appearance all the more phantasmic, in that it can be sketched at all. Unlike other descriptions of the East End from the period in question, this is not some orientalized savage landscape but an unquiet topography offering no knowledge about itself and not encouraging interest: 'nobody goes east, no one wants to see the place; no one is curious about the way of life in the east' (*ASCM* 29). Nothing, arguably, could be in greater contrast to the usual late nineteenth-century obsessive fascination with the figure of the east, however that comes to be troped and transformed in discourse. At the same time though, there is that sense of possession, figured in the comparison with 'British Columbia'. The East End is an imperial territory, and yet wild for all that; it is, moreover, 'an utterly unknown town', despite its population in the 1880s of two million, to which statistic Besant draws our attention (*ASCM* 28). There is a curious effect here in the tension between statistic and the absence of knowledge, the anonymity of place. The East End cannot be rendered except through the abstraction of a number or the lack of history, awareness, or cultural memory by which it could be said to be as much London as any other district. It thus comes to hover as a liminal and negative site due to the insistence on its ineffable condition, a place for which no language will quite do, even though there is a certain apprehensive familiarity about it.

If considered in the context of other fin de siècle representations of London to which I shall turn shortly, where the city is menacing, threatening, monstrous and uncannily gothic in its *Grand Guignol* effects, Besant's passage is strangely at odds in its assertion of nothingness. We might respond to Besant's urban nothingness by borrowing what could be taken as a criticism from an interview with Jean Baudrillard, who asserts that 'we can't begin with nothing because, logically, nothingness is the culmination of something'. However, continuing from this

Baudrillard announces an interest in the radicality of space but admits that 'the true radicality is the radicality of nothingness', continuing to ask 'is there a radical space that is also a void?'[11] I would propose, as a partial response to Baudrillard's question, that the East End is precisely, in Besant's imagination, such a radical space and, simultaneously, a void. In the light of Baudrillard's comments, we can read that what Besant makes plain is that the condition of abject London is not merely a condition of poverty:

> It is the fashion to believe that they are all paupers, which is a foolish and mischievous belief . . . Probably there is no such spectacle in the whole world as that of this immense, neglected, forgotten great city of East London. It is even neglected by its own citizens, who have never yet perceived their abandoned condition. They are Londoners, it is true, but they have no part or share of London; its wealth, its splendours, its honours exist not for them. They see nothing of any splendours . . . the city lies between them and the greatness of England. They are beyond the wards, and cannot become aldermen; the rich London merchants go north and south and west; but they do not go east. Nobody goes east, no one wants to see the place; no one is curious about the way of life in the east. Books on London pass it over . . . If anything happens in the east, people at the other end have to stop and think before they can remember where the place may be. (*ASCM* 28–9)

Belief, perception, and sight punctuate the passage, but these offer nothing; rather they offer the absence of truth, image, and understanding. Here we read the 'radicality of nothingness', a nothingness that is marked through negation and the figure of the 'beyond', as well as through the absence of access to the possibilities of power from within the East End, and the invisibility of this area and its inhabitants from the outside. Other Londoners do not even hold the East End in active memory; a cultural amnesia maintains the erasure of the other London's remnants and reminders. Thus, Besant is forced to work with absence, with otherness, with all that is beyond what might be described as the everyday networks of signification. In Besant's passage, the nothingness by which the text gets underway is arrived at through the culmination of misperception and non-reception. There is thus a registration here of a kind of abject-sublime. Inexpressible not because wonderful or terrible, but because it exists beneath the barest limits of figuration, this other London is awful and inexpressible in any positive sense precisely because it is so terrifyingly anonymous at the level of the everyday. In this, Besant's text usefully demonstrates for us the limit – and, undoubtedly, the crisis – that representation of London has reached, at least in terms of the languages deployed to map and figure the city.

This, the earliest example on which I wish to draw, clearly does not produce an obviously malevolent or malignant London. Equally clearly, there is a development in the discourse of the city from that found in the work of either Mayhew, with its sentimentalized, personalized depictions of poverty, or that of Engels, in which a phobic response driven by anxiety in the face of the incomprehensibility of 'size' determines the distortions of a largely numerically or statistically oriented representation. Besant works with languages of the urban which open a view of social space as void, all the more terrible for the possibility that one is thereby afforded a screen onto which to project the worst aspects of the other city. More than this though, with regard to urban representation, Besant's language gives the lie somewhat to other literary and documentary projects of social revelation and witness, such as Mayhew's *London Labour and the London Poor* (1864) or Andrew Mearns' *The Bitter Cry of Outcast London* (1883), which rely for their ideological efficacy on the belief that 'to write truthfully about the city seems to entail a commitment to the visible'.[12] At its limit then, narrative projection becomes a kind of pragmatic performative (to borrow a phrase of Jean-Luc Nancy's[13]), where, in the absence of knowledge, an absence of narrative, memory, history, or representation, London's other becomes the place without place, where from the comfort of known London, the city's refiguration takes place. That this occurs serves several purposes, at least. On the one hand, if, in the textual, public, or ideological imagination, the East End can be made to assume a khora-like function, by which, in being a mutable shape, it can come to be shaped by anything that comes to fill it, it can become the place where anything and everything that is monstrous can and does happen. (We need only consider in passing the power of the Jack the Ripper narratives, or that of the Ratcliffe Highway Murders,[14] both during their times, and subsequently down to the present day, to understand such performative persistence.)

On the other hand, and perhaps as a consequence of the maintenance of the East End's 'non-existence' as Besant perceives it, the work of the pragmatic performative narrative is to generate a phantasmic topography of the city. Such a topography occludes, marginalizes, and erases the quotidian realities and horrors of poverty, of working-class and immigrant experience. Such mystification throughout the last twenty years or so of the nineteenth century clearly authorizes a resistance against the comprehension of London's others. Simultaneously, it also may be read as making possible the promotion of countless phobic discourses having to do with class, race, foreignness, and sexuality, to name but a few; anything in fact which can be read, or rather mis-read, as being a potential threat to the 'proper' urban self. Such a threat is always about incursions into community and the erasure of corporeal and psychic limits, whereby the not-self, in this case the East End Londoner, always holds the power of transgressive incursion into and through the propriety of individual and collective London identity. And identity is at stake because, despite the absences of which Besant speaks, the reader knows only too well that it is the space and place known as 'London' that is always at stake, always up for grabs. Transgression and disruption of identity are always closer than we think, for they are never truly separate but always a part of us.

We see this in the extracts from my next well-known example, Robert Louis Stevenson's *The Strange Case of Dr Jekyll and Mr Hyde* (1886).

It chanced on one of these rambles that their way led them down a bystreet in a busy quarter of London. The street was small and what is called quiet, but it drove a thriving trade on the weekdays . . .

Two doors from one corner, on the left hand going east, the line was broken by the entry of a court; and just at that point, a certain sinister block of building thrust forward its gable on the street. It was two storeys high; showed no window, nothing but a door on the lower storey and a blind forehead of discoloured wall on the upper; and bore in every feature, the marks of prolonged and sordid negligence, blistered and distained. (*JH* 6)

A typical feature of fin de siècle urban writing is that sudden entrance onto a 'bystreet' or passageway, inevitably quiet but intimately adjacent to a busy district. The alley leads, equally typically, to a courtyard. The projection of the building into the courtyard, the wall described as a 'blind forehead', and the stained and blistered aspect: all are resonant for those familiar with Dickens' later descriptions of city architecture, particularly those in *Our Mutual Friend*. However, it is not only a certain intertextual reference or formal reiteration which is at work. (Were it only this, one could equally address Thomas Hardy's representations of buildings in *The Mayor of Casterbridge*.) As with other late nineteenth-century architectural representations of the less salubrious areas of cities, the quasi-anthropomorphized figuration is obviously suggestive of moral corruption and sexual disease. That I am saying nothing not already well known and acknowledged serves to illustrate two issues. On the one hand, the language of urban representation is undeniably exhausted; on the other hand, this has less to do with representation of or response to the condition of London as such, than with the generation or projection of a particular effect.

We witness Stevenson deploying yet other all-too-familiar tropes in the following passage in another section of the narrative: here in a description not of the East End as had been the case with Besant's novel, and as is to be read in *Dorian Gray*, but in a location much closer to the London of authority, society, culture, and power, Soho:

> It was by this time about nine in the morning, and the first fog of the season. A great chocolate-coloured pall lowered over heaven, but the wind was continually charging and routing these embattled vapours; so that as the cab crawled from street to street, Mr Utterson beheld a marvellous number of degrees and hues of twilight; for here it would be dark like the back-end of evening; and there would be a glow of a rich, lurid brown, like the light of some strange conflagration; and here, for a moment, the fog would be quite broken up, and a haggard shaft of daylight would glance in between the swirling wreaths. The dismal quarter of Soho seen under these changing glimpses, with its muddy ways, and slatternly passengers, and its lamps, which had never been extinguished or had been kindled afresh to combat this mournful reinvasion of darkness, seemed, in the lawyer's eyes, like a district of some city in a nightmare . . .
>
> As the cab drew up before the address indicated, the fog lifted a little and showed him a dingy street, a gin palace, a low French eating house, a shop for the retail of penny numbers and twopenny salads, many ragged children huddled in the doorways, and many women of many different nationalities passing out, key in hand, to have a morning glass; and the next moment the fog settled down again upon that part, as brown as umber, and cut him off from his black-guardly surroundings. (*JH* 23)

In this description of Soho, the drifting fog, incongruously rendered as both chocolate in colour and akin to a funeral shroud ('pall' might possibly recall or be haunted by Blake's 'London'), moves wraith-like around the streets, the city becoming transformed. The fog not only obscures the city, *it becomes it*: neither material nor immaterial, neither transparent nor opaque, neither wholly there nor not there, yet all of these simultaneously, London is translated from within itself. It is phantomized performatively through the very language that articulates it. Nothing is fixed in this representation, the image being one of ruins and traces, a series of 'changing glimpses', wherein all identity is unfixed and Soho appears to Utterson 'like a district of some city in a nightmare'. The phrase, 'mournful reinvasion of darkness' captures both the funereal aspect intimated by other words in the passage and also captures the precarious condition of the city's identity. It is worth noting that the passage appears to waver between empirical description and phenomenological reception, channelled through the figure of the lawyer. Is this a sign of writing's historicity? Are we witnesses to a moment of inscription caught between modalities of perception and representation? Or is this an oscillation that belongs to that pragmatic performativity, whereby the mutability of the city is such that it pervades not only the act of representation but also passes from the external world of the narrative to the mind of Utterson? This is not clear. But in a manner, we hardly need to provide an answer; for both gestures are equally telling, with regard to the question of what London imposes on the text at a given moment. What should be noted is that the passage seems so inescapably familiar, all too predictable in fact.

The second paragraph maintains the work of the overworked trope, but adds to this in typically fin de siècle manner. There is an explicit adumbration of poverty, the foreign, the sexual, addiction, the other, with the references to the 'low' French restaurant, the women of different nationalities in search of habitual drink – the reference to the 'morning glass' would appear to confirm this. But how do we know that they are of different nationalities? This assertion is, I would argue, all the more violent for being imposed so swiftly, so arbitrarily, and there is in Stevenson's gesture an assumption of shared knowledge concerning the identity and condition of Soho. The scene is disturbing, however, not for what it reveals; that is too banal, too familiar. The discomfort it imparts is due in large part to the way in which it is so clearly stage-managed, with the fog lifting like a curtain at the pantomime just long enough to reveal all the hidden threats at the heart of the city, before descending once more.

The nightmare city, the city of endless crepuscular hallucination is also captured in the work of Henry James, even though there are no obvious horrors stalking the streets of James' London (with the possible exception of Hyacinth Robinson and the anarchists of *The Princess Casamassima*):

> There is a certain evening that I count as virtually a first impression – the end of a wet, black Sunday, twenty years ago, about the first of March. There had been an earlier vision, but it had turned to grey, like faded ink, and the occasion I speak of was a fresh beginning. No doubt I had mystic prescience of how fond of the murky modern Babylon I was one day to become. (L 241)

From an essay entitled 'London' produced in 1888, written just six years after Besant's novel, and two after *Dr Jekyll and Mr Hyde*, James' text arrives with an inescapable sense, if not of *déjà vu*, then of *déjà lu*. The distinct sense in these three brief sentences – brief for James, that is – is one of an unwilled and fleeting image impressing itself on the mind's eye. The revenant impression, one in a series, is recalled across time to arrive on the page from that 'wet, black Sunday'. The visitation, one which is not originary but is itself the trace of that earlier trace, a memory of an impression, conjures for James another 'vision'. As James writes, he does so not only of the imprint of the city but also of a particular translation effect at work in this phantasmic inscription. Anamnesis returns the representation not as itself but as 'faded ink'; a fresh writing is employed to delineate an older mark, even as the ghost of that mark haunts the present act of writing. This multiplies the oscillation already at work between the double memory of what can be counted effectively as two 'first impressions' and the gesture of staying the passage of anamnesis' traversal across the writing subject in the process of retrospective rapport with both the impressions and the effect engendered within the younger, other self. This is so because the writer is, of course, also a reader, doubled, doubling, and dividing himself. That there are two 'first visions', the one less significant because less distinct, is itself significant inasmuch as James appears to admit that one can assign no originary moment or source for the arrival of the city's phantasm and the response it produces in one. Teleological retrospect authorizes the gesture of doubling and division thereby signalling the work of difference in the performative dimension of writing, memory, and the projection of, in this case, the urban subject. As a result, in an instant of temporal disorder as fleeting as the impressions of the 'murky modern Babylon' there can be made the claim, however belatedly, of 'mystic prescience'. I would argue that the prescience and implied temporal disorder offer a self-conscious gesture, authorizing the writer to produce an image of himself as a distinctly London figure, as belonging to, written by, the strangeness of the city.

So, James' text, though not a story belonging obviously to the late Victorian gothic or sensation genre, nonetheless does have recourse to the language of such genres, while also playing in specific phenomenological and psychological registers that can be associated with much London writing during the period in question. His representation of the city and its spectral power is in evidence further on in the same essay, as James describes the generation in him of a sense of anxiety or abjection, possibly the uncanny even:

> A day or two later, in the afternoon, I found myself staring at my fire, in a lodging of which I had taken possession on foreseeing that I should spend some weeks in London. I had just come in, and, having attended to the distribution of my luggage, sat down to consider my habituation. It was on the ground floor, and the fading daylight reached it in a sadly damaged condition. It struck me as stuffy and unsocial, with its mouldy smell and its decoration of lithographs and wax-flowers – an impersonal black hole in the huge general blackness. (L 244)

While obviously used in a quotidian manner in the context of the passage as a whole, and certainly with reference to the earlier notion of 'mystic prescience', 'foreseeing' takes on an especial resonance here (as, it might be averred, does 'possession'). The impression is disquietingly unfixed: daylight fades, mould grows, and the flowers are mere imitations. There is a sense of apparitional motion, and of being caught in some liminal moment and space, between life and death, between one state and another, while the room, with its lack of identity, darkness, and its being a void of sorts, is presented as merely a synecdochic figure for that greater 'general blackness' of London in general. James continues:

> The uproar of Piccadilly hummed away at the end of the street, and the rattle of a heartless hansom passed close to my ears. A sudden horror of the whole place came over me, like a tiger-pounce of homesickness which had been watching its moment. London was hideous, vicious, cruel, and above all overwhelming; whether or no she was 'careful of the type', she was as indifferent as Nature herself to the single life . . . It appeared to me that I would rather remain dinner-

less, would rather even starve, than sally forth into the infernal town, where the natural fate of an obscure stranger would be trampled to death in Piccadilly and have his carcass thrown into the Thames. I did not starve, however, and I eventually attached myself by a hundred human links to the dreadful, delightful city. (L 244–5)

From the first line of the passage immediately above, it is apparent that James' room is situated in one of those alleys off busy thoroughfares so popular in late Victorian London texts. The noise is oppressively inti-mate in the opening sentence, the alliteration of 'heartless hansom' curiously forceful, especially given its imagined quasi-living state. In the delineation of horror and anxiety that – uncannily – anticipates the con-siderations of fear, dread, and the process of the uncanny within being, James juxtaposes the monstrosity of London with the ferocity of jungle animals. He does so in order to transform the city into an unnaturally natural location, where the condition of the city is to be, as nature, 'red in tooth and claw', to recall Tennyson's Darwinian echo, which returns here, in the late 1880s, with social-Darwinian overtones, with London becoming the impersonal, all-devouring abyss. The horror of place is related closely to the uncanny, at least in the Freudian sense of that word, because the abject sensation of the subject produces the corollary of homesickness, through the startling illumination that the city could not be less familiar, less comforting. What then follows is no less violent, though perhaps somewhat more surreal; the jungle-city becomes a hellish landscape where the anonymous individual is oblit-erated, 'trampled to death', and disposed of in the river, all of which is related as though this were an everyday occurrence.

However, London is not simply place, not only a Dantesque stage, even if the city's modernity is hellish for James in its totality. Indeed, neither is it assignable a stable ontological determination, nor is it reducible to a single representation, whether mimetically or analogi-cally, as we see in the passages above, where the figure of ghostly locale gives way to that of jungle, before, in turn, being transformed into a dream-like purgatory. Not one identity, both less and more than this, London exceeds and overflows both itself and the power of adequate representation, so that all that can be said of it is that it is, at one and the same time, 'dreadful, delightful'. The Jamesian recognition of the city's sublimity is then acknowledged again, in the same essay, when it is remarked that a 'small London would be an abomination, as it for-tunately is an impossibility, for the idea and the name are beyond every-thing an expression of extent and number' (L 245). One cannot 'know' or comprehend London as a totality, and James, of all the writers of the fin de siècle being considered here, begins to perceive the necessity of an other language – or a language of the other – if it is possible to write London in response to that which the city imposes, that demand and call articulated by London. James is not Besant; he does not proceed by negation, as if working through some gesture of quasi-Kantian apprehension of the sublime. The very idea of the city, its proper name: both signify that which cannot otherwise be signified in directly representational, mimetic, logical, mathematical, or ontological terms. 'London' stands in as the name for what cannot otherwise be articulated directly, and one apprehends the city if at all only through a kind of indirect approach, through the spectral poetics of indirection of which we have already spoken.

In *The Sign of Four* (1890), Arthur Conan Doyle has no such intimation of the necessity or possibility of another language, his urban discourse being somewhat similar to that of Stevenson's in its atmospheric and topographical troping. Concerning the Strand in Chapter 3, we read of the 'dense drizzly fog [which] lay low upon the great city' (*SF* 21). In an image reminiscent of the opening page of *Bleak House*, the mud-coloured clouds and mud-covered streets suggest an undifferentiatable landscape. The lamps are 'misty', their light 'feeble', the pavement 'slimy'; the air is 'vaporous', and there is a semi-fluid 'shifting radiance' about the entire scene. The crowds moving through the Strand are spectralized, undifferentiated and endless; they move 'eerie and ghostlike' in and out of shade and light (*SF* 21). The motion of the cabs is a 'continuous stream' and so echoes the motion of both the anonymous, inhuman crowds and that of the almost palpable air. As Utterson, the lawyer, had seen the procession of the nightmare city from a cab in *The Strange Case of Dr Jekyll and Mr Hyde*, so Dr Watson also observes the city's endless, ghoulish parade from the safety of a hansom. Thus the individual subject is subject in part to the terrors of fluid impersonality, where all dissolves into everything else in a constant, unstaunchable flow, transgressive in its suggestion that every being, every identity, every ontology or representation is subject to an excess which erases the boundaries of the discrete or the proper. However, it is important to note that the individual subject witnesses the monstrous, apparently organic flow of London from within the relative safety of the cab, the horror of the megalopolis, its endlessness, being apparently containable by the frame of the cab's window.

The city is thus both threatening and partially containable, the intimation being that the subject can be thrilled and terrified by the grotesque illimitable pulsation of the city space, and yet maintain a voyeuristic distance *and* proximity, as if being involved in some private peepshow. Indeed, one might even posit the cab window as analogous with a screen across which move successive, uncanny tableaux, all of which are all the more fascinating *and* terrifying because they intimate for the voyeuristic traveller a not-quite-human world. The registration of the city's phantasmagoria through the movement of the cab-screen attests to an increasingly common mode of attention in the second half of the nineteenth century, one in which 'perception is fundamentally characterized by experiences of fragmentation, shock, and dispersal'.[15] In addition, it has to be acknowledged that with this scene, as with all the others addressed in the chapter, a strange act of reading in ruins is taking place through which, 'it is possible to see one crucial aspect of modernity as an ongoing crisis of attentiveness' (Crary *SP* 14). This crisis, I would argue, is but one aspect of the crisis of representation and also the crisis *in* representation. The reading of such scenes offers a threat to the subject, whose eye is the medium of transference, but who is barely there otherwise, and who is placed under the threat of erasure by the plenitude and velocity of the city's heterogeneous traces. James is anxious about his possible obliteration: Utterson is only his 'lawyer's eye', his professional identity being that which both authorizes his journey and protects him from the otherness of Soho; anything may, indeed, *must* be witnessed in the legal eye, and in the name of the Law. In Conan Doyle's narrative, Watson, the professional medical man, is reduced to utilitarian technological function, becoming a mere recording device for forensic detail, almost at a loss to hold on to representation, given the rapidity of movement registered through the cab window.

Watson's function is not exhausted, however, and Conan Doyle acknowledges the specificity of location through a shift in representation when the doctor's cab crosses the river, going south. Obviously enough to anyone familiar with the topographical and economic divisions of London, this means a change in what one witnesses. South of the river, we are on what Iain Sinclair calls, in his introduction to another Holmes tale, *A Study in Scarlet*, the 'dark side of the Thames'.[16] If the Strand had offered the city as phantasm, a place of ghosts and also a disquieting illusion within the mind's eye, South London is rendered in a more material, yet no less monstrous manner:

> We had . . . reached a questionable and forbidding neighbourhood.
> Long lines of dull brick houses were only relieved by the coarse glare

and tawdry brilliancy of public-houses at the corner. Then came rows of two-storeyed villas, each with a fronting of miniature garden, and then again interminable lines of new, staring brick buildings – the monster tentacles which the giant city was throwing out into the country. At last the cab drew up at the third house in a new terrace. None of the other houses was inhabited, and that at which we stopped was as dark as its neighbours, save for a single glimmer in the kitchen-window. On our knocking, however, the door was instantly thrown open by a Hindoo servant, clad in a yellow turban, white loose-fitting clothes, and a yellow sash. There was something strangely incongruous in this Oriental figure framed in the commonplace door-way of a third-rate suburban dwelling-house. (*SF* 23)

Whereas motion had unseated the stability of representation in the earlier scene, here it is the repetitive, somewhat brutal anonymity of regimented terraced housing that is read as 'forbidding'. The banality of domestic dwellings is contrasted to the 'coarse glare and tawdry brilliancy' of the public houses, a description suggestive of a relationship between illumination and morality. It might be said that the illumination is double: both literal and figurative, it serves to illustrate and throw in dramatic relief the 'human condition' through the employment of those judgmental adjectives, 'coarse' and 'tawdry'. What takes place here precisely is an illustration of the invisible, through that implied relationship between lighting and morality (or the lack thereof). The houses are therefore impersonal, indistinguishable forms that stand in for the anonymity of those who live within them, whose only 'notoriety' is illuminated, in turn, through the sketch of the public houses. A graphic representation is forced through the spectral trait of the words, of what works within them, upon the reading subject. A generative force is at work, which, while never presenting or representing as such, nonetheless puts into effect an economically situated commentary. The lives of the Londoners in such a scene are never addressed directly, but a presumed aspect of such life is opened for us, as if such life were too terrible to represent on the page. And this, I would argue, is performative rather than constative, or certainly more than merely constative. The limitation of representation allows for a performative gesture that overdetermines location, without giving the reader access to sufficient information to read for him- or herself. Having none of the hallucinatory quality of the earlier scene, the present moment relies on a telegraphing stroke that tells us how to read the city in this particular place. That so much of this area of South London is 'third-rate', 'dull', 'interminable', produces a somewhat violent contrast to both the image of brick buildings which stare and the description of the area as being only the most recent result of the spread of London's 'tentacles'. In this latter image, London clearly becomes a monster or, perhaps, a disease, reaching out, touching, and leaving its demoralizing traces everywhere. Finally, the reader and narrator encounter the singularly 'incongruous' figure of the Asian servant, whose bright clothing and origin so clearly set him apart, and yet whose presence serves as another reminder that this is an other London, and one which cannot be read easily, or with any assurance.

Of course, the disquiet engendered by 'this grey monstrous London of ours' in the minds of certain of its subjects is not always fearful; or, if fearful, then at least tinged with an uneasy pleasure of sorts, having, as Oscar Wilde remarks through Dorian Gray, an 'exquisite poison'. Dorian has a 'passion for sensations' (*PDG* 73) and London provides a surfeit of these, being very much a world of the sensory and sensual. In Chapter 4 of *The Picture of Dorian Gray*, London *is* its people, some of whom 'fascinate', while others 'filled me with terror', though all encourage a 'mad curiosity'. London is comprised of 'myriads of people, its sordid sinners, and its splendid sins . . .' (*PDG* 73). In the language of some voyeuristic ingénue, Dorian continues:

> I went out and wandered eastward, soon losing my way in a labyrinth of grimy streets and black, grassless squares. About half past eight I passed by an absurd little theatre, with great flaring gas-jets and gaudy play-bills. A hideous Jew, in the most amazing waistcoat I ever beheld in my life, was standing at the entrance smoking a vile cigar. He had greasy ringlets, and an enormous diamond glazed in the centre of a soiled shirt. (*PDG* 73)

Once again, the movement of the subject in fin de siècle London writing is to the East End of London, to a world of almost hypnagogic illusion, where nothing is real. It is this quality of irreality that four years after Wilde's novel, Arthur Machen in *The Three Impostors* describes as a world of 'chiaroscuro that had in it something unearthly', in which crepuscular London 'casual passers-by . . . flickered and hovered in the play of lights', rather than standing out as 'substantial things', while lights appear in windows with 'semi-theatrical magic' (*TI* 9). However, Wilde's theatrical, unreal city is notable in its description for that impression of intertextuality, playing as it appears to do – or are these merely more phantasmic traces within the phantasmic urban location?

– between the disquieting, gaudy theatre reminiscent of Wordsworth's groundless London of *The Prelude* and the dirty Jew, a figure belonging equally to Dickens or Du Maurier (to identify only the most obvious texts) whose monstrosity is figured through the play of synecdochic elements: the waistcoat, the cigar, the ringlets, the diamond, and the soiled shirt. Wilde's passage is remarkable for nothing so much as its play on cultural, racial, and urban stereotype. It plunders shamelessly the register of anxieties of middle-class Victorian Londoners in its performative projection of a groundless London 'tainted' by strangeness and foreignness. While in previous passages cited it had been the French, women, and a 'Hindoo servant', here we have that archetypal figure of otherness, the Jew.

The singular specifics aside, it is important to note that Wilde's writing, like that of the others already discussed, engages in a performative gesture, and this can be read from the intertextual and stereotypical dimensions. For again, we are not reading a constative representation so much as we are being asked to imagine a phantasmic London projected into our minds (as is the case in Conan Doyle's text), which, in its predictable literary and cultural recognizability, produces the appropriately programmed frisson of delight *and* terror akin to that felt by Dorian in his voyeuristic observation. The city is monstrously, potentially abyssally absurd only because the traces from which it comes to be generated are so familiar from other literary models. Reading London in Wilde's case suggests not reading the city but reading onto some imaginary space a network of textual tropes. Tangible, material effects are produced because the reader is placed between texts, and projected onto in this positioning as the subject of an absurd urban formation. The structure of urban representation in the 1890s is absurd precisely because it engages in what we can now, following Baudrillard, describe as a hyperreal play of simulacra, or what Rainer Nägele has called 'the phantasmatic instrumentalization of language . . . [which] produces as its complement the phantasm of "real presences"'.[17] *The Picture of Dorian Gray* is not so much an example of the ways in which a writer will draw on prior texts, as it is an example, albeit a highly singular one, of a text locating itself as one nodal location within an already existing network of texts performing a monstrous and absurd, often abyssal London.

Arthur Machen captures London's phantasmic absurdity in his novel already mentioned, *The Three Impostors* (1895). Somewhat more engagingly perhaps than Wilde's narrative, here urban strangeness is projected through the counterpoint of street music and street sounds: 'the runs and flourishes of brave Italian opera played a little distance off on a piano-organ seemed an appropriate accompaniment, while the deep-muttered bass of the traffic of Holborn never ceased' (*TI* 9). The city clearly both joins in with the music and produces its own melodic effects. Machen renders the oddity of effect economically through the rendition of opera on a piano-organ. However, Machen's text is not merely concerned with the production of comic effects, so much as it can be read as partaking in the by-now-familiar disruptive juxtapositions in which fin de siècle city writing partakes repeatedly, as the following passage demonstrates:

> I got into one of those quiet places to the north of Oxford Street as you go west, the genteel residential neighbourhood of stucco and prosperity. I turned east again without knowing it, and it was quite dark when I passed along a sombre little by-street, ill-lighted and empty. I did not know at the time in the least where I was, but I found out afterwards that it was not very far from Tottenham Court Road. I strolled idly along, enjoying the stillness; on one side there seemed to be the back premises of some great shop; tier after tier of dusty windows lifted up into the night, with gibbet-like contrivances for raising heavy goods, and below large doors, fast closed and bolted, all dark and desolate. Then there came a huge pantechnicon warehouse; and over the way a grim blank wall, as forbidding as the wall of a gaol, and then the headquarters of some volunteer regiment, and afterwards a passage leading to a court where wagons were standing to be hired; it was, one might almost say, a street devoid of inhabitants, and scarce a window showed the glimmer of light. I was wondering at the strange peace and dimness there, where it must be close to some roaring main artery of London life . . . (*TI* 10)

The quotation functions for the reader through a dependence on familiarity with the echoes from that network of particular London texts, such as those to which I have already referred. There is the sudden entrance onto quiet locations devoid of the signs of human life, yet still intimately close to busy main streets, stereotypically described as 'arteries', in a partial translation of the city into a gigantic body. There are the architectural accents and details – the gibbet-like contrivances, the grim blank wall – suggestive of prisons and punishment. The still and quiet is not simply this, but is remarked on, and thereby rendered performatively, as strange. Interestingly, the passage maps the streets and their features as the narrator walks through them, so that the narrative figures as it traces a topography, but one without precise coordinates. For, despite the naming of principal streets, which run, respectively, East–West and North–South, the narrator remarks that 'I did not know at the time in the least where I was'. Here is an act of mapping that is all the more strange for being both partially locatable *and also* disorientating.

VII

This last sketch of Machen's double gesture, simultaneously offering topographical coordinates in the form of street names and his narrator-subject's sense of unfamiliarity, should, perhaps, give us pause in the conclusion of this chapter to ask some broader questions, which will refold back on the interests thus far articulated before proceeding. To put it bluntly, what is happening in fin de siècle London texts? What shared contours and processes can we discern with regard to the act of writing the city? And why are these available as so many shared acts that remark the limit of a particular moment in urban representation? Let me trace possible answers through a series of formulae, all of which acknowledge the generation of a process from within particular acts of narrative construction. As a bare narrative minimum the London text relies on a relation between the delineation of location, the act of representation of that location, and commentary concerning what takes place within and as a result of the location, whereby representation produces a contextualized action as belonging to, part of, location. Location as symbolic function determines the choreography of narrative action and the events of the narrative, in turn, serve to inform the reader as to the condition of location. Yet within each of these three figures there is discernible a shadow-function at work, which I give here as corollary *and* other-within. These figures can be traced as follows: location *and/as* dislocation; representation *and/as* misrecognition; commentary *and/as* proscriptive performativity. In each of these a series of tropes is deployed, along with motifs, images, and metaphors, whereby the familiarity of such figures, and of course the figures themselves, serve to stage a fictive city. For all that, it is so apparently recognizable, this metropolis is nonetheless neither a reception of nor a response to London, to that which the city can inscribe on the subject open to the arrival of the multiple traces of its otherness. Such performative staging as we see in fin de siècle writing prohibits through enactment the reader's reception of any other aspect of London. It enacts such a proscription because the motifs of proximal foreignness and intimate monstrosity are reiterated within a pervasive economy of self-replication and intertextual self-referentiality, all of which are suggestive that this is all there is to London and London is just this monstrous identity (a monstrous identity all the more uncanny in being so coherent). To borrow a phrase wholly out of context from Bernard Steigler, in such writing as I have considered in this part of the introduction, 'everything is already identically the same' (*TT* 124) in these texts, so that no access to the city is possible. London does not write here and neither is it written, strictly speaking; it becomes – it is always already – written, if not, perhaps more accurately, overwritten, as the proper name, metonymy, and synecdoche, for the cultural anxiety and fear of the other, of others. The mapping of London is translated into a topography of terror, having more to do with giving location to that which haunts the cultural, historial psyche.

This is not to say anything new of course. Critics of the late Victorian period have known this for a long time. But what is fascinating is the way in which London as site, as stage, is so energetically, repeatedly produced, again and again, as both location and source, so that representation of the city is always misrepresentation in the service of ideological overdeterminations. London is rendered as the place par excellence of voyeuristic horror, whether economic and social, as in the case either of Besant or Morrison, or else phantastic, atavistic, or gothic, as in the other examples. (Not that the socio-economic and the gothic are absolutely separable, as I have sought to demonstrate.) While the terrors of the gothic were already well known, it is arguable that never before the end of the nineteenth century had a single site or topography so effectively served as the focal point for the exploration and expression of cultural anxiety, as had London. In this topographical and ideological intensity (and intensification), the language of representation comes to be revealed as reaching particular limits. Dread, fear, anxiety: all produce and translate alterity and heterogeneity as what, following Benjamin on the hell of modernity, I would term the *same-everywhere*. At the moment in which this happens, reading no longer takes place, representation admits to a paucity of the imagination, and language as response to the other begins to assume an inarticulacy in the insistence and frequency of its repetitions. In its repetitious reproduction of the same-everywhere, such inarticulacy admits not so much to social atavism as the seemingly atavistic fear from within the (bourgeois male) subject in the face of that which appears all the more wholly other, because there is no language, no mode of representation or ontological framework by which to control it.

While I discuss such fears in Wordsworth, de Quincey, and Engels, in *Writing London*, it seems to me that fear or anxiety in the face of the city as other reaches fever-pitch by the end of the century concomitantly with the breakdown in mimetic or directly representational modes of discourse. This is particularly so with regard to London, precisely because what the city imposes is simultaneously in excess of any ontology, and so is irreducible to any mode of discourse intended to generate or convey a coherent meaning. Fin de siècle writers, such as those with whom we have been engaged, open themselves to an abyss of the not-self as the absence of their reflection anywhere in the city is allied to a voyeuristic impulse that drives the search for reflection further. This is a drive which reveals the impossibility of locating, in Derrida's words, 'a pleasure of the same . . . the mastery of the dissimilar . . . the reduction of the heterogeneous' (*TP* 113). Yet despite or because of the recognition of representational failure, what takes place in the fin de siècle with regard to the production of stable meaning appears as an act of mechanistic urban reproduction. This is reminiscent – at least to this reader – of the masturbatory machinery figured in Marcel Duchamp's *The Bride Stripped Bare by Her Bachelors, Even (The Large Glass)*. Through such self-generating writerly technicity – whereby writing polices itself in its imaginary productivity and performativity rather than giving itself over to the reception of a *poiesis* of the other – the city, controllable through the delimitation of its tropes, is maintained in the process of generating fear in response to its images. Such reproducibility – the reproducibility of the image, of the fear, of the component parts of a certain pre- and overdetermined structure – is a process of stage-management effected insistently through occlusion and erasure. That which is obscured, denied, made invisible, is threefold – otherness, memory, and difference: otherness as non-threatening, memory as vital to community, and difference and heterogeneity as merely the conditions for the maintenance of the taking place that is the city's condition. The spectral memory and historicity of the city, its many ruined narratives, are suppressed in favour of a formal literary haunting denying the alterity and heterogeneity of a true London poiesis, which it is the aim of this volume to open to analysis.

II. Crises

2
'That particular psychic London': the uncanny example of Elizabeth Bowen

And yet, what do I see from the window if not hats and coats that could conceal spectres or automatons?

René Descartes

Writing is eventful; one might say it is in itself eventfulness.

Elizabeth Bowen

[T]he image has to be present and past, still present and already past, at one and the same time. If it was not already past at the same time as present, the present would never pass on. The past does not follow the present that it is no longer, it coexists with the present it was. The present is the actual image, and *its* contemporaneous past is the virtual image, the image in a mirror.

Gilles Deleuze

I

Elizabeth Bowen is a writer responsive to what she has called in *The Heat of the Day* a 'particular psychic London' (*HD* 92). While this novel addresses the condition of the city and life in London during wartime, the psychic and phantasmagoric aspects of the city are Bowen's constant concerns, even as the spectral nature of urban materiality in its relation to the uncanny and anamnesis come to inform her act of writing the city text. Although Bowen ostensibly writes of a recognizably 'real' and apparently somewhat representable world, the force of the city is perceived through fragmentary details, ruins, and remainders belonging to what might best be described as the 'schemata of dreamwork', to use a phrase of Walter Benjamin's (*AP* 212). Or as Maud

Ellmann has it, 'the furniture of realism is shattered by the violence of Bowen's style'.[1] This shattering effect is irreversible. Once having taken place, and having imposed its violence on the reader, the ruination of representation cannot be reconfigured. The city, its buildings, its people, its domestic interiors and external public spaces: all undergo a critical transformation that admits of a multiplicity of haunting traces on *and* as the urban scene.

Bowen's 'style' (a style without coherence, style in ruins we might say) is also defined by Ellmann as a fragmentary art form appropriate to a fragmentary world (*EB* 146). This announces itself in part through a 'surreal intensity' (*EB* 147), which is achieved, in turn, through 'the porousness of architectural and psychic space' whereby the ruins and fragments can circulate (*EB* 153), without a return to a cohesive whole. Furthermore, the amaterial signs of haunting unveil themselves; they disappear and return from within the 'contours of the banal' as a kind of narrative 'threshold magic', to borrow from Benjamin once more (*AP* 212, 214), which serves to focus the reader's attention with a disquieting intensity that disturbs the complacent certainties of realist, mimetic art. Through such intensity, which also amounts to moments of narrative suspension, there is foregrounded a crisis in representation concerning the city, its historicity, and its subjects. In order to open this to a partial reading, Bowen's short stories and novels attend to those fleeting, transient moments of urban impression that compose and comprise this idiomatic configuration of the city. She registers such estranging and ephemeral traces and signals of the city as they have inscribed themselves at specific times and during particular events, and which subsequently come to be filtered through the sensibilities and perceptions of those inhabitants of the city who articulate the singular experience and mediation of London. That this is so is seen to be the case, whether one is speaking of an interior or a specific external London location. Indeed, what takes place in being open to Bowen's psychic London is a strange and haunting passage between the internal and the external, between the inanimate and the living, between the individual and all of London.

II

We can see such processes at work in a short passage from *The Heat of the Day*. The description of furnishings from Stella Rodney's flat in the novel offers the reader the suspension of narrative and, with that, the uncanny disfigurement of the representation of domestic space. Moreover, it opens out from this, by analogy, to the eerie suspended animation of all London, as the act of writing brings the city almost to a halt in a brief moment of psychic reflection. We read, initially, of the room's 'unreality' (*HD* 54). In the wake of Eliot's *The Waste Land* with its apostrophic naming of London as the 'Unreal City', there can be no doubt that this is a modern London interior. Its modernity is in both its suspensive, disquieting unreality and a strangely anachronistic rupture within the scene. (To pause parenthetically for a moment: the analogical echo between Eliot and Bowen is not merely fanciful, I feel, if one pauses to consider the emphasis placed by both writers on the city's dead as a phantasmic flow. Eliot admits to the countless dead flowing over London Bridge, finding a resonance in Bowen's image of the dead, who 'made their anonymous presence . . . felt through London' (*HD* 91); it is the sense of this flow that becomes more and more insistently foregrounded as the act of writing London continues throughout the twentieth century, and as is seen in Duffy, in Ackroyd, and in Sinclair.) This perception of unreality, which might belong as much to Stella Rodney and her son Roderick as it does to the narratorial discourse, is strengthened almost immediately by the announcement that the sofa is 'without environment' (*HD* 55).

As Bowen continues, 'it might have been some derelict piece of furniture exposed on a pavement after an air raid or washed up by a flood on some unknown shore' (*HD* 55). While the first hypothetical supposition provides a context for reading the sofa's abstraction from its surroundings, the second image only serves to magnify the furniture's odd dislocation, its 'derelict' or ruined condition. In either case, the sense of the domestic is irrevocably haunted by a violence that is at once both real and surreal, and therefore all the more uncanny precisely because the unhomeliness is a condition of what should appear in all its domestic familiarity. It is precisely in the focus on the sofa, ripped from the very domestic context in which it stands, that the interior, the conversation between Stella and Rodney, the narrative, and the world of the novel, all come to be suspended, as the reader is given access to the psychic lives of mother and son. If the world is 'impoverished' for Stella and her son as Bowen suggests (*HD* 56), then such impoverishment is figured both allegorically and uncannily through the absence of environment of the sofa and the ruin that it becomes as a result of this lack.[2]

Bowen suspends narrative, producing a kind of ghostly suspended animation through an intensity of attention directed towards those domestic details that should be completely familiar, which should belong to the unobserved paraphernalia of inhabited space and those contours of the banal. The minutiae of the domestic demand our response because they no longer function habitually; as Bowen remarks, not only do Stella and Rodney stop speaking, nothing in the room speaks either (*HD* 56). Time itself is suspended, and hence becomes visible; minutes, which usually flutter mysteriously like a 'fire burning', 'seemed to be at a stop' (*HD* 56). Within this disturbing hiatus, where the inanimate and living are alike transfixed, neither alive nor dead and therefore truly spectral, Bowen effects a further ghostly drift: from metaphorical to real fire. In this transference, one particular aspect of the uncanny is foregrounded in Bowen's description of the electric fire: '[t]he actual fire's electric elements, vertical hot set lips, grinned away at the empty end of the room' (*HD* 56). The absence of life in the room is contrasted sharply in this somewhat prosopopoeic animation of the fire, which, in being attributed lips, grins disturbingly both within the room and, across the threshold of the space, at the reader also. Recalling the uncanny sensation attributed to automata acknowledged by Freud[3] in their giving body to a liminal suspension between life and lifelessness, between the human and the machine, the fire is all the more disruptive because while neither one nor the other, yet it is suggestive of both. While Bowen will later remark that 'in the unfamiliar the familiar persisted like a ghost' (*HD* 98), with regard to interior London spaces it is undeniably the case that the opposite persists all too hauntingly. For it is through the intensity of focus that we feel the 'sheer "otherness" of surroundings' (*HD* 318).

Why, it might be asked, is this estranged domestic space so particular to London? One answer is put forward: 'no other city's built-up density could be so strongly felt' (*HD* 200). Across *The Heat of the Day*, such density of resonance is registered; one might connect, for example, the grinning vibration of the fire to the registered sense of 'London giving one of her sleepy galvanic shudders' (*HD* 65). There is clearly a relation between interior life and the external world, between inanimate objects and the semi-organic condition of the city; and of course in the oscillating shuttle between the psyche and the city, that 'general rocking of London and one's own mind' (*HD* 91). In the particular scene on which we are focusing, however, all awareness is focused through the distortion of detail, in which every aspect of domestic unreality functions synecdochally. The suspension of narrative progression allied to the ruination of a domestic interior is further emphasized by Bowen's emphasis on the silence, 'black-out registered' (*HD* 56), by which figure we are transported invisibly through the window into the streets. The very identity of silence is 'imperfect', being a 'resistance to sound – as though the *inner tension* of London were being struck and struck on' (*HD* 56; emphasis added). Indirection, analogy, spectral transport: through these flows the city is disclosed; although not seen as such, as that which is *inner*, the city is made available through analogical apperception. The play between inner and outer, visible and invisible, that which is material and immaterial, 'heard and unheard' (*HD* 56); all tension is trapped between the hiatus of the minutes in Stella's flat and the 'ticking over' of London (*HD* 56), as if the city were one huge idling machine. And from this, we are returned to the room, in which lack is once more emphasized through the absence of 'apprehension of time' (*HD* 56). Yet – and here is the paradox – the sense of the city as uncanny and haunted place, a particular psychic place, is felt most forcefully (is it not?) in the fact that the absence of temporal apprehension, the halt to the fluttering of minutes, is brought to view so demandingly. Thus, *inner tension*, felt everywhere, and everywhere as a singular experience, acknowledged in the focus on the domestic interior, by which London is known but not shown analogically.

III

Such narrative suspensions are readable as, and informed by, so many movements, motifs even, of the play of traces – inscriptions arriving from elsewhere as ghostly remainders constituting and yet disordering the scenes and locations that they mark. It is in the psychic economy of the city's narratives that imagination and memory find their correspondences at the analogical and allegorical levels,[4] whereby such levels permit access to the otherwise encrypted resonances of the city, in the refiguring of both its locations and its various pasts. Irreversible and ineluctable fragmentation takes place as the condition by which the narrative of the city, its architecture and interiors, may be staged in allegorical and analogical fashion. Thus we read that the writing of London for Bowen performs, as much as it implies, what Benjamin, in speaking of allegory, terms 'the renunciation of the idea of harmonious totality' (*AP* 330), even as 'the infirmity and decrepitude of a great city' (*AP* 332) is articulated apophatically through the transitory motion of the city's remainders.

From place to subject, such traces and their motions discompose and exceed both the stability of urban identity and the identities of, primarily, the city's female inhabitants, offering a ghostly telegraphy of endlessly circulating and punctuating countersignatures to the principal figure that is the city always already haunted by such analogous work. Bowen's ruinous inscription of London thus exemplifies one of the ways in which cities and their subjects may enact singular, reciprocal moments of affiliation that endlessly fold, unfold, and refold. Such motion is described in part by Elizabeth Grosz: '[c]ities have always represented and projected images and fantasies of bodies, whether individual, collective, or political. In this sense, the city can be seen as a (collective) body-prosthesis or boundary that enframes, protects, and houses while at the same time taking its own forms and functions from the (imaginary) bodies it constitutes'; there is thus what Grosz describes as 'a relation of both productive constraint and inherent unpredictability'.[5] Constituted through the shifting and kaleidoscopic impressions that are indelibly imprinted by the city, the Londoner's identity is, therefore, at best provisional, precarious, even in those very instances and places when it is perceived or experienced most intensely. Bowen's London thus resonates through the contours of its identity, and those of the women and men who dwell there, through a simultaneous, if paradoxical, fragility *and* intensity.

That London for Bowen is 'psychic' suggests a greater emphasis on the imaginary and phantastic or phantasmatic, on the phenomenological also, rather than on the corporeal. That the city is conceptualized in this manner intimates that its representations amount to the constellated interactions of, and between, so many phantasms, projections of or upon the imagination. I write 'of *or* upon' because there is readable a seemingly endless semi-fluidity, a continuous making and unmaking, the origins of which are indecipherable, strictly speaking, either inside or outside any of Bowen's female subjects. The haunting traces of London cross and recross any discernible psychic boundaries. Bowen's writing of the city is a phantasmagoric work, where its subjects are interpellated by its haunting call, even while their apperceptions of the city mediate the flow of urban sensibility through its more concrete coordinates. This is captured in a moving image from *The Heat of the Day*: 'most of all the dead . . . made their anonymous presence – not as today's dead but as yesterday's living – felt through London. Uncounted, they continued to move in shoals through the city day, pervading everything to be seen or heard or felt . . . The wall between the living and the living became less solid as the wall between the living and the dead thinned. In that September transparency people became transparent . . .' (*HD* 91, 92). The revenance of 'yesterday's living' dissolves boundaries that are both psychic and material, while invoking and issuing a call from the otherwise unimaginable totality of London's historicity as network of material and immaterial traces. The phantom 'signature' produced by mnemonic inscription of the city caused by the effects of bombing during the autumn of 1940 figures a singular violent image for all the city's dead. However, this is not to suggest that London is merely, in any simple fashion, *just* immaterial or unreal, or that the work of haunting is merely a metaphor for capturing a sense of the city at war. Bowen is also intimately attentive to the material spaces, the structures and absences (whether human or built), as well as to the rhythms of the city. For example, a window is noticed by its 'non-existence' (*HD* 93). She traces these through the often metonymic and synecdochic implied relationships between architectural details, topographical locations, what was once to be encountered and which is no longer there, and the sense of the city as a phantom whole. She responds to the various conjunctions and disjunctions of London, often as, by occasion, these chance to come into contact, and interact, with one another.

It is frequently the case, furthermore, that Bowen writes the city, if not as being anthropomorphized, then, at least, as being semi-organic; though not human, it has signs of life and also afterlife, of reality and unreality. Indeed, it is very much the incompleteness of the sense of anthropomorphization that lends to Bowen's writing an often uncanny resonance, as though London is itself the ghost of something neither quite alive nor dead, as well as being a city of ghosts. As evidence of this, we witness 'the unstopping phantasmagoric streaming of lorries, buses, vans, drays, taxis', which 'set[s] up an overpowering sense of London's organic power' (*HD* 91): phantasmic and organic, a city written by spectral flow, and also, as a result of this circulation within its body, projected as some immense inhuman entity. Neither living nor deceased entirely, London appears, after a fashion, as both unnatural, moving between states of identity, and as a naturally occurring phenomenon in Bowen's writing, inflected as it is so repeatedly by the weather, by plant life, and by temporal movements beyond those of clock time. Thus, the city is often comprehended through what inevitably takes place according to the motion of seasons in conjunction with locale. Bowen's writing therefore exemplifies the point made by Hubert Damisch, that cities, 'in the course of their uncontrolled development, can begin to resemble something natural'.[6] However, what is 'unnatural' or, perhaps more properly speaking, unhomely or uncanny, in Bowen's London, is the extent to which fragments of the 'natural' so insistently impose themselves in the images of the most 'built' areas. (Perhaps it is worth considering, albeit in passing, that in Bowen's writing 'nature' is merely a potent metaphor – or even a monstrous example of catachresis – for the inhuman, psychic London's unconscious articulation of an irresistible and irrecuperable alterity.) Finally, the other aspect of Bowen's text to which I wish to direct the reader's attention in this chapter is the way in which Bowen's urban text mobilizes a performative relation between writing and the city, which in part has been illustrated already. The phantomatic condition of London admits to its *graphic* state. For the author, the city just is the performative motion of an ongoing writing, where that graphic encryption is 'never finished, never complete', to borrow Damisch's auto-performative phrase (*SNC* 34), but which comes to be read as rein-scribing the violence of its writing through the focus afforded by the catastrophe and event of war.

IV

The principal short story with which this chapter is concerned is 'Ann Lee's' (*CS* 103–11), the story of a visit by two women, Mrs Dick Logan and Miss Ames, to a hat shop, the name of which is also the title of the story. We should linger around particular details of this, the earliest of Bowen's stories, first published in 1924; the act of writing London so far sketched in this chapter is readable through this short story as being wholly engaged, and is witnessed in even the briefest of extracts from this tale. The narrative of the story is as follows: during the visit of Miss Ames and Mrs Logan to Ann Lee's, a man enters, a Mr Richardson, who insists upon an appointment apparently previously made with Ann Lee. A strange, implicit violence fills the shop. Purchasing hats, Mrs Logan and Miss Ames leave, in search of a taxi in the foggy twilight, only to encounter the man from the shop as he passes them at the close of the story. Whatever had taken place remains unexplained. However, as Bowen herself puts it of another scene, from *The Heat of the Day*, '[i]n fact, the scene at this day and hour could not have been more perfectly set for violence . . .' (*HD* 23). Our attention is drawn, therefore, to a setting haunted by a possibility that is never brought into being, but which effects an uncanny oscillation within the given reality. Such a gesture of immanence speaks to what may be read as always already traced in the chance events of the city, awaiting only the appropriate occasion.

Such apprehension is encrypted by Bowen in specific ways having to do with the related information concerning location and the represen-tation of the internal and external particulars of shops and houses. We are told of the hat shop that:

Ann Lee's occupied a single frontage in one of the dimmer and more silent streets of south-west London. Grey-painted woodwork framed a window over which her legend was inscribed in far-apart black letters: 'ANN LEE – HATS.' In the window there were always just two hats . . . a black curtain with a violet border hung behind to make a background for the hats. In the two upper storeys, perhaps, Ann Lee lived mysteriously, but this no known customer had ever inquired, and the black gauze curtains were impenetrable from without. (*CS* 103)

There is about this passage, which opens the short story, a motion between precision and imprecision, an attention to minimal factual detail on the one hand, and a more or less tacit admission, on the other, that while the facts may be given, while detail may serve a certain mimetic project up to a limit, there is that about the shop, its owner, and its location, which is not merely imprecise, but unknowable. One is told of the single frontage, the hats and their unchanging number, the shop's legend and its location, the woodwork of the window painted grey, the black, violet-bordered curtains; the reader is also offered an implied vertical perspective indicating the three storeys of the building. Precise architectural information is presented, signs are reproduced (even though they make explicit no more than is already inferred, a certain occlusion, perhaps, being effected through presentation), and the assertion that 'there were always just two hats' makes available a certain doxical history attesting to constancy, if not permanence. However, there are also other elements in the opening lines that function contrapuntally. There is the absence of precise location, the impenetrability of the curtains, and, of course, the enigma concerning Ann Lee. That which is enigmatic is doubled. It is not only that no one knows whether the proprietor lives above her shop; no one has inquired, at least no one who is known to have been a customer. Ann Lee's home is the subject of undecidable, irreducible conjecture. What is all the stranger, and imperceptibly resistant for this reason, is the adverbial 'mysteriously'. Does it refer to the insoluble mystery of where Ann Lee lives, or to a supposition, also to be read, that Ann Lee lives *mysteriously*? Bowen's word is arguably performative here, for it enacts its own condition, remaining undecidable in powerfully affirmative manner and emptying the certainty of all constative function from itself in the process.

Knowledge and non-knowledge hold sway, apparently equally. Yet, more than two terms for different epistemological orientations in dialec-

tical relationship to each other in this passage, they are intimately intertwined, each as the ghostly apparition emanating from within the other,
and as the other of the other. Such an abyssal disfiguration is redoubled
further in the passage by the structurally disjointing – architextural –
tracing of frames, a tracing which does service as a performative framing
in its own right: there is the window, the border of the curtains, the
curtains themselves as frame for the hats (which are, of course, within
the frame of the window). As iterable form (frame), colour (black), and
item – is it not suggested that there is the curtain framed by the window
framing, in turn, the hats, and also the impenetrable drapes of the
windows belonging to the upper two storeys? – reduplicate, so any certainty that the facts might present or, more accurately, re-present is registered in the process of failing. Even the proper name is reiterated
between different locations, and with different purposes: for there is the
title of the story, the shop, for which the name acts as synecdoche, the
sign, naming shop and proprietor (and story), and then Ann Lee herself,
the last of the Ann Lee's to appear in the text, the one who names the
shop and for whom the shop – and, again, the story – are named. The
act of reading reinscribes framing as the architectural projection serving,
opening onto, undecidability, in a disruptive, unhinged manner. There
is thus what Avital Ronell calls a 'finity of knowing',[7] a limit which is
not the end, not some articulation of closure, but only the place of
passage, the structural location across which one moves, and is opened
onto a dim apperception of what remains undecidable.

   Which leads me back to the question of location and the very first
sentence of the story, to the vagueness announced both in and as 'one
of the dimmer and more silent streets of south-west London', streets
that are also referred to as 'those miserable back streets' (*CS* 105), where
the events take place on 'an afternoon in January' (*CS* 103). It is at the
suggestion of Miss Ames that she and her friend go to the hat shop.
However, while the reader has already been presented with the image
of the shop, the narrative folds back on itself, to describe how, en route
to Ann Lee's 'Miss Ames . . . hesitated beneath the names at the street
corner, wrinkled up her brows and said she hadn't remembered that
Ann Lee's was so far from Sloane Square Station' (*CS* 103). Once more,
the precision of location and the implied information of street names
is undermined as the shop evades momentarily the two women. The
effect is all the more pointed for its being related to the failure of
memory, so that, despite place names, the map of the city becomes
blurred. Around, and emerging from within, both mimetic determination and mapping, Bowen's prose – the cadences of which might be

defined as *rubato* – offers a sense of somewhat uncanny slippage in the city, a material *dérive*. Bowen's writing of London is marked by 'constant currents, fixed points, and eddies' belonging to what Guy Debord termed in 1956, 'the psychogeographical relief'[8] of the city. What is particularly engaging about 'Ann Lee's' is that the drift takes place materially in the agency of the letter, marking the text prior to any phenomenal perception on the part of any characters. Indeed, the fact that Miss Ames does not remember the shop having been so far from Sloane Street Station, the fact that the city appears to have shifted around her, is, I would argue, indicative of this pre-phenomenal materiality. Thus, we come to read that London is not comprehended through a conscious act of navigation or walking. Writing the city just is one aspect of the city, rather than being a representation of it: the writing performs this material mapping, a cartography of urban contours, echoing with their own ebb and flow.

Bowen is not only a writer of externals, however. She has occasion to cross thresholds so as to offer the reader internal spaces, the coordinates and accents of which counterpoint the streets. It is remarked of Miss Ames and Mrs Logan, when they enter the hat shop:

> their first sensation was of pleasure as they pushed open the curtained door and felt the warm air of the shop vibrate against their faces. An electric fire was reflected in the crimson patch upon the lustrous pile of the black carpet. There were two chairs, two mirrors, a divan and a curtain over an expectant archway. No hats were visible. (*CS* 103)

To recall and rework a remark of Paul Klee's on the function of art, Bowen's writing does not so much represent the visible, as it makes it appear. It is, therefore, discernible neither as solely constative nor mimetic but, instead, as materially performative and phenomenologically phantasmatic. As with the external description of the shop, the internal space is articulated as hovering between discernible element, that which is taken as materially *there*, and the material registration of immaterial impression. This modality, which I would argue is dominant throughout, and essential to, any figuring or mapping of London in Elizabeth Bowen's fiction, is akin to Peter Schwenger's commentary on the readerly visualization of fictional worlds as being determined by 'a sense of . . . play, of figure and ground flickering in and out of each other'.[9] In the context of this reading of 'Ann Lee', 'figure' and 'ground' might be replaced with 'phantasm' and 'reality'. Interweaving the objective reality of furnishings and architectural detail with sensory experience, the passage just quoted establishes a phenomenal perception apparently shared by the two women. Sensation, vibration, reflection, warmth, pleasure, and the radiance of the carpet's pile, are the coordinates that map what Maurice Merleau-Ponty calls the 'subject of perception', and we comprehend from this citation how the 'perceiving subject is the *place*'[10] (emphasis added) where the world is made visible. However, the perceiving subject is neither Mrs Logan nor Miss Ames, nor, indeed, both women conjointly, but the reader. The act of reading stands in for the subjective place where – to use an admittedly awkward phrase – place takes place performatively. Thus the city and consciousness of the city are traced as inseparable in Bowen, whether by the city one refers to representations of streets, details of the weather, of a location or of architectural features, or whether one is speaking of the inner spaces of buildings on which Bowen lingers, such as in the present example. Bowen's act of urban inscription acknowledges how 'sensation is a reconstitution', to cite Merleau-Ponty once more (*PP* 215), but it is a reconstitution that leads us to comprehend what Ernst Bloch has called 'the spectral and still ineffable nature of consciousness or interiorisation'.[11] Bowen's haunted city consciousness, incapable of marking any distance between experience and memory, announces the extent to which it is spectral because, 'since sensation is a reconstitution, it presupposes in me sediments left behind by some previous constitution' (*PP* 215).

The interior of the hat shop appears, then, as more than mere description. Indeed, its appearance is also an instance of the return of those sedimented sensory traces, and it is in this direct appeal, an appeal that is also an apparition, which marks place as uncanny. Whether this is fictional or not, whether we know or have visited this place or not, we find ourselves addressed by what seems strangely familiar. Elsewhere, Bowen utilizes season, month, weather to produce this estranging relationship, a sensation of always-haunted dwelling. Wherever we are in Bowen's London, whether in a house we have never had occasion to enter, in Regent's Park, responding momentarily to the sound of traffic, or turning into a side-street in St John's Wood, writing as reconstitution imposes a disturbing recognition, and a memory of the city that was never ours. And, to borrow a formula for acknowledging the undecidable from Merleau-Ponty, it is impossible to say, finally, whether it is either London or the process of writing the city, whether it is 'the look or . . . the things' (that is to say the processes of writing/reading or the objects themselves),[12] which generate the impression of the haunting, and haunted, awareness. For what both the representations of the interior and the exterior of Ann Lee's hat shop effect is the tracing of an intimate proximity, an enfolding, between subject and setting, between the phantasm and the real. The visible and the invisible are not autonomous, separable, or dialectical terms for Bowen. Rather, the visible is what comes to appear from within the invisible, as an oscillation across, and also suspended at, a threshold.

One singular manifestation of traversal and suspension is caught in the interior description of Ann Lee's by the fleeting marking of the passage with colours, the crimson and black. Bare reference to colour (violet, grey, black) has already been made in the representation of the shop-front. Serving as, at once, the most intangible manifestations of the clearly visible – one can see colour but not hold it or touch it *as such* – and, simultaneously, as the most materially objective elements – again, one can see colours directly but not warmth or sensation – belonging to the immaterial sensory world of the shop's interior, the colours are located at a dual threshold or, more precisely, in between two thresholds: between the material and the phenomenal, between the real and the phantasmic, and between the visible and the invisible. More than merely located, the colours resonate, resulting from and causing other oscillations. It will be noticed that the crimson is already a reflexion, the visible sign of invisible heat electrically produced and displaced, represented indirectly, away from the bars of the electric fire.[13] (It should be remarked in passing that, in reading of internal spaces in Bowen's narratives, the reader will often have her attention drawn momentarily, perhaps interruptively, to the presence of inanimate technology such as electric or gas fires, telephones, and clocks, of which more below.) Through that reflexion, the reading subject is positioned so as to reflect on what comes into view as the part of the process of reflexion: the otherwise invisible lustrous condition of the black carpet, the colour of which materializes in contrast to its reflexiveness. Bowen's trope of reflexion in this passage is apposite in a number of ways, as a momentary glance at the *Oxford English Dictionary* should serve to show: meaning, of course, the process of throwing back light or heat, there is also a more obscure sense, that being a reflexive influence on the mind, while the etymology of the word signifies a bending or folding back. In a sense, this is precisely what the effect of colour makes possible, a folding or a bending back onto both the visible and the invisible. More than this, in this particular instance, I would argue, there is also a folding and refolding, a reflexion between the scene and the reading subject. Thus, Bowen's application of colour figures the very work of writing itself and is, here, in the signs 'crimson' and 'black' not mimetic. Marking the page, colour moves back and forth between the 'internal' space of the narrative and the 'external' location of the reader, erasing in the process any delimitable location. Entertaining, as Paul de Man puts it, 'no notion of reference or semiosis' as such (*AI* 128) – *we* impose the association between 'crimson' and 'warmth'[14] – colour is one singular example of the elements, the marks that compose materiality of Bowen's city-text. Yet, to stress the point once more, the city's materiality is uncanny, and also spectral; to employ a phrase used elsewhere in this volume, it is a 'materiality without materialism and even perhaps without matter' (TR 281), as psychic London and its psychogeographic coordinates persist for the author in – perhaps only *as* – a kind of afterlife (recall the interior from *The Heat of the Day*). To borrow from T. J. Clark's assessment of Cézanne, Bowen's urban project 'stakes everything on the possibility of re-creating the structure of experience out of that experience's units . . . But the very radicality of the project . . . [is registered in the way that] it fetishizes the singular, it discovers the singular as exactly *not* the form of "experience". It shows us a way of world-making in which the very idea of a "world" . . . is not drawn from some . . . "out-there," and therefore (potentially) "in-here"'.[15] And it is the phantom passage between the 'out-there' and the 'in-here' that is always at work everywhere in Bowen's text, and in her London also.

The fetishization of the singular threatens to engulf, as is attested, I believe, by the manner in which this analysis has found itself caught up in closer and closer attention to ever-smaller details, particularly around the signs of the liminal, the marginal, and other examples of thresholds. An abyssal opening takes place, whereby (to recall a remark of Benjamin's to which I allude elsewhere in this volume) 'the sense of "the abyssal" is to be defined as "meaning" [and] such a sense is always allegorical' (*AP* 271). And, it must be added, analogical also, where the movement of reading proceeds from unit to unit in a process suggesting the possibility of a nanotextual abyss. I find myself arrested by the mechanisms of Bowen's 'representation', even as its operation intensifies if not accelerates. Indeed, it is the case that narrative representation is readable as arresting itself through its own intensity and density, as interrupting or calling a momentary halt to – and breaking with – the process of becoming that 'appears' or becomes visible in any act of representation. In some disquieting quasi-synaesthesic moment, the names of colours behave as though they are purely figural, as though they are caesuras. Yet, if the colours can be read in such a performative manner, they also erase simultaneously the very threshold that demarcates discernible location, as I have already suggested; thus one is faced with the experience of the aporetic. For, while it may be that 'all representation is narrative by nature', as Louis Marin has it,[16] Elizabeth Bowen reveals that any narrative representation supposedly grounded in the comforting reassurances of mimesis will always, in its nervous attempt to grasp what cannot be re-presented as a presence, go too far, and so reveal that it can never go far enough, exhausting itself in the process. There is perhaps a tacit acknowledgement of this exhaustion in the matter-of-fact enumeration, following the play of reflexion, of 'two chairs, two mirrors, a divan and a curtain', culminating in that 'expectant archway'. The world seems reduced to a brute ontic inventory, relieved only in the apparently anthropomorphized architectural detail.

I say *seems* with good reason, for it is very much the case that there takes place here a figural doubling and division of simulacra from within any supposed representational stability, as can be read in the fact that there are *two* chairs, *two* mirrors. This doubling of objects echoes that of the hats seen in the window, while the single curtain adds to the curtains already seen from outside. It might also be suggested that the reflective capability of the mirrors hints at the abyssal framing already commented on with regard to the shop-front. Thus, again, there is both a figural traversal and momentary suspension between exterior to interior, which is also caught in the structure of the archway. Such an architectural feature always draws attention to its status as boundary, to the possibility of its being crossed and its always remaining to be crossed. This is further reduplicated when Lulu Logan and Letty Ames are interrupted in the process of trying on hats: 'The outer door was open and a man was standing on the threshold, blatant in the light against the foggy dusk behind him' (*CS* 106). In this violent moment, the internal and external worlds are no longer separated absolutely. For Bowen, London at large will always find a way into the city's interiors, commercial or domestic. Interruption takes place, furthermore, both within the narrative and *in* the narrative for the reader, the caesura of the entrance effectively erasing the distinction between locations just made. In the opening of the door, the instance of the framed suspension of passage – and passage suspending narrative – takes place, taking place every time it is read, though never for a first time, as the performative force of language erupts from within the narrative description of events. This suspended transition or, perhaps, transitive suspension between one state and other, is also caught, on the one hand, by the acknowledgement of the shop's artificial illumination – revealed indirectly through the 'blatant' revelation of the anonymous figure – and, on the other, by the natural passage (dusk) between day and night, the former implying visibility, while the latter doubles the partial obscurity of the visible, through the figure of the fog, a figure which paradoxically makes clear the very fact that we can see that we cannot see.

Which brings me to the final passage from 'Ann Lee's' bearing directly on Bowen's London and the inscription of that city:

> There were no taxis where they [Mrs Logan and Miss Ames] had been promised to find them, and the two walked on in the direction of Sloane Street through the thickening fog . . . When they came to the third corner they once more hesitated, and again lamented the non-appearance of a taxi. Down as much of the two streets as was visible, small shop-windows threw out squares of light on to the fog. Was there, behind all these windows, some one waiting, as indifferent as a magnet, for one to come in? . . . As they stood on the kerbstone, recoiling not without complaints from the unkindness of the weather, they heard rapid steps approaching them, metallic on the pavement, in little uneven spurts of speed. Somebody, half blinded by the fog, in flight from somebody else. They said nothing to each other, but held their breaths, mute with a common expectancy.
>
> A square man, sunk deep in an overcoat, scudded across their patch of visibility. By putting out a hand they could have touched him. He went by them blindly; his breath sobbed and panted. It was by his breath that they knew how terrible it had been – terrible.
>
> Passing them quite blindly, he stabbed his way on into the fog.
> (CS 111)

On a first reading, there is little enough, it might be said, about this extract that would justify reading it as being more concerned with London than with the story's characters and narrative climax. However, to step back from reading the city as merely stage-setting or background here, and to attempt to disengage from a reading that insists on the signs as having a primarily mimetic function, there is to be distinguished a materiality of the letter in the shaping of this climactic narrative moment, which is dependent on the coincidence between the elements of the urban landscape, the time of day, and the weather, typical of Bowen's comprehension of what can happen in London in that combination of events we name coincidence. Such coincidences are in fact composed of a topography of conjunctions, the contours of which echo beyond the immediate narrative event to intimate that which can take place at any time in the city in innumerable ways. This is, furthermore, allied to '[t]he suspensive modality of the possible',[17] which, articulated in this instance as a rhetorical hesitation in the middle of the passage, also needs to be addressed. Bowen's sudden question – 'Was there, behind all these windows, some one waiting, as indifferent as a magnet, for one to come in?' – interrupts the singularity of the narrative through positing the possibility of countless other singularities. Each window, suggestive of an anonymous figure, frames the possibility of other narrative trajectories. Windows both punctuate and frame; while they are instances of images within the narrative, they also offer the possibility of a snapshot or vignette of the other; they re-mark themselves as thresholds awaiting traversal, an irreversible movement that disrupts the present narrative within which they are embedded. Synecdoche for architecture and image, then, as well as for individual buildings and lives, for myriad shops, homes, the innumerable human encounters therein as a result of points of intersection and the passage across thresholds, the windows suspend the narrative in a moment of time overflowing with the immanence of mathematical sublimity. This is only one example, however. The suspensive modality of the possible erupts and interrupts in countless ways in Bowen's comprehension of London but is not merely a rhetorical strategy. Rather, it should be apprehended as a response on Bowen's part, a response inscribed as a tropic mechanism, to that which the city writes as its very own possibility.

Then of course, we notice that there is discernible the drift once again, between what might or might not be seen, between the visible and invisible – figured in 'Ann Lee's' conclusion by the 'visible', 'visibility', and 'blindly' – and between what can be known and what remains beyond the realms of perception and understanding. Despite, or perhaps because of, the partial blindness accompanying the fog, there is a sense of 'surface geometry' to this passage, of moments of stasis and movement across planes, and, equally, as a result of this purblind activity, chance intersections, suddenly vectored events immanent with violence and other narratives. This is mapped serially through various reiterated figures and tropes: there is the fog, several times; it is as if a single reference to the fog is insufficient, intensification through repetition is required in order for there to take place the atmospheric obfuscation indicated by the adjectival qualification of the fog's first mention. Putting this in another manner: the reader can only comprehend the extent to which fog prevents one from seeing; by being able to see clearly, as it were, the effect of limited visibility through serial references concerning – and performing – the thickening of the fog. There are other instances of reiteration: there are taxis or, more precisely, their absence; there are negations (taxis are not there, twice); there is blindness, visibility, 'somebody' or 'some one' appears repeatedly, every anonymous figure being one other in a potentially infinite series or, at least, every other invisible figure in London at any given moment; and then there is the repeated troping of reiteration itself ('once more', 'again'). There is also the work of a series of the most minimal of locations, partial forms or structures, generated out of, and in turn marking, the act of walking. Such movement both articulates and propels the narrative, moving between narration and that which is narrated, between memory and action. Thus there is traced the unreadable map of the city hidden in fog. We see this in the movement of the two women towards the unspecified place where they have been promised they would find taxis but do not. The minimal locations or forms become listed as punctuation of their walk: the kerbstone, the 'third corner', shop windows observed along however much of the streets as can be seen in the fog from the corner, and the one named referent, Sloane Street, for which the women are heading.

The urban space is traced by a complex of rhythms – the various instances of punctuating iterability are, themselves, rhythmic – belonging to both narrative and text, of which the act of walking and the act of writing as memory of the paths taken in walking are merely the most obvious. There is registered both the urban space and the time it takes to move through that space when slowed by limited visibility, which motion is thereby also made uneven, a series of related stops and starts. Beginning with that unspecified location, the only coordinate of which is the absence of taxis, 'they walked on'; we are told that 'they once more hesitated', then, 'they stood on the kerbstone', 'they heard rapid steps approaching them'. The steps belong to somebody 'in flight', a figure 'scuds', moves past the two women 'across their patch of visibility', and, in passing, moves in a stabbing motion 'into the fog' to disappear from sight. The women's halting progression – even breathing is brought temporarily to a standstill – is counterpointed by the velocity of the 'square man' (whose own sobbing, panting breath offers rhythmic response).

Passage thus takes place, at different, differing, discontinuous, yet related velocities and in different directions, both in and through this area of London and across the final lines of the story. In lieu of any possibility of representation, given the fact that little can be seen in the fog, the lines once more assume a performative effect, as the relational polyrhythmic pulsation *just is* this figuring of London, responding to and shaped out of the city's psychic condition or what might also be termed, in the words of Gilles Deleuze, its 'pure virtuality'.[18] The city is indirectly received through the resonance of this virtuality, where 'the virtual image . . . is not a psychological state or a consciousness; it exists outside of consciousness, in time'; hence, the processes that collapse the distance between the urban world – which, though never there as such, performs in revenant fashion, as its patterns and flows return constantly in excess of the particulars of any story – and the reader.

V

> The aesthetic is nothing but a return to images that will allow nothing to take their place; the aesthetic is nothing but an attempt to disguise and glorify the enforced return.
>
> Elizabeth Bowen

Whatever goes by the name of London can only be approached if one understands that name as an 'identity', which is mobilized by what Andrew Bennett and Nicholas Royle describe as 'the necessary logic of multiplicity', and which in turn therefore comes to be recognized as a 'fictive or phantasmagoric conglomeration, a self already subject to a dynamically proliferating logic of foreignness and fictionality' (Grosz *AO* 156). Such a proliferating logic must, equally necessarily, be auto(re)generative, informed by excess and loss, overflow and absence, whereby 'any notion of order, system, community, knowledge and control . . . entails a notion of excess, expenditure and loss' (Grosz *AO* 156). Structured by alterity and revenance, Bowen's city-text reiterates its traces everywhere in a manner that is disruptive, hence the impression, already discussed, on narrative of polyrhythmic cadences and plenitude that never settle into a fixed or fixable representation of the city. Rather, they remain at work in that figure of city space, described by Henri Lefebvre in his 'rhythmanalysis' as an 'open totality',[19] through the material traces of what Bowen calls, above, the 'enforced return'.[20] These two figures – open totality and enforced return – provide with congruent felicity possible names for the peculiarly disconcerting force that arrives through the images of the revenance of the city's dead and the phantasmagoria of the city's traffic. Strangely, there is an uncomfortably uncanny consonance in these image events; for both figures are those of *poiesis* and *tekhne*, both are acts of making as apparition, of

making appear. And what appears through them is of course the amaterial articulation of London; and this is a London which is hauntingly
inhuman, but nonetheless subject to that mnemotechnic inscription
whereby stable identity is erased through passage and transport,
whether temporal or spatial, whether through return or circulation.

What returns and circulates is clearly never present as such; it is suggestive, however, of an excessive disturbance in the field of vision, a
moment in the present of the narrative where that present, where the
real implied in representation, is unsettled from within, through the act
on Bowen's part of bearing witness to the phantoms, and also through
memory's involuntary revenance. At the same time, the present is
unveiled, through that return, as itself nothing other than an image
belonging to the 'phantasmagoric conglomeration', so that the city is
perceived as a constellated series of virtual and associative images. There
is thus generated a strange suspensive density to the city (already
acknowledged), as is seen in the following spectral scenario from 'In the
Square' (*CS* 609–15):

> At about nine o'clock on this hot bright July evening the square
> looked mysterious: it was completely empty, and a whitish reflection,
> ghost of the glare of midday, came from the pale-coloured façades
> on its four sides and seemed to brim it up to the top. The grass was
> parched in the middle; its shaved surface was paid for by people who
> had gone. The sun, now too low to enter normally, was able to enter
> brilliantly at a point where three of the houses had been bombed
> away; two or three of the may trees, dark with summer, caught on
> their tops the illicit gold. Each side of the breach, exposed wallpa-
> pers were exaggerated into viridians, yellows and corals that they had
> probably never been. Elsewhere, the painted front doors under the
> balconies and at the tops of steps not whitened for some time stood
> out in the deadness of colour with light off it. Most of the glassless
> windows were shuttered or boarded up, but some framed hollow
> inside dark.
>
> The extinct scene had the appearance of belonging to some ages
> ago. Time having only been thrust forward for reasons that could no
> longer affect the square, this still was a virtual eight o'clock. One taxi
> did now enter at the north side and cruise round the polish to a
> house in a corner: a man got out and paid his fare . . . In spite of the
> dazzling breach, the square's acoustics had altered very little: in the
> confined sound of his taxi driving away there was nothing to tell him
> he had not arrived to dinner as on many summer evenings before

... Some windows of this house were not shuttered, though they were semi-blinded by oiled stuff behind which the curtains dimly hung: these windows fixed on the outdoors their tenacious look; some of the sashes were pushed right up, to draw this singular summer evening – parched, freshening, and a little acrid with ruins – into the rooms where people lived. (*CS* 609)

A narrative reflecting in its details the effects of the Blitz, the opening lines of the short story unfold in a manner intimating both excess and loss; in doing so, they eerily exceed their own descriptive processes through a ghostly doubling of the scene, from within itself and yet as other than itself. Time is already doubled at the very beginning of the story, the light of the late evening being a spectral manifestation of its daytime counterpart. This reflexion of an other moment in time, of this other instance of illumination returning *in*, *through*, and *as* only that reflexion – reflexion of reflexion – causes the presentation of the present to quiver in an abyssal solicitation of the implied architectural solidity of the square, which becomes filled to the point of overflowing in an excessive instant paradoxically suggestive of both suspension and motion. Despite the fact that the scene belongs to a 'present' after bombing, a moment acknowledged with the apparent precision of clock time, and the London square can only appear as it does as a result of this technological assurance, the beginning of the second paragraph suggests another scene, the double of that being witnessed, and having returned from some unlocatable past. There is yet another temporal rift opened. Time is 'thrust forward' – by what? one is tempted to ask, and why this disturbing quasi-personification of the temporal, suggestive of unwillingness? – while the square, out of joint with time, persists, and can only be experienced in a virtual instant. We thus read (in) a moment of stasis, suspended animation troubled by prosopopoeia, amounting perhaps to a trembling that shatters the frame of reference in its very representation, and so brings to light that ghostly force described by Andrew Bennett and Nicholas Royle as the simultaneous 'concatenation of events [that] is also, at the same time, determined by convulsions of reading. A dissolution: mobile, fluid and uncontainably still, uncontainable still' (*EBDN* 157).

Other tropes are put to work in the service of the spectral energy. The two paragraphs are inflected repeatedly by loss, negation, and absence: the square is 'empty', the grass is kept cut, paid for by 'people who had gone', 'houses had been bombed away', there is a 'breach', which reiterates itself as a 'dazzling breach' (as if reiteration of absence amplifies light); wallpaper colours are exaggerated into hues 'they had probably never been', steps are seen 'not whitened for some time', windows are 'glassless', some are not 'shuttered'. The sheer intensity through accretion of that which is not there is singularly palpable. One experiences absence and loss as a reading of the urban space, but one also simultaneously reads that space as their experience. The force and effect of spectral accumulation might best be described as phantom-picturesque, a wavering, perhaps utopic modality haunting the interstices between the picturesque proper and the sublime, in which the play of light and colour only add to the shimmering, hallucinatory impression of this suspended moment in time where that which is not returns insistently and unendingly to haunt that which is. (Without seeking to rush to any systematization of the ghostly effect, to this quasi-modality of the phantom-picturesque one might ascribe the effects of weather and season in Bowen's London.) The resonance of the unseen calls the act of representation to bear witness, to act as a medium, and thereby, to make the point again, to open the present from within itself to its other, every successive temporal moment doubling and dividing, coinciding with itself. The actual image is thus ghosted – and exceeded – by its virtual image, the immediate present of the narrative ghost-written by the traces of its past, and creating in this way a revenant circuitry that attests to the uncanny virtuality of any narrative.[21]

Structural totality, temporal order, and architectural form are thus disordered, the square itself broken into and then replayed through the various figures of framing that reduplicate abyssally a form of replay and reflexive repetition, causing the reader to pause at the following reflexion: 'This had been the room of a hostess; the replica of so many others that you could not count' (*CS* 610). The singular image becomes, once more, the occasion for that 'suspensive modality' of iterable sublimity which has been seen at work in 'Ann Lee's', as too have framing and the dismantling of the frame, which are to be noted here in windows, shutters, blinds, doors, balconies, corners, steps, and other architectural and structural features. It is important to note, then, that, while 'In the Square' clearly is a narrative generated by the war, the ways in which Bowen writes London relies less on an immediate historical context – though the war is, of course, undeniably significant in the shaping of narrative concerns in stories such as 'In the Square' and 'Careless Talk', and in novels such as *The Heat of the Day* – than on the various possibilities or, to use her word, the 'eventfulness', that writing London animates. War intensifies and amplifies the effects – in 'The Demon Lover' (*CS* 661–6) 'silence' is 'intense'; it is 'one of those creeks of London silence exaggerated this summer by the damage of war' (*CS* 666) – already underway in Bowen's writing. However, the 'arrested violence'[22] of exposed wallpapers is only different in degree rather than in kind to that of the intrusion into the hat shop; its singular manifestations belong to the encrypted tropology by which the city is traced. To take another encrypted example of that which serves as a coordinate in the psychic mapping of London, we should turn to the trope of silence, encountered twice in the citation from 'The Demon Lover', and another figure intensified through the experience of war but belonging generally to Bowen's London. The figure of silence occupies a small but significant place in the city-text, occurring in both *The Death of the Heart* and *The Heat of the Day* also, and marked by the city in particular ways, as both the citation from 'The Demon Lover' and the following, from *The Death of the Heart*, show: 'The silence of a shut park does not sound like country silence: it is tense and confined' (*DH* 73). As already witnessed in the discussion of silence in *The Heat of the Day* at the beginning of this chapter, London silence, like its darkness, is idiomatic, singular (*DH* 230). It is also rhythmic, and punctuates experience. In *The Death of the Heart*, in Regent's Park, Anna and Portia, though not together, hear the same brief pulses of silence at the same time: 'They heard silence, then horns, cries, an oar on the lake, silence striking again, the thrush fluting so beautifully' (*DH* 123–4). The experience of London is traced in its mingled taxonomy of sounds and absences of sound. In *The Heat of the Day*, '[s]ilence mounted the stairs, to enter her [Stella's] flat through the windows from the deserted street' (*HD* 23). Crossing thresholds, silence is precisely that spectral figure of the city, dissolving boundaries, yet moving between and thereby connecting the different spaces of London as one of its countless signatures.

Signatures of the city can also arrive as dates. Such punctuating marks appear within narrative, and seem to belong to a wholly reasonable device in the service of representational verisimilitude. Yet, their arrival also suspends particular narratives, giving place to the psychic pause and the contrapuntal uncanny motion that emerges from within, thereby fragmenting the mimetic whole. In 'Ann Lee's', it was 'an afternoon in January', while in 'In the Square' it is 'about about nine o'clock on this hot bright July evening'. 'Recent Photograph' begins: 'The streets were silver in the sunshine; London in the April morning glowed like a pearl' (*CS* 211–20; 211), a line in which the formal elements of alliteration and sibilance, assonance and simile mark representation materially, as though prose itself were etched, imprinted as in a gelatin print, such as that alluded to in the title. In 'The Demon Lover', 'it was late August; it had been a steamy, showery day: at the moment the trees down the pavement glittered in an escape of humid yellow afternoon sun. Against the next batch of clouds, already piling up ink-dark, broken chimneys and parapets stood out' (*CS* 661). In 'Tears, Idle Tears', 'May sun spattered gold through the breezy trees; the tulips though falling open were still gay; three girls in a long boat shot out under the bridge' (*CS* 481–7; 481); and, in 'No. 16', 'The thaw had left London glistening, supine, sunny. From the gardens, the snow, swept up into mounds, had not gone yet. Jane had come on buses from Battersea Park; she was not a Londoner . . . Everything, in this maze of trees and doorways . . . gave her its message or mystery' (*CS* 547–54; 548). And as a final example, *The Death of the Heart* addresses a London winter and spring. We read at the beginning of the novel: 'That morning's ice, no more than a brittle film, had cracked and was now floating in segments . . . A sort of breath from the clay, from the city outside the park, condensing, made the air unclear . . . Bronze cold of January bound the sky and the land-scape; the sky was shut to the sun – but the swans, the rims of ice, the pallid withdrawn Regency terraces had an unnatural burnish, as though cold were light. There is something monstrous about the height of winter' (*DH* 7). At the beginning of Part Two, begun '[e]arly in March', we read that

> the crocuses crept alight, then blazed yellow and purple in the park. The whistle was blown later: it was possible to walk there after tea. In fact, it is about five o'clock in an evening that the first hour of spring strikes – autumn arrives in the early morning, but spring at the close of a winter day. To the person out walking that first evening of spring, nothing appears inanimate, nothing not sentient: darkening chimneys, viaducts, villas, glass-and-steel factories, chain stores seem to strike as deep as natural rocks, seem not only to exist but to dream. Atoms of light quiver between the branches of stepping-up black trees. It is in this unearthly first hour of spring twilight that earth's most agonized livingness is most felt. This hour is so dreadful to some people that they hurry indoors and turn on the lights – they are pursued by the scent of violets sold on the kerb. (*DH* 123)

Suspension immediately takes place following the whistle being blown; the shift is made clear in the formal movement from past to present tense. The hour of spring striking is caught performatively, as, with the shift to present tense, everything is animated, whether natural, architectural or technological. The city comes to life in all its details; in every aspect of its image there appears a vitality, albeit a somewhat strange life, as organic form tied to temporal patterns. But this is not a wholly comforting image of city and nature in concert: for there is that illusion – witnessed by whom? – of dreaming architectural forms, themselves already cast somewhat organically. What is remarkable in this response to the spring is the uncanny condition of sentience and animation pervading the 'natural' and the built worlds alike, so that one has forced upon one the recognition that atmosphere and season are coextensive with the constructed environment of the city.

Thus, London as psychic place; as animate and yet inhuman; as phantasmagoric archive and the place of involuntary memory, the very demands of which bring about the crisis in representation. It is not exactly that everything has a voice, to recall Leopold Bloom; we can, however, suggest provisionally that everything does have a signature, and in this is comprised the 'signature-system' of the city's singularity. London is therefore understood in Bowen's writing as the endless operation of ghostly, spectral, and phantasmic inscriptions; it is a city of differential movements and their rhythms, and also the duration of these. At the same time, there is also to be read, through the insistence of the city's cadence and pulse, an irreducible tension in Bowen's writing – that *inner tension* which opens an unsuturable gap, even as it traverses and translates the spaces between supposedly discrete identities – between that materiality without matter and the aesthetic and mimetic dimensions of narrative representation. Through this process, the former remains both incommensurable with and inexhaustible by any analysis of the latter. All representational stability is thrown into ineluctable crisis, the crisis of haunting that demands a response. It is as if, in being open to that which a 'particular psychic London' imposes on one, in answering the call issued by this city, Bowen has anticipated Adorno's desire for a radical cinematic naturalism which would develop its narrative according to 'an associative stream of images, deriving its form from their pure, immanent construction'.[23] Bowen's psychic London is figured as and through that pure immanence of the network. Through the currents of the network the otherwise unspeakable events in the city's material history come to find a place on which to leave their signatures, and these in turn are echoed in the endless play between temporal movement and suspension, in order that we might pause long enough to witness the arrival and return of the spectral city.

3
The insatiable crisis of memory: Maureen Duffy's *Capital*

. . . it is an *echo* that speaks.

Rainer Nägele

Neurotics are often very reliable prophets.

Elissa Marder

Perhaps all cities at all times have been, are surreal.

Maureen Duffy

I

This chapter offers a reading of poet and novelist Maureen Duffy's *Capital*,[1] the second work in her London trilogy, which I would like to describe, at least initially, as a chorographical text.[2] Though given relatively recent attention in the work of Gregory Ulmer, and bearing a passing resemblance to the Situationist International's concept of psychogeography, chorography is an Early Modern discourse, the most famous extant example being Michael Drayton's self-styled 'topo-chrono-graphical' poem, *Poly-Olbion*, printed in 1613. The purpose of chorography for Elizabethan intellectuals was to map the various historical, folkloric, and cultural resonances which could be unearthed in one location, specifically at the county level, as a means of producing a mythical and ideological identity that acknowledged singularity while showing analogically the resonance, both temporally and spatially, between local and national identity. It was also, often, an act of writing, which, like psychogeographical texts of the twentieth century, aimed to generate complex and unanticipated relations in the reading of place, vertiginous dislocations of undifferentiated identity in the service of cultural mythologization. Frequently tied to early modern cartography, the chorographical intent was largely hegemonic. In the twentieth century, however, Duffy's text functions differently; informed as it is by a spirit of place, it appears as the articulation of dissident, ambivalent, insurgent events.

To comprehend this, and the spectral work by which the text produces identities for, and from within, London, we should start with the title. *Capital* is undeniably a multiply resonant title. It signifies both the capital city and 'capital', material wealth. More than this, *Capital* announces behind its title another work of the same name, all too obviously, that by Karl Marx, even as, equally evidently, Duffy's work produces a material history of the capital that is irreducible to, and in excess of, any consideration of capitalist economics. In this light though, it is important to recall what seems equally all too obvious, that, while London is the capital city, within it is another city, the City, location of the Bank of England, amongst many other leading financial institutions, and therefore the place *par excellence* of the control of capital. Yet, while the title echoes with each of these, it also speaks indirectly of the cost of thinking London as only the place of the production and management of capital, or as the capital city. The title of Duffy's novel speaks volumes, and those volumes are all the occluded texts of the narratives of countless Londoners, who have existed within the capital, who exist and live on beyond material existence in *Capital*, and who return in the place of the text in excess of anything articulated directly in the name of the novel. For if Duffy's title is available as the signature of a particular polyvalence, it also inscribes itself within its own limits, while simultaneously being traced by an undecidable excess beyond polyvalence, by everything else belonging and subject to the capital, to capital, which calls to be remembered, but which only arrives through this title, under the guarantee that this title signs apophatically. Moreover, without wishing to sound too fanciful, we should consider the material condition of the book as analogy for the material condition of the city: a capital has no existence without the millions who have lived and died and who live and work within it, who make it operate, and – quite simply – make it appear in any given *now*. *Capital* has no existence without the countless voices, more or less anonymous, of those who are *Capital*, and who both make the novel and make its narrative appear, in any given *now* of reading.

II

Duffy being the least 'visible' of London novelists addressed in *Writing London – Volume 2*, it is perhaps necessary to offer a brief outline of *Capital's* structure and narratives: Duffy's novel is divided into Prologue, Epilogue, and five sections, unfolding through three principal narrative strands. The Prologue and Epilogue take place in some undefined future moment for London, which has become a decaying, yet overcrowded wasteland populated only by apparently barbaric refugees. Duffy's framing narratives for *Capital* are therefore reminiscent of the apocalyptic images of London in texts such as Anna Laetitia Barbauld's *Eighteen Hundred and Eleven, A Poem* (1812) or Richard Jeffries' *After London* (1885), and so partake of, as they situate themselves in, a certain narrative counter-tradition concerning the city. To take this point further, it can be said that Duffy's novel is not simply reminiscent of previous apocalyptic London narratives; in structuring itself in this manner, it resonates within and thus belongs to the counter-tradition, an insurgent event-text as I have already suggested.

The five sections indicate alternative identities for London, and are titled 'The City of the Dead', 'New Troy', 'Respublica Londiniensis', 'Babylon', and 'Cockaigne'. Each of the section titles provides alternative names and identities for London. More than this, I would argue that each title offers not merely proper names or identities *for* the city, but figures different, singular and alternative Londons. 'The City of the Dead' is possibly the most generic, while 'Babylon' is the most culturally familiar, also being significant in the context of Duffy's text as the place – and taking place – of uncontrollable multiple tongues, irreducible to meaning. 'Cockaigne' is a mythical place, apparently found in Celtic reference to London (*L:B* 164), and popular in medieval culture as a land of luxury and pleasurable excess. 'New Troy', appearing in print as early as the twelfth century in the work of Geoffrey of Monmouth, is also the name given to London in John Milton's censored and incomplete *The History of Britain* (1670), a work of republican historiography in which Brutus, the great-grandson of Aeneas, founds London under the name of *Troia Nova*.[3] Thus, each 'London' is available as a result of the gathering, under the sign of the proper name, different cultural, historical, and textual memories in excess of that name, even while the narrative trajectory follows a linear historical movement.

The three narratives of *Capital* are as follows: there is the third-person narrative of Meepers, an amateur historian and squatter who works as a porter at Queen's College, London, and who believes he channels the dead of London's past. There is also the narrative of an unnamed academic historian, whose research interest is the eighteenth century, and whose story is told, appropriately given the period of his research, in epistolary form to an also unnamed lover. Also the editor of an academic journal, the historian first comes into contact with Meepers shortly before the beginning of *Capital*, having being sent by Meepers, and having rejected, an article on London during the Dark Ages. Subsequently, the men's lives become intertwined. Meepers' interests in those aspects of London's past, which, in the historian's initial assessment, 'didn't really count as history'(*C* 21), gradually begin to possess the historian and, in turn, he becomes more responsive to the city around him. The events of the novel's present take place during summertime, the historian having opted to teach, while his partner has gone to the United States. Finally, there are a series of brief narratives, moving through the history of place as materialized narratives of otherwise invisible memory or acts of bearing witness, from those of an anonymous prehistoric woman belonging to one of the earliest groups of *Homo sapiens* known as Swanscombe Man, skull fragments of whom were first found in Swanscombe near London in 1935 and 1936, and Neanderthal man. Both live and die in settlements near the Thames, and these are followed by a series of vignettes concerning successive Londoners, including a transvestite King Elizabeth, and the flea that brings the Great Plague of 1665. The episodic stories are interpolated between the narratives of Meepers and the historian until, near the end of the novel, all three narrative strands are interwoven. In one of the three final episodes concerning relatively minor characters from the stories of both the academic and Meepers, Martha, who has come into contact with both the porter and the historian, wanders with her son, Ben, around Westminster Abbey. She reflects on both the unknown soldier and, in the words of a hymn Martha recalls from school, ' "some there be which have no mem-or-ial" ' (*C* 214).

III

Now, a brief orientation around the terms of my title – *insatiable, crisis, memory* – as a means by which to approach Duffy's visions of the city. The *OED* tells us that the *insatiable* is a condition of never having enough, never being replete; one can never satisfy one's desires. Meepers embodies, corporealizes, the insatiability of the phantoms of anamnesis, and their insatiable demand to be heard, to be acknowledged in the name, and as the spectral revenants, of London's occluded pasts. The oldest senses of the word *crisis* have to do with decision or judgement, or otherwise signify a token or sign by which to make a judgement or decision, which can only be taken when there are no grounds for decision; and so one is forced into a decision as a result of the experience of the aporetic, in the absence of determinable phenomena, evidence, reasons, or rational calculation. Hence *crisis*. Duffy's presentation of the brief lives of mostly anonymous Londoners involves the reader in a condition of constant, insatiable crisis. Implicit in the arrival of each narrative is the demand for response, even in the most minimal form of bearing witness, and, within this, the demand for opening oneself without calculation or limit to the phantoms of London, to the spectral machinery of the city.

But what of memory? This is not so straightforward. Apropos of the fraught attempt to respond to the city's memory, the urgency of the dilemma is expressed by Meepers: 'we may become what we think we have been. But also . . . if we have misinterpreted once we may be doing so again' (C 153). Considering memory as always already a translation, the information we receive might be, already, in error. But how would we know? Given the fact that Meepers, encouraged by the historian and his colleagues to seek an answer to the future of the city by feeding all his data into a computer, dies shortly before the computer programme is run, it is arguably the case that any effort to programme the future – and in this act to suppose that there can be *an answer* that terminates the insatiable call – is in itself an act of misinterpretation, a violent act which, in failing to remain open to other Londons to come, produces consequences which are dire in the extreme. When the historian asks '[a]re we elements in an unstoppable historical process or can we foresee and redirect?' (C 77) he posits the location of the undecidable between two questions to the pull of which Meepers succumbs in the effort to reach a decision, without any possibility for logically determined conclusion. Moreover, despite the absence of evidence by which to calculate the identity of the city, there is always that which cannot be anticipated – as with the crisis produced through the disorientating force of the unexpected arrival of vision, in excess of all empirical data. The historian is subject to such a crisis:

> I suddenly saw the city as a series of anonymous concentric rings each further and further from the centre point which is always I or in childhood me: department, faculty, college, university, city, each increasing the depth of anonymity and isolation, wrapping the gauze layers tighter and tighter until all sound and sensation are padded

away. Only the eyes are left free to blink and water as they stare at a world that they can't make meaning of by themselves.   (*C* 93)

The city appears as its own meaning, without any accessible meaning beyond an image which places phenomenologically the subject of the city at its heart, the implication being that there is no one centre, but eight million locations at least from which the city may be witnessed and which, in turn, London informs. And this is to take account only of a particular *now*, without being able to apprehend any other gaze, gone or to come. The overwhelming sublimity of vision and the crisis it produces in the subject transforms the viewing subject, the historian, into a bandaged figure, mummified perhaps, but equally, transformed into an invisible man, whose only act is to bear witness.

At another time, bearing witness to the city, again involving the historian, involves not sight but the arrival of London sound and sensation: 'It's very late. I sit here above the city feeling it breath round me in the dark and the ether even more full of radio chatter than it used to be' (*C* 69). That the city breathes and yet is also produced through radio chatter, suggests an uncanny hybrid identity, neither wholly technological nor wholly organic, and in this recalls Bowen's images of London, with its anonymous ghosts and the phantasmagoria of traffic moving in a circulatory flow, suggestive of London's organic power, as Bowen suggests. Unlike the computer, the purpose of which is to process information to a particular end, the radio merely channels, the image of radio phone-ins intimating potentially endless relays, interrupted by, flowing to and from, momentary coordinates and connections in a radically unmappable rhizome. Referring to late-night callers on radio phone-in shows, the historian acknowledges that 'they're the just moderators for this city, anonymous as itself' (*C* 69). Each voice *is* the city and, reciprocally, London has no identifiable identity, even as it is the countless transmission of voices, an excess of signals, hauntological resonance irreducible to ontology. Radiophony is one technology of the spectral that, by analogy, produces a singular figure for London's phantom technicity generating an unstoppable series of calls.[4] Disembodied, invisible signals arrive, innumerable ghosts and mediums of the city's constant becoming, and mediated by a technology that refigures the spectral machinery of the city, to which in another manner Meepers is already attuned, being the receiver of an occulted radiophony. The historian recognizes the signals of the city, even if he cannot say what these mean. Or rather say, he bears witness to the fact that the signals *just are* the city, its meaning. As the image of concentric circles attests, everything about London for the historian has to do with surface pattern; it is his apperception in the form of vision and signal that figures the city's networks and structures, without data available for analysis. (And, in passing we might note how, while Meepers receives the signals of the city's past lives, the historian is open, despite himself, to that which takes place synchronically.)

These are but a few examples of crisis through which we read the novel foregrounding the undecidability of London. With regard to the idea of history as an unbroken linear movement, *Capital* challenges this concept by showing how crisis takes place when the present no longer holds, when one understands that the past is always in the present as a virtuality, as is the future.[5] Moreover, conventional wisdom concerning historical time is further undone if one takes the position argued by Bernard Steigler in an exposition of *Dasein*, that 'my past is not my past; it is first that of my ancestors . . . inasmuch as [*Dasein*] exists, it is never finished, it always already anticipates itself in the mode of "not yet" . . . existence is what extends itself . . . between "already" and "not yet"' (*TT* 5). This is the rhythm of becoming and uncanny simultaneity that haunts Meepers' words, just cited, and which also motivates both the historian's question and Meepers' own concerning London's future, a question, he admits, belonging to both the past and the future, 'with a gap of fifteen hundred or two thousand years between the asking' (*C* 151), to which I shall return.

As with the ghostly voices of the city, memory arrives therefore as pulse and signal. These are generated by the phantom relay-machine of crisis' unending affirmation, often in moments of a disordering near-simultaneity. Such disordering of presence is registered in *Capital* as immediately personal and also impersonally historical. On the one hand, the house in which the historian lives is next door to that in which Meepers had been raised, while the historian's house is also in the square, in the gardens of which Meepers squats in the garden shed at the beginning of *Capital* (*C* 150). Thus, no location is ever simply itself – other histories touch upon and flow through place. On the other hand, a route travelled by a police car invokes several instances of London time that trace the present for Meepers: 'Once again he was . . . whirled . . . along the Roman Road that lay vibrating under the modern tarmac skin of the burning tyres, over Llugh's river, by the bowed bridge past the abbey where bony prioresses lisped in provincial French . . . through vanished Aldgate and the blizzard ash and flame of a thousand fires long out, by cheapened London Bridge broken down for ever . . .' (*C* 148). Every time memory arrives or returns, always coming as an iteration, there is, we might say, no time like the present; but then neither are there pasts or futures – *as such*. Unlike the narration and discourse of history, which is always supposedly the economic reckoning of the appropriate in the erection of a retrospective architectonic justification of itself as sign of the subject's supposed mastery of the past *qua* past, memory is the sign of an *apparitioning*, to borrow Hélène Cixous' word.[6] It is the revenant of an ineluctable and insatiable crisis: a coming without coming, a call for decision without calculation, before the subject, as the other of the subject's or culture's identity, as the other of history. Or, putting this in another, aphoristic mode: 'one phantom recalls another'[7] and this is what is witnessed through the narrative of the journey of the police car.

Duffy's novel is structured therefore by the pulsing flux of memory as the weave in the relation between being, place, and temporal revenance, as the articulation of that constant becoming figured between the 'already' and the 'not yet'. *Capital* addresses the role cultural memory plays in the generation of urban structure, particularly as this concerns the lived, and shared, experience of Londoners in the city of London throughout the history of settlements that, eventually becoming transformed into the city, have occupied the site around the River Thames for the last 250000 years. This becomes manifest in various ways throughout the novel. In the second of the historical narratives, we read that 'Neanderthalensis stood shivering at Whitehall' (*C* 29); he picked and ate berries near Piccadilly (*C* 27); and 'at the corner of Glasshouse Street on the site of the Regent Palace Hotel he paused to lean on his flint-tipped spear . . . A few feet below, the sharp handaxes of millennia before lay quietly together on a bed of London clay' (*C* 27). Here we have a series of impossible juxtapositions figured through the concatenation of place-name, prehistorical moment, activity and artefact, all of which together serve to undo temporal stability and commonsense comprehension of place. This displacement is further exaggerated by the reference to those artefacts already ancient in the time of Neanderthalensis buried in the 'London clay'. Given that the 'present' of the narrative is that of Neanderthal man, the disconcerting effect of the proper names of mappable locations lies in their arrival from the future; this, I would argue in passing, is heightened in the acknowledgement of the nominal particularity of the soil itself. In this manner, Duffy confounds discrete moments in time. In the narrative staging of structural anachrony, no one moment is privileged, while implicitly every instance of the city's time is immanent with every other, every 'now' becoming shot through by the marks of other times and, importantly, the memories of others, all of whom clamour for our attention. London thus becomes available as a singular site, composed of countless other singular sites, all of which are, on the one hand, microcosms of the urban macrocosm in their spatial and temporal resonances, while, on the other hand, every singularity is itself neither a centre nor an origin, but, instead, the narrative revelation of an intensity, that chance gathering of other singularities. Such structuring does not operate only within particular scenes, or from one scene to another through the occurrence of iterability. It is also there as the very form of the novel itself, where each of the 'historical' vignettes arrives with a dislocating and interruptive force between the narratives of Meepers and the historian. The past takes place *now*, while *now* is itself doubled, in both third- and first-person, arriving so as to disturb the historical progression of narrative from past to present. This is what London imposes: an identity of remnants and vestiges, which ruins narrative and historical continuity, compelling us to perceive and respond as the very text of *Capital* perceives, indirectly, in different rhythms and different registers, without the desire to see the city whole.

The conflation of hitherto perceived distinct and supposedly isolated temporal images is only one technique for making appear the memory-traces of the city, in an act at once the communication of textual form as both *tekhne* and *poiesis*. Memory arrives therefore and, in so doing, constitutes an unveiling or act of unconcealment, entailing the responsibility we have not only to what is legible but also to the question concerning how reading takes place. We witness iterable transformations: 'Tools evolved: the stone or bone notched with menstrual or hunting days became the computer' (*C* 182). A 'file of horses' in Hyde Park becomes a 'Stubbs in motion', but one which is strangely anachronistic; in an example of the Benjaminian dialectical image there is temporal conflation through olfactory commingling: 'A sharp smell of horse dung and grass clippings mixed with the car exhausts' (*C* 76). In this, another example of the dialectical image or image event, both the earth, that 'London clay', and a computer are acknowledged as memory banks (*C* 130, 157); the former attests, of course, only to the insatiable demand for reading and its impossibility, while the latter promises, for some at least, a conclusive analysis. As the historian admits in a remark which undermines in principle the institutional premises of his discipline, 'it's hard to tell with only a fragment' (*C* 160), which phrase, I would suggest, is a suitable aphorism for the insatiable crisis of memory, that confrontation with undecidability and the ethical demand of the other through the architexture of the city perceived, in Hubert Damisch's words, as 'the seemingly infinite, inscrutable network of itineraries inscribable within it' (*SNC* 28).

What should be clear is that Duffy's perception of cultural memory concerning what she calls 'the obliterating city' (*C* 38) is not predicated on some nostalgic sense of uninterrupted continuity of community progressing towards the present. Instead, as the multiple, discontinuous narratives of *Capital* make plain, memory is always fragile, evanescent, its erasure always possible, even as its signals are unstoppable. *Capital* illustrates this in several ways. Meepers, who is referred to as the 'custodian of the dead' (*C* 117), remarks of London soil that it 'isn't kind to the prehistoric dead. They dissolve' (*C* 33). At the same time, however, he also recognizes the earth as 'the memory bank that would give you the right answers as long as you asked the right questions in the right way but whose subtle structures could be so easily and irrevocably destroyed' (*C* 130). Here we see the problem, which is one of decision, of judgement. It is not merely a matter of careful archaeological perseverance, though, and nor is it necessarily simply the work of a particular metaphor in Meepers' imagination. For we read that '[h]e couldn't help it if the bones poked through the pavements under his feet; plague victims, there was a pit hereabouts he was sure, jumbled together, massacred Danes weighted by their axes to the river-bed, the cinders of legionaries in porphyry and glass urns gritting beneath the soles of his thin shoes'. The spectres of at least three supposedly distinct, different temporal moments and differing cultures in the memory of the city arise in no particular order, their arrival dictated only by place. This chorographic flow takes place despite its recipient. The passage continues:

> It was the living who passed ghostly around him, through whose curiously incorporeal flesh he moved without sensation while the dead pressed and clamoured, their cries drowning out the traffic . . . They had found mammoth bones here, he remembered, when they were digging the first underground in the 1860s . . . An archaeopteryx flapped like a garish broken parasol from the tower of St Mary's blotting out the clockface. Sweet Thames was running out with the tide . . . it was no longer profitable, after nearly two thousand years . . . (*C* 17–18)

As a result of so many ghostly appearances, Meepers is forced to recall another memory-image, where the historical moment is multiplied anachronistically yet again in the chance topographical concatenation of mammoth bones and the building of the underground. This leads immediately to another anachronistic vision, of the archaeopteryx flying from the church tower. The image is all the more arresting in its simile of the parasol, and the juxtaposition of the reptile with the clock, while there is the faintest echo of Dickens' estranging vision of a megalosaurus climbing Holborn Hill at the beginning of *Bleak House*.[8] The echo of the literary – another symptom of the city as example of its cultural productions – is taken up in that reference to the 'Sweet Thames', which gestures towards the sixteenth and twentieth centuries, to the refrain from Spenser's *Prothalamion*,[9] and to that other echo of Spenser, found in 'The Fire Sermon' from Eliot's *The Waste Land* (*WL* 70). The drifting image in turn invokes the recognition that the river is not natural but has an economic history tied closely to the fate of London, in a phrase where 'tide' operates both literally and metaphorically. What we are confronted with therefore is a series of closely interwoven images, echoes intimating greater historical and cultural networks of association, all of which call up other memories, even as they are themselves memories encrypted as the traces of the city's alternative identities. There is produced a perception which recalls 'all the temporalities of place, the ones that are located in space and in words'.[10]

Indeed, to take this further, place is only 'completed through the word', as Marc Augé has proposed suggestively, so that in Duffy's registration of this phenomenal transition London arrives and arises in a number of ways between the materiality of place and the materiality of the letter. On the one hand, it arrives, in such a way as to imitate 'a "rhetorical" territory shared with everyone who is capable of following [its] reasoning' (*N-P* 124). Initially, it appears that Meepers is capable of this, while the historian is not. There occurs, however, an effect of translation between them as a result of the changing chorological perceptions of the two men. Increasingly, place becomes a question of data for Meepers. The city's *reasoning* is, however, not dependent on research, but on being witness to the chance of apparitioning. And of course one cannot be prepared for this. In coming into being in a manner that confuses historical time and refuses rational mastery, the 'movement of appearing', Jean-Luc Marion asserts, 'ends by bursting on the depthless surface of consciousness like the impact of a gift ... What gives itself *shows itself*.'[11] The gift of the other, this motion of giving, is constitutive of the movement of apparitioning, as the city makes itself available for apprehension. Despite himself, the historian gradually receives such gifts, through a number of visionary epiphanies concerning the spirit of the city; the 'reasoning' pertaining to London's identity is poetic, not logical or economic, and the exchange of urban apprehension between the two serves perhaps to explain the use of third- and first-person narratives: Meepers, whether he knows it or not, is consigned to a narrative past tense, while the historian, finding himself responding to London's resonances, continues, without name, to say 'I', remaining merely one more articulation belonging to the city and so having a chance – though no more than a chance – of spectral survival.

What is given is exemplified, made startlingly apparent for the historian, following a visit to the flat of two of his students, Jenny and Robin, who live, to a certain degree, in hardship: 'Suddenly I had a vision of assorted pockets like this all over the city . . . The Paris of Abelard and Villon must have been like this' (*C* 124). This particular echo is one that is taken up by Duffy in the third novel of the London trilogy, *Londoners: an Elegy*, in which the narrator, Al, who is writing a biography of Villon, reflects that '[i]t's perverse to be at heart a mediaevalist in the computer age, to have an imagination with a five-hundred-year time warp, to see the Paris of Joan of Arc and the London of Marie Lloyd as one eternal city . . .' (*L* 15). As elsewhere in Duffy's staging of the city as phantasy, vision operates by analogy; it is 'topochronographical', to recall Michael Drayton's term. The historian's understanding of the lives of Jenny and Robin calls to mind for him the lives of countless other city dwellers, past and present as the phrase has it. Such multiple, heterogeneous apparitioning, as constelled memory of London, thus constitutes itself for the reader in a performative *givenness*, giving itself from within itself as echoic other. It also serves to suggest through those moments in Meepers' perceptions where the dead are 'pushing up through the ground, standing on each others' shoulders and calling him not to leave them out' (*C* 213), to aver that place is 'never completely erased' (Augé *N-P* 77), though demolished or built over. And perception has an intimate relationship with memory, writes Bernard Cache, for it 'places us immediately within memory, where the present is determined by the past . . . memory preserves the past in its singularity'.[12] This is of course illustrated by the historian's revelation, as intimated through his use of the proper name.

The city is therefore both echo chamber and palimpsest, the reading of which is far from simple, opening us to reception and calling us to response through its technicity. Memory, we come to see, is always the expression of crisis, because its irreducible complexity escapes and exceeds any conscious will to respond adequately in the face of the tropological discontinuity and ruin of London that it causes to appear. Such excess, perhaps the only sign of the city's terrible sublimity, is caught in the historian's phrase 'this vast tel' (*C* 79). The historian's choice of term for the city – 'tel' – is, I'm tempted to say, risking only a partial pun, telling. Shortened from the Old English *getael*, meaning number, it arrives in the remark as the sign of that ghostly relay that marks all language; moreover it has added significance, sharing its etymological roots with *tale*. The enunciation of a tale is always enumeration or reckoning, therefore, but the city's tales, its numbers are uncountable, unrepresentable. While singular examples arrive, giving us to think, they must also make us remember that we cannot be mindful of every narrative. In our recognition of responsibility, we recognize our betrayal of the ethical dimension, for while 'the simple concepts of alterity and singularity constitute the concept of duty as much as that of responsibility . . . As soon as I enter into a relation with the other . . . I know that I can respond only by sacrificing ethics, that is, by sacrificing whatever obliges me to respond, in the same way, in the same instant, to all the others', as Derrida reminds us.[13] *Insatiable crisis* indeed – and Duffy marks this in the historian's final missive; having come to apprehend London, he chooses to leave, flying to his lover, his other, writing to her, 'you are my city' (*C* 208).

IV

Attempting then to think the pasts of London, to receive its signals, and be responsive to each and every one of its memory traces, always involves us in a confrontation with this abyssal excess beyond polysemy, as well as with the undecidable, as already implied, putting us in the position of sacrifice and betrayal. Memory traces arrive, return, but how we receive them, if we receive them at all, is never certain, never orderable, certainly never comfortable. It is always a matter, undoubtedly, of being prepared to move amongst Meepers' 'living dead' (*C* 56). Especially pertinent therefore in the unfolding of Duffy's rhetoric of the city-text is that sense of relentless ethical call issued through the traces of memory already adumbrated, to which Duffy, knowing the impossibility of the demand, nevertheless seeks to bear witness through affirmation of the ineradicably haunted condition of London. This assertion is itself an echo, a spectral resonance of every other avowal, those affirmations of every other Londoner whose names are lost to history, occluded or erased in a present where 'clerks' terraced cottages . . . were [now] desirable residences for designers and television script editors and advertising men' (*C* 40). The involuntary return of the city's other resonates in a thought which, unwilled, suddenly springs to mind for Meepers: '[w]hat was he thinking of? Something tugged at a memory of ragged boys mudlarking through the pockets of corpses stranded by the ebb' (*C* 98). Again, the memory is double, carrying both the mudlarks and their prey, figures of a grim aspect of the city's symbiotic structure, and merely one example of London's 'centuries of detritus and excretion' (*C* 99). However, those who call to be remembered are not simply the dead, they are also those without identity and voice in the city's present, such as the 'gaggle of cleaners', without whom, 'dust and trash would gradually silt [the city] up. The gleaming offices would film over and dull, the lavatories block, the basins scum, the carpets and floors be overwhelmed in a tide of waste from flowing baskets' (*C* 97). In order to allude at least to the possibility of indirect apperception, Duffy's singular affirmation of the city's memories and its inhabitants takes the shape in part of a non-hierarchical symbiotic form or open structure, summarized in another of her novels, *The Microcosm* from 1966. In this, every Londoner is 'a unit in the complex structure of the city which is forever changing and expanding, thrusting out a part of itself which will break away from the main mass to begin a separate existence as satellite town or suburb with its own nucleus'

casting off dead cells only to replace them as dust is swept into the orbit of a star, the sweepings of distant places drawn irresistibly to its magnetic centre; the outer skin constantly renewed as buildings crumble, streets are bull-dozed away, new blocks rise. Each cell has a life of its own yet it is part of the total life of the city.[14]

As is seen in the quotations concerning the cleaners and the mudlarks, the intimate connection between attraction and repulsion, decay and renewal, survival and waste, is clearly significant, addressing as it does the flux of energy within a given structure over time. The text, in responding to and tracing the condition of the city, can, like the urban form itself, 'be understood', as architect Luis Fernández-Galliano argues, 'as a *material* organization that regulates and brings order to *energy flows*; and, simultaneously and inseparably, as an *energetic* organization that stabilizes and maintains *material* forms'.[15] How might this be thought in terms of impersonal anamnesis? For Fernández-Galliano, energy stored as form through repeated transformations means that matter 'remembers' and forms, therefore, 'the material basis of collective memory' (*FM* 66). This introduction of the discourse of memory into that of architecture and, by extension, the reading of topography and the city-text, 'entails a parallel evaluation of the persistence of . . . exis-

tence . . .' (*FM* 67). Taking fully into account the temporal dimension of
the argument just presented and recalling Duffy's ebb and flow of energy
and form in the presentation of the urban organism, there can be no
doubt that her text is equally clearly informed by the instantaneity and
simultaneity in every instant, every *now*, of spatial and temporal relationships, so that any analysis of Duffy's mapping of London and the
lives of its inhabitants requires that we understand, in the words of Peter
Ackroyd, that 'there are different worlds, and different times, within the
city' (*L:B* 777). Herein is acknowledged the importance of an otherwise
ungraspable totality that a certain projection of the city makes possible.
Henri Lefebvre clarifies this in the following citation, in which urban
topography and multi-temporality conjoin. Lefebvre asks: 'what about
totality?' only to answer, '[d]ialectically speaking, it is present, here and
now. It is absent as well. In every human act . . . all moments are contained . . . But these moments . . . require a form for their elaboration.
Although close by in this sense, totality is also distant: lived immediacy and horizon . . . Urban society puts an end to the things that make
totality impossible . . .'[16]

Lefebvre's formulation, signalling the simultaneity of presence and
absence, immediacy and horizon, and, by implication, all time, every
event, in every act, announces a totality that can be imagined, though
only indirectly. As the examples of the multiple and heterogeneous temporal and cultural folds of Duffy's text aver, the image of the urban totality operates through what Edmund Husserl has termed in his *Cartesian
Meditations* 'analogical apperception',[17] rather than via any representation, which is always inadequate to the oscillating echolalia and glossalalia of London. To stress the point once more, *Capital* attempts to
grasp this conception of urban totality as this is enacted through Duffy's
registration of those different worlds and different times. The temporal
and the topographic are always intimately enfolded through those serial
singularities of each narrative instance. It is through the response to the
singular that Duffy 'proposes memory as a precious mediation between
individual and social life' so as to ' "give voice" to subjects often
neglected and ignored', to borrow Mieke Bal's definition of memory as
performative.[18] However, Duffy's engagement is not with a particular
individual's memory of London; she does not privilege particular voices,
even though, perhaps inevitably, greater focus is given to the dialectic
between Meepers and the historian. It is important that we see these
figures as merely two more Londoners, two more traces standing in for,
without representing directly, other voices, other lives. They are figures
in the relay of memory's discontinuous oscillation, 'opening to us a view

of what is called spirit', as Henri Bergson remarks; so that it is given to us to perceive, with regard to the city's identity 'that *there is in matter something more than, but not something different from, that which is actually given'.*[19] Consciousness, comments Bergson, 'is born of the mere interplay of material elements' (*MM* 72). Is this not what we perceive? Is this not what comes to appear, in the act of reading, as we open ourselves to such interplay? Certainly this is what takes place in the coming to apperceptive awareness on the part of the historian and what is understood by Meepers, although insatiable obsession appears to get the better of him. For us as readers, both figures are figures of alterity, each constituting the singularity of a givenness, which by analogical transfer we apprehend, even as, by analogical translation and appresentation, they apprehend the city as this collectivity of otherness. Rather, developing from the figure of the city as endlessly evolving organism, containing not multitudes but multitudinous singularities, Duffy projects London as the bearer of memories, as so many traces signifying through the '*radical differentiation of apperceptions*' (Husserl *CMIP* 111) all the city's living and the dead, what the novel calls 'this flume of swirling people' (*C* 79). And in this fashion, London's memory is figured most forcefully, most disquietingly, in *Capital* as the memories of the city's past and present contaminate and disrupt the temporal order of the novel to the extent that all that takes place in this 'present' is 'predicated upon, "directed" by, memory', to cite Bal once more (*TCH* 186).

V

Memory is, therefore, 'not a possession we have at our disposal', to recall the words of Gaston Bachelard.[20] Duffy's text recognizes that memory has an agency of its own, that no subjective, human agency or consciousness can overpower. While the subject of memory has been addressed throughout this chapter, I want now to focus this attention a little further, turning to, and drawing on a number of theoretical reflections on the condition of memory, as this condition is exemplified within the structure of Duffy's novel. With its many episodic and vestigial narratives, *Capital* is disquieting, dangerous even, because, as an alternative poetics of the city's epochs rather than a history, it enacts, in the words of poet David Jones, 'a kind of *anamnesis* . . . an effective recalling';[21] but this is a recalling of what we can never have known, and so the epochal remnants give us pause through a relay of memories, by which 'something arrives and comes to be known' albeit indirectly.[22] What comes to be known most immediately is that 'the past does not belong to the past but to the present', as Didier Maleuvre avers,[23] while 'always and everywhere, the phenomena of time appear first of all in a discontinuous progress' (*DD* 65). What is called the present becomes translated from within itself by an ineluctable projection of so many serial and near-simultaneous instances of *now*.[24]

We see the place-ness of memory, if I can put it like that, in both the historian and Meepers' phenomenological responses to London, which are variously allegorical and archaeological, allusive and archival. Place-memory informs both men's reception and analyses, their crises of perception, their lack of comprehension, and their insatiable desire to know. Despite the historian's belief that '[t]ime and distance so diminish things' (*C* 48), his sense of the city is one of an often oppressive proximity. At first, the city is a 'drowned Atlantis under deep waves of mugginess and fumes as if the dew' was a 'damp ocean shroud over the streets' (*C* 29). A truly spectral figure, being a memory of that which has never existed, Atlantis points to the power of place-memory, even when there is no place as such. The Atlantean analogy appears initially an odd figure, coming as it does from someone associated with historical detail, but Duffy's historian is strangely adrift, being without a name and having only the sketchiest of identities provided by the acknowledgement of his existence by colleagues, students, and, of course, Meepers. The metaphor of drowning pertains to both a sense of fluidity and that which pervades the air, being reiterated by the historian several more times (*C* 30, 48). In his comparison of the atmosphere, between that of the city of Wordsworth and Blake and that of his present moment, though the air is cleaner there is still a sense of overwhelming personal pollution, in part because the 'deadliest fume is invisible' (*C* 30). Much of the historian's sense of the city lacks solidity. The leaves are seen in 'waves', while the sunlight is a 'wash' (*C* 48). The perception of the fluid and watery condition of London recedes for the historian, but comes to figure in Meepers' urban phantasy. Reflecting on the mudlarks, he apprehends the secreted layers of the riverbed, like an organic, temporal archive, 'broadening and raising ... so that a whole waterfront lay under the waves under centuries of detritus and excretion' (*C* 99). Following this passage, he desires to be able to explore the strata submerged beneath the river waters, but regretfully acknowledges that he must salvage the city's past only on dry land. At the close of 'Respublica Londiniensis', London in rain is for Meepers a vision of a 'lead skin of water' (*C* 164), a disquieting image that is simultaneously both solid and fluid, and yet neither solid nor fluid entirely. Finally, in the moments of his dying, Meepers has a vision of the 'waters of the Thames' shrinking 'back to show wharves and quays with ships riding the tides' (*C* 213). There is a monstrous transference here in Meepers' final scene, as he breaks into a sweat, subsequently vomiting, his body giving way to the expulsion of its own fluids.

The historian's response to the city is to register insistently London's almost tactile imposition. He remarks of its oppression that 'you have to shout not to be absorbed or smothered' by the city's noise (*C* 79), while pavements are 'choked' (*C* 26); there is a 'constant subdued tumult' (*C* 79). He chooses at one point to take the bus home rather than the underground, which, he anticipates, 'would be stinking and steaming' (*C* 48). There are 'eight million people in this city and we are forced up against each other' (*C* 93), but then he admits that '[e]ighteenth-century London was pretty cramped too' (*C* 126). Meepers also acknowledges the crowdedness of London, perceiving 'its millions of ant bodies busying around him' (*C* 38), an image which denies singular aspects to the living that he accords the dead, who 'nudge and jostle' him as he crosses Russell Square (*C* 56).

For the historian, then, we see that the historicity of London is precisely that of materially overwhelming sensual, rather than rational, force, a constant surfeit of, and assault on, the senses. The historian's response is, however, not that different from Meepers, the difference being that the former responds to the living, while the latter usually reacts only to the dead, who are, for the historian expressible in terms of periodic identification and therefore maintained at a certain distance. This might lead us to hypothesize a lack of historical imagination on the part of the historian, an inability to translate the 'not yet' of the living into the 'already' of the dead. It is, we might suggest, impossible for the historian to comprehend the very nature of being, a condition for which his academic training has no language. The heterogeneous traces of being's multiple alterity, where every other is wholly, singularly other irreducible to any 'mass', 'crowd', or 'group', is unavailable to formal historical representation. The condition of being only gradually comes to be revealed to him in ways that escape normative historical modes of production. The city cannot be comprehended through statistics, data, or facts. The press and proximity are available only to sensible apprehension or phenomenological apperception for the historian, not empirically verifiable information or events. Coming to awareness is an act of learning to read history's others, history's difference, those traces or signs that escape historical representation, and therefore appear insignificant. For example, '[a]fter the Great Fire a plant had grown up amid the charred ruins, as rose-bay willow-herb had covered the bombed sites. London rocket it was called' (*C* 204). Here we read two historical moments of destruction and the chance occurrence of regeneration, in the seventeenth and twentieth centuries. While it is interesting to note that the latter of the two plants is accorded a London identity, what is perhaps more important to note is that, for Duffy, there is rhetorical power in the figure of iterable recurrence as an otherwise undecipherable sign of the city. Of course, there can be offered a rational explanation of the occurrence of plant life's resurgence amongst the city's ruins, yet this does not quite explain or account for everything. There is, or at least might be, in the presentation of the double figure an uncanny, poetic pulsation that might best be perceived as speaking of the spirit of place, through this narrative staging. Yet we cannot say for sure. The figure arrives in a manner that makes it impossible to decide, being irreducible to any positive statement.

VI

Memory is clearly that which refuses to be consigned to some mausoleum or museum. It is, in its affirmative resistance, always the announcement of what we understand as the past's refusal to be assigned location. It is in its motions irrational; it arrives as it will, despite our conscious effort to control its flows. Never about itself, memory, a series of traces and signs, will always demand a response, an act of witnessing, a reading and an interpretation, a solution to its teasing encryptions, hence Aristotle's appellation of the images, icons, or imprints both of and in memory as so many *phantasmata* in their discontinuous temporal motion.[25]

Despite all efforts to read the comings and goings of such phantasms 'as though the compulsion to recall could be purged',[26] any solution can be therefore only ever temporary; we can never satisfy memory's call. Unstaunchable flow, without direct access to discernible origin, memory is simply this: the ungovernable constellation of crises, of tokens or signs of singular crises, being simultaneously decisions, judgements, testimonies; demanding endless decision or judgement, such demands, by their very nature, are insatiable. What we name memory therefore *just is* an inadequate nomination for what cannot be determined, a signifier as the recognition of the crisis in naming. One phantom recalls another, you remember, and this is not simply a question of the past, for in the words of Jacques Derrida, 'the question – and demand – of the phantom is the question and the demand of the future and of justice as well' (Ar 24). To take one more example from *Capital*, the haunting to come is recognized when Meepers says of the importance of urban memory 'the real question is of the future not the past. Or perhaps I should say it's the same question with a gap of fifteen hundred or two thousand years between the asking. Does it survive? ... The city, this city' (C 152). Acknowledging the persistence of the question in this moment of uncanny iterability, memory – in the form of the question, as that after which the question labours – opens onto, even as it receives a spectral arrival from the future, presenting that which in its manifestation interrupts the quest for certain knowledge, throwing that search into crisis through the encounter with the aporetic.

If Duffy's novel is then fundamentally a *mnemotechnic of the other*, as I take it to be, it is, in being this, also readable as a polemical act. *Capital* effects an intervention and interruption in an amnesiac present where the past is memorialized and mystified. Duffy, it might be said, understands that the past is not what it was. Having been made into a theme park comprising so many acceptable, cleaned buildings, historical walks, memorial crypts, experiences, renovations, and other government-sponsored projects, the past today is ontologized in the name of 'heritage'. For this reason, one amongst many, *Capital*, first published in 1975, is now in 2004 an ever more uncannily prescient and provocative, singular example of the urgency of anamnesis' call in the face of ideological forgetting that underpins the notion of heritage and which obliterates the very real political changes made *for and in the name of* working-class Londoners, during the middle third of the twentieth century. For Duffy, London has its double, an other both poetic and political. This figure, this other London, is not simply dialectical or oppositional, even though it frequently is this, as can be illustrated in the following two passages from *Londoners*, in which the narrator Al becomes the willing medium for acts of urban anamnesis: 'Who was it?' Al asks himself, 'Herbert Morrison, who wanted his ashes scattered on the Thames during a sitting of the LCC?'[27] This memory reveals little enough, cryptically presented as it is. One has to know of Herbert Morrison and what LCC stands for; but, once known, an entire other history is recalled. Morrison had been the architect of the most successful period of local London government, and leader of the London County Council for thirty-one years. A disciple of Fabian Sidney Webb, who, in the 1890s, had 'drafted the influential *The London Programme*', Morrison and others realized what Roy Porter has described as 'a Fabian dream of municipal socialism run by experts for Londoners' good'.[28]

However, this is not simply a recollection of socialist transformation, for the question poses itself somewhat eschatologically, so that local government and last rites are tied intimately in this vision of alternative London. Al continues in a similar vein:

> It had such glamour that old set of initials to conjure up the ghost of Keir Hardie, and *Fifty Years a Borough*, the story of the growth of radical London with its monuments in schools and paving stones, chest clinics and grants to sixth formers to make its children stay on, swimming baths and libraries like some mediaeval Italian republic, our own city state caring for its people, one of the intertwined strands in our Lighttown, so that it isn't just Mammonsberg. (*L* 155)

The letters *LCC* are themselves powerfully evocative, their force being in their hieratic function as much as in the political memories they have the power to conjure. The letters act as a mnemonic device, which provoke an act of anamnesis as affirmative resistance to the myth of capitalist might with its implication that London is only material in a narrow sense. As significant as the political legacy traced here in the form of place-memory is the revenant figure of Keir Hardie,[29] which leads metonymically to that untimely comparison between Fabian London and the image of the Italian city-state, so as to suggest *Respublica Londiniensis*. That the political left effects changes to both social and cultural life in a number of different ways is clearly indicated in this passage, so that education, health, and leisure are encompassed. Yet, that is not all; for it is important to note that Al remarks of this alternative political history that it is merely 'one of the intertwined strands' of London's alternative histories, the city being not solely the place for the production of capital.

There is in Duffy's brief memory image an insistent complication of our understanding of the capital. It is never only the seat of government and the centre of financial power, and if Al's mediated recollection is insistent, this is undeniably due to the crisis concerning the struggle for London's memories. The city, at one moment described as 'Kafkaesque' and at another apprehended through a music-hall song (*L* 85, 13),[30] is comprised of many other traces, as the second extract from *Londoners* unfolds for us: 'It's dark outside and the rain has come back. The rush hour flows down from St Paul's in a muddy Styx of struggling bodies and cars.' Transformed into an semi-obscuring flow, recalling those watery images that mark *Capital* and being evocative once more perhaps of Dickens' opening to *Bleak House* or one of Doré's etchings, the City is translated mythologically. The passage continues: 'Paul's is a gaunt sepulchre for Donne's bones against a sky of smoking clouds. Clerks and typists and bookkeepers froth through the drizzle from Mammon's heart to Cannon Street and London Bridge as they've done for over a century, homewards to their suburban teas, through Eliotesquerie to Betjemania . . .' (*L* 63). Against the fact of capitalism and its simultaneous dominance on the city and its imposition of anonymity on its workers is the memory of the City's poets. (Reciprocally, it is the responsibility of the city poet to open the work of poetry to work in the city.) While the movement of the workers leaves a century-old trace, the marks of the poets extend back on the same site to the seventeenth century. Is this the work of dialectic, or, as in the previous citation, where last rites and ghosts arrive to recall a politics of community, is there that at work here, through the signs of myth and poetics, a resonant excess irrecuperable to ordered representation? As I remark above, dialectic is at work, but this is not all. Duffy's doubling of London is abyssal, as already argued. The excess of figuration resides not only as the oppositional discourse. For, even as there is the magical countersignature of *LCC* related directly to memory, and Keir Hardie's force is as a spectre haunting London – the spectre, if not of communism, then certainly socialism – so in Al's persistent use of 'Mammon' as the name for the materialist, capitalist exploitative city, there is the Aramaic word for wealth, personified in medieval mythological and theological writings as the demon of covetousness. The overflowing sign, the counter-text, is encrypted within representation, an alternative memory that haunts the very act of representing place, thereby throwing that image into crisis.

Unavailable therefore to any controlling ontology, image, or narrative, London is instead, a multiple, potentially infinite and abyssal poetic and monstrous figure, as I have sought to demonstrate, implying the ungovernable totality of memory that takes place insistently, over and over again. In the structure of the novel so many alternative traces may be read as a rhetorical troping and repetition, a kind of cultural and historical *epanalepsis*. But it is not a word, phrase, or clause that comes to be repeated – unless that word by implication can be taken to be the name of the city – but urban memory itself, which arrives as the unruly echo that reiterates with a vengeance. In making appear and reappear the occluded memories and ghosts of London's lives, *Capital* puts to work the city's insatiable projections as so many singular symptoms of London's phantasmic topographies and architextures, as these echo with the spectral traces of its otherwise forgotten. History is not necessarily a nightmare from which I am trying to awake; it is, however, a narrative telos, which Duffy's city ineluctably exceeds.

III. Punctuations

IV. Interventions

4

Peter Ackroyd and the 'endless variety' of the 'eternal city': receiving 'London's haunted past'

Sometimes it even seems to me that the city itself creates the conditions of its own growth, that it somehow plays an active part in its own development like some complex organism slowly discovering its form. Certainly it affects the lives, the behaviour, the speech, even the gestures of the people who live within it.

Peter Ackroyd

I reflected upon these stupendious Works, vast and of a manner Colossale, and of the curious Signs cut upon their Stone. I gaz'd upon the Shaddowes of fallen Collumnes until my Spirit itself became a very Ruine and so, as I proceeded further in my Books, it was a surety that I studied part of my self.

Nicholas Dyer, *Hawksmoor*

I

My title is a somewhat obvious, not to say awkward, patchwork of citations. Yet the citations serve a telegraphic function with regard to those perceptions of London pursued throughout this book, as the articulation and presentation of the city comes to be understood through the texts of the twentieth century on which the present volume focuses. Endlessness, variety, the eternal, the past, haunting, and, inferentially, inheritance, reception, and the relation between city and subject: all speak – and figure – that which is shared between Elizabeth Bowen, Maureen Duffy, Peter Ackroyd, and Iain Sinclair in their perceptions of and responses to London. Alluding then to what is shared amongst the writers with which *Writing London – Volume 2* concerns itself, the two

quotations arrive from Ackroyd's writing. They serve to imply a cluster
or constellation of already mapped interests in and responses to the city
beyond the immediate focus of Ackroyd's texts. These are echoed in
turn, supplemented through the imaginary and spectral, phantasmic
work of the epigraphs, which serve to illustrate Ackroyd's concerns
with London and what he perceives as its spiritual or sacred continuities, especially as those are projected through particular privileged
London subjects. With such a configuration in mind, and with an
eye both to the structural and historical interactions and the referen-
tial, echoing density in mind, it is on *Doctor Dee* and *Dan Leno* and
the city's 'apotropaic magic' (Benjamin *AP* 335) that this chapter
concentrates.

Before proceeding, it is necessary to offer an *apologia* for what has
been omitted in this chapter. Arguably, most if not all of Ackroyd's
novels speak of inheritance and continuity with regard to London and
Londoners. Certainly one could address *Hawksmoor*, *The Great Fire of
London*, *The Plato Papers*, and *The Clerkenwell Tales*. This is true, and of
these other novels, *Hawksmoor* would appear especially to demand
attention, given the way in which it toys playfully with the idea of
continuity's resonance down through the centuries, as this comes to be
embedded in the very fabric of the stones from which particular
churches are built as a result of necromantic practice. However, apropos
Hawksmoor I would aver that temporal revenance is the principal motif,
under the signs of which motion London is subsumed for the purpose
of the narrative exploration of what might best be described as the persistence of evil. Furthermore, my choice in this chapter is dictated in
part by the impossibility of addressing each novel in sufficient depth,
and to suggest that 'what Ackroyd does' with regard to London is best
exemplified through *Dee* and *Leno*, as well as through particular aspects
of certain of Ackroyd's biographies, to which I turn in the second part
of this chapter.

An objection might be raised also that I have not addressed *London:
the Biography*. My reasons for this should be explained. While I speak to
the relation between London and its subjects in certain of Ackroyd's
other biographies, I have refrained from analysis of *London: the Biography* because, as with aspects of the work of Iain Sinclair, there is a sense
in which *London* is unreadable. Everything – everything and all the rest
– is undeniably there, everywhere throughout each chapter and from
chapter to chapter; but like the city for which it is named, which it in
turn invents, through the innumerable traces to which it responds

so faithfully, Ackroyd's biography of the city can, I believe, only be acknowledged in momentary reflections, through responses and acknowledgements appropriate to its own ruinous, excessive condition. As with the city, so the biography: so many ruins, remains, fleeting, iterable phantom figures, arriving, demanding response, calling for acts of bearing witness to the city's countless voices and anonymous lives, and yet reminding us all the while that such response entails an impossible responsibility, if we are indeed to be faithful to both London and *London*. There is that, in short, about both book and city, which affirms itself through resisting ontology, identification, or representation. Writing the city intervenes in such teleological or hermeneutic impulses, affirming in the process the work of difference, alterity, trace, inscription, anamnesis: this – and *only* this performative *poiesis* and technicity of a true writing – is what makes possible the chance for even the most inchoate apprehension of the city in all its absences and excesses.

This is what I perceive to be taking place in Ackroyd's writing of *London*, which might accurately be described as a failed attempt at *apocatasasis* – the restoration of everything. There is a density *and* a velocity to the motion of traces and ruins of the city's memories in that book that pre-empt and enfeeble any critical recuperation or stasis implicit in representation. It is as if, in *London: the Biography*, Ackroyd has recognized that his 'method' of composition (a 'method' that must exceed any programme) must follow that desired by Walter Benjamin in the *The Arcades Project*, which is that 'everything one is thinking at a specific moment in time must at all costs be incorporated into the project then at hand' (*AP* 457), and that this in part can only be arrived at through a practice of what Benjamin calls 'citing without quotation marks', a practice 'intimately related to that of montage' (*AP* 458). Such citations are not merely those adapted from the writings of other authors on London, even though these do surface frequently. Ackroyd's architecture extends beyond the merely intertextual in its mapping of the city, operating as it does through a structural embedding of countless ruins of others' texts. There is also to be witnessed the citation of the city itself, the citation of 'the most heterogeneous temporal elements . . . coexist[ing] in the city' (Ferdinand Lion, cit. Benjamin *AP* 435). It is remarked that '[w]hoever sets foot in a city feels caught up as in a web of dreams, where the most remote past is linked to the events of the day' (Lion, cit. Benjamin *AP* 435). The significance of response to entanglement in a web and the phenomenological apperception of this entanglement as experience of the city cannot be stressed here too strongly, for so too, is the experience of the good reader who sets foot in *London*. Such an event is unreadable; so, while Ackroyd might be perceived as apprehending Benjamin's desired method, it is also to be recognized that it is impossible to fulfil any such desire. One can only respond in the event and in effect to the fragmentary pulse without capturing it. No reading therefore; instead, momentary eruptions from *London* throughout the chapter, as these might be appropriate to specific subjects being considered.

But to come back to where we began: from what I have said, it can be seen that Ackroyd is clearly one of those authors who inherit and mediate a particularly concentrated and singular apprehension of place and its subjects. This is marked by, manifested through, on the one hand, attention to the interplay between materiality and memory. On the other hand, it is mapped through a rhizomic opening from a singular source – as 'the plane tree at the corner of Wood Street and Cheapside' (*L:B* 666) – to countless other trajectories and traces in the imaginary map of the city. The singularity of the plane tree is instructive in our understanding of Ackroyd's writing. Having persisted for centuries, it marks a continuity the meaning of which is undecidable, strictly speaking: it is at once suggestively symbolic and yet without any significance beyond its survival Moving from this tree, which becomes the singular occasion for an entire chapter in *London*, Ackroyd is moved to remark that '[a]ppearances may change, but form remains constant' (*L:B 667*). What that form may be is inaccessible, because every apparition will necessarily be different from every other. And thus it is possible from the inaugural observation of the tree for Ackroyd to conclude that the 'continuity of London is the continuity of life itself', a remark offering a continuity between the visible and invisible, the material and the spectral, without there necessarily being any transcendent or metaphysical value attached (*L:B* 672). His writing may be read as being articulated to greater or lesser degree through narratives at pains to map 'the relation of spirit with matter', to borrow a phrase of Henri Bergson's (*MM* 76). This mapping, I would argue, affirms, with regard to the response to London (and to cite Bergson once again), 'the reality of spirit and the reality of matter' in 'the relation of the one to the other' through memory (*MM* 9). Particularly, memory is understood here as so many echoes, to recall Rainer Nägele, who produces a reading of Baudelaire's conception of memory's echoes 'not as a reconstruction of the past but as fragments and refractions of loss . . . [leading to a perception of a new poetics, that of] a construction with the pieces of destruction, not a reconstruction' (*ET* 10). This in turn, argues Nägele, is part of a 'poetics of correspondence' in the urban space, as that correspondence makes possible connections between place and place, between place, its ghosts, its traces, its palimpsests across time, and what takes place through the echolalia of the city in any given location.

What emerges in such a reading or response to the acts of writing London is a sense of both inheritance and broken filiations, where the pasts of the city arrive as so many active ruins and fragments of urban anamnesis. The arrivals invariably take place for Ackroyd through privileged subjects of the city, whether fictional or real, whether famous or, today at least, relatively obscure. Such subjects provide a singular, momentary provisional identity to the city, which cannot be generalized. Such Londoners make possible a certain glimpse of London via a narrative gesture akin to *prosopopoeia*. The force of revenance transforms the present irrevocably, and it does so precisely through the Londoner who gives face to the phantasms of the past, and so bears witness in mediumistic acts of *poiesis*. Furthermore, that which returns and informs London's excessive identity and the process of writing the city is not merely archival or archaeological. In Ackroyd's words: 'this variety, this heterogeneity, is of more than just historical interest – it can include and empower anything that strays within its bounds. This is why London writing is always open to new themes and concerns' (*TC* 341–51; 348). In particular, this openness is acknowledged through the figure of the subject who, already haunted by the city's landscape, becomes empowered, through an awakening, as the result of the receipt of, and response to, the visionary arrival. In the texts, we read how London is phantasm, an assemblage of phantasmagoric traces, so that the city's act of revenance opens the subject up 'as a landscape, even as it closes around him as a room' (Benjamin *AP* 417) in the visionary affirmation. What Ackroyd calls openness in writing is a matter of interanimation, so that the vision may have the chance of being recognized. In his writing, 'it is not', as Walter Benjamin has it, 'that what is past casts its light on what is present, or what is present its light on what is past' (*AP* 462). Rather, through the concatenation of London and Londoner, there is disclosed what Benjamin terms the constellation that accedes to consciousness as legible, transformative image.

II

Before turning to *The House of Doctor Dee* and *Dan Leno and the Limehouse Golem*, it is instructive to attend to particular aspects of Ackroyd's biographies, and to remarks made in lectures and essays on London. In 'A Manifesto for London' Ackroyd makes the self-evident but necessary statement that 'London is an infinite labyrinthine city . . . a megalopolis, a world space to be surveyed by satellites.' Importantly, he adds to this the directive that 'attention should be given to the inner rather than the outer areas. The historic trend has always been outward . . . but the citizens must reclaim their old territory' (*TC* 386–8; 387). As inspiring initially as the sentiment might be – and I am wholly in sympathy with it – there are few real signs of this, perhaps, idealist vision. However, the 'reality' of the vision – if I can put it like this – is made manifest in writing, if not (yet) in London itself. Writers such as Ackroyd attune themselves to and reclaim the inner areas of the city in ways that are often resistant to the logic of ordered representation, historical accuracy, or even factual detail. As we will see in both *The House of Doctor Dee* and *Dan Leno and the Limehouse Golem*, anonymous London voices arrive to affirm aspects of the city's otherness, while also speaking *as* otherwise forgotten, occluded Londoners, the 'poor and the desperate' for example, from whose shadow 'the city is most recognisable',[1] or the vagrants and children[2] in *Hawksmoor*, who are sacrificed, literally, to the rebuilding of the city's churches after the Great Fire of 1666. The symbolic violence of this narrative device whereby Ackroyd speaks indirectly of the politics and history of London power in one historical moment and also as a spiritual continuity between the seventeenth and twentieth centuries is too obvious to warrant further comment here. Suffice it to say, Ackroyd's resistances are achieved through gestures of such excess and continuity, as well as through troubling comic and parodic moments, narrative and mythopoetic strategies, irreconcilable paradox, and through the work of analogy rather than mimesis. The city is thus figured through a sensibility of disorientation, excess, laughter, and, not infrequently, violence and darkness, which no reading can domesticate or rationalize, as I am at pains to illustrate.

Giving attention to the inner areas of the city there is to be acknowledged in London, particularly working-class London as Ackroyd shows in *London: the Biography*, an independence, a culture of dissidence, and a history of 'spiritual radicalism' (*TC* 286), to borrow a phrase used in both Ackroyd's review of Sinclair's *Lights Out for the Territory* and to describe William Blake. London also has the power to create a 'mood of aimlessness and excitement' (*TC* 286), a power which, says Ackroyd, is ineluctable, and because of which the pedestrian comes to mimic 'the movement of time in the city itself' (*TC* 287). The double question of London time and its alternative sources of power is significant, while at the same time it is acknowledged that as there is no *single* London so there is *no one time* for London. In different areas, time moves at different speeds (*TC* 665), while 'there are still areas of London where time seems to have come to an end or ceaselessly to repeat itself' (*TC* 665). It has to be said that the concern with temporality and power, already illustrated with reference to both *Hawksmoor* and *London*, is neither Ackroyd's alone, nor merely a conceit read by Ackroyd as belonging to Sinclair as a result of the latter's knowing indebtedness to Guy Debord and the Situationist International, particularly their notion of psychogeography (see the following chapter). Nor is this simply a so-called postmodern affectation, supposing it were even that. One can find an apprehension of such ineluctable pull, through time and in any given place, in Eliot's *The Waste Land* and throughout those novels and essays of Virginia Woolf's addressing London. Ackroyd is doing no more here than offering a sense of the ways in which the city has a spirit and energy, while also alerting us to the ways in which that spirit or energy reiterates itself over time, imposing itself on the London writer intent on 'finding his inheritance' (*TC* 287). As he puts it of Sinclair, but in a manner equally applicable to his own textual productions, 'the great aim . . . is not to discover or to describe, but to recollect'. Such acts of writing produce 'a dialogue with the dead in which only one can speak . . . understanding of place is a refraction of all the memories associated with it' (*TC* 287).

Clearly then, Ackroyd is speaking of writing London as performative response rather than detached observation, a process, as we have insisted, of *poiesis* rather than mimesis: an active, constantly unfolding act of making, rather than a mode of production subordinate to a telos of representation. This is captured in the following commentary: 'I am not . . . talking about a dead or irrelevant past. I am trying to disclose a definite pattern of continuity . . . I am invoking a living inheritance that has everything to do with the spirit of place and with the nature of the city' (*TC* 346). The act of writing London is then a double act: of reading as rereading and rewriting, of invocation and disclosure of the hitherto invisible, whereby what comes to be remarked is what is already at work, and which, in returning, appears as the traces of multiple cultures, histories, and events. Therefore, no act of writing can ever control itself or its subject, if it is open in its reception of the city. Even while the 'luminaries of London are always trying to find a way of confronting [the] darkness on their own terms' (*TC* 288), writing the city becomes an act – indeed it is already haunted by this possibility – of receiving the city in all its flows as we have already remarked, as writing is the place where urban intensities come to take place in particular, singular ways. Such city writing always engages in a transaction with what Michael Moorcock has described as the 'alarming flotsam of London's endless flux'.[3] Writing the city is always already *just this uneasy negotiation*, an ebb and flow across the boundaries of the self, those borders becoming erased in the city's constantly revenant becoming, whereby there is created 'out of the world of time a city that has a manifold and perpetual presence' (*TC* 288).

Such a manifold and perpetual presence is not a presence at all, of course, but rather the effects and signs of an unimaginable, impossible totality or continuity; or, as is remarked in my introduction, the impossible, as that which arrives. If London is to be inherited, translated at all, it must be received as the gift of the apparitional, through the taking place of analogical appresentation, and in acts of writing, which are also acts of anamnesis (as already argued), often figured in the singularity of a particular subject. Whether that subject is John Dee, Nicholas Hawksmoor, William Blake, or Dan Leno, the purpose for Ackroyd is to employ the figure as both medium and screen. The subject is not an archetypal or stereotypical Londoner (it would be impossible to produce such a generalized figure). Rather, the subject is a writerly trope, a figure of prosopopoeiac singularity, through which London projects and onto which the traces of the city are written. Ackroyd comprehends this when he says in an interview: 'in a city of 7 000 000 people, one could write 7 000 000 novels, and that's just the initial number – the reason why London is so amorphous is because it is also so endlessly imaginable; as a physical city it is unimaginable, but for the visionary, or a particular type of person, his or her London becomes the world'.[4] And we might add, the only way imaginable of addressing this world is, on the one hand, to acknowledge the impossibility of such a task while, on the other, to indicate London in the most indirect manner imaginable – through the narrative of a single subject, as Ackroyd has done with the biographies of More, Blake, and Dickens.

The biographies of Charles Dickens (1990), William Blake (1995), and Thomas More (1998) all make evident Peter Ackroyd's sense of the potential interconnectedness between the subject, the act of writing, and the city of London, along with the continuity of spirit, a spectral inheritance on which he insists, and which is the motivating force within the mnemotechnic assemblage that is *London: the Biography*. Indeed, in a certain sense the three biographies are as much biographies of the city as they are biographies of the lawyer, statesman, and martyr, the poet and visionary, the novelist and entertainer. To put this another way: More, Blake, and Dickens are on occasions within their own biographies 'translated' by Ackroyd. From being the principal subjects, they become singular figures, who in becoming-prosopopoeic give face and access to the city's continuities. In this, through its ostensible subjects, each biography anticipates *London: the Biography*, and thus might be read in part as a microcosm of that text, if not of the city itself: for each explores a single life, a single facet in a particular historical moment, but does so with the awareness that each life is but one of the countless millions of London lives. At the same time, the narratives of the city appear across the biographies. In this, each figure serves to function as the plane tree or the Thames, as do specific examples of silence or the example of Fetter Lane; which last example offers both a knowable material location and a material signature; we read the sign of transhistorical persistence and the city's constant becoming, 'this lane of perpetual change', which for Ackroyd maintains memory, insuring that no one dies in London while London is always there (*L:B* 237). Indeed, what the human cannot give to the mapping of London, the inhuman or inanimate can: a trans- and intertemporal flow and revenance. London thus asserts itself in and as so many momentary surges, appearing, vanishing, and reappearing, intruding to interrupt and punctuate the writing of a life. With the earlier biographies, the biographical subject disappears into the textual movement of the city momentarily, as 'biography' unfolds itself from within, becoming temporarily other. And it is precisely this gesture of response to the city that finds its most excessive, exhausting articulation in *London: the Biography*, where chapter after chapter is encountered as the gathering of so many countless, serial and iterable tropes, motifs, events, occurrences, occupations, and, of course, subjects.

The iterability of London's scenes, figures, events, phenomena, and traces that appear from biography to biography, and within *London*, as each chapter, each sentence takes on the guise of a singular manifestation of every other chapter or sentence, intimates both temporally and spatially a sense of London's regenerative power, a power which returns ineluctably, thereby overflowing the limits of any particular narrative or historical moment. The history of silence, Ackroyd tells us, is 'one of London's secrets' (*L:B* 81). Silence provides an image of the city but not just any image, not simply an image amongst images: for it is what Frédéric Neyrat names *l'image hors-l'image*: the image without or outside-image, outside-the-image.[5] In being this phantom effect, the image-without-image marks or writes the place – in this case London – as always apprehended after the event by what has come to pass or taken place. Hence Ackroyd's response in *London* to London: writing in ruins, acknowledging through the structure of the *après-coup* the serial iterability of phenomena and events as so many caesuras in the continuity of becoming that is London. Silence offers the spectral figure *par excellence*: it is an 'ambiguous presence' that paradoxically 'may also suggest absence of being' (*L:B* 81). In its undecidability, silence exceeds an ontology of silence to haunt the streets and the reader, its every experience and every commentary haunted by the unceasing shuttling motion that undoes definition from within its very possibility. Anachronistically, we 'hear' this silence. We receive its image-outside-image in the event of reading, by which each moment of silence haunts us – never more there than when it is not there except as the trace of itself, an 'itself' which has no self. More than this, the question is not merely one of an occluded history of silence; there is also a historicity to silences, of which there are more than one, each singular historicity being the sign of the symptom of the phantom, of that which is neither there nor not there but which returns. The silence of the sixteenth century is theatrical, as is that of the nineteenth, though with a difference; in the sixteenth century silence is also 'unnatural'. In the eighteenth century, silence takes on the form of localized punctuation of place, taking place as a topographical counterpoint to another place. Silence is both contemplative in the Victorian period but also capable of producing anxiety. Yet, what marks the continuity of London silence for Ackroyd throughout the history of the city is the way in which it informs the sacred sites of London (*L:B* 81–5). In this, silence allows for a suspension of time, a moment of timelessness in which the London subject might be open to the revenant vision of the city.

But to return to the biographies of particular London subjects in the light of this discussion of the work of silence: whether it is in the tracing of walks or routes through the city of More, Blake, and Dickens; whether it is in the act of naming the streets, wards, or boroughs; whether it is in displaying the life of the streets, the vendors, stalls, shops, marketplaces, or the countless anonymous figures who cross and recross the streets through which More, Blake, or Dickens walk, the act of writing; London always performs for Ackroyd the condition of the city itself in singular fashion and without offering access to any general image or representation, whether in the fifteenth, the eighteenth, or the nineteenth century. Thus, in the act of writing the city, Ackroyd's understanding of the continuity of spirit is articulated: London may change, but the city remains in some manner the same, remaining the same in being always already mutable, protean, articulated through the play of difference. It returns to itself but never quite as it was; it is always haunted by its previous forms and manifestations, any of which return to disturb any present moment. London takes place *as* place only in our recognition of the absence of form or image, which is to say the place of figuration envisaged as *processus*, in which, through which, is projected and performed a certain ruination, carried by figuration, as the ruin of ontology.[6] And it is this process, and this ruin, which the good reader, the good Londoner is open to, which he or she receives.

Ackroyd's multi- and cross-temporal and intertextual resonances are performative furthermore in this figural manner inasmuch as the text builds, through allusion and reference, the acknowledgement of other structures, other texts, into its own structure as that structure's possibility. This in itself hints at the possibility of a haunting urban continuity, and is given expression in both *Blake* and *The Life of Thomas More*. For example, we read that 'it is one of the features of London of this period that ruins were to be found among the modern buildings as a perpetual reminder of the city's past' (*B* 33), while, of Londoners' speech, 'through such tags and apothegms it is possible to glimpse a true permanence of continuity within English culture . . . a tradition of speech enduring for almost a thousand years' (*LTM* 20). Thus, Ackroyd can suggest that 'Londoners [of Blake's time] . . . were in fact like Londoners of all times and all periods' (*B* 33). Between architecture in ruins and the recurring fragments of language which persist in the everyday speech of the city, Ackroyd traces that sense of 'tradition' or 'continuity' which is so often perceived in his writing in a more general manner and is assumed to be that which Ackroyd creates. As the constant return of catchphrases suggests, there is a textual continuity, if by continuity we can infer a ruined or discontinuous continuity, one which is transformative, which translates itself from within itself. This sense of continuity or connection may well be the expression of a desire for connection through an act of seeking to read the traces as being in some way connected. As the first example of ruined architecture makes clear, the desire for the textual tracing is written into the very fabric of the city itself, as the space of the city knowingly alludes to its own resonant historical traces.

Writing's relationship to architectural structure and the topography of the city, its ability to trace in words the map and the space, refigures the city's own constant development and reinvention. At the same time, it performs the urban rhythm as Ackroyd weaves together architecture and text, topography and inscription. For example, as a means of placing ourselves in relation to both London and Ackroyd's own writing, we are informed that Dickens' godfather, Christopher Huffam, lived near to Nicholas Hawksmoor's Limehouse church (*D* 67). Although the Hawksmoor mentioned here is the historical figure and obviously neither Hawksmoor nor Dyer from *Hawksmoor*, nonetheless the resonance between the historical and the fictional remains in place, as it does when the architect's words are cited to describe William Blake's education as belonging to the 'hidden tradition of "English Gothic" ' (*B* 51). Nicholas Hawksmoor is as important a figure as William Blake, Charles Dickens, John Stow (*LTM* 4, 8, 10, 25, 112, 116, 234, 326), Thomas More, or the author of *London Lykpeny* in this hidden tradition described by the architect, a tradition always intimately connected to London (at least for Ackroyd, where Englishness and belonging to London are seemingly synonymous or, at the least, reciprocally resonant concepts). This 'hidden tradition' is most expressly encountered in the acknowledgement of the city being filled with 'angels and prophets' for Blake (*B* 33), or the darkness of the city, which for Dickens, was integral to the being of the city, and to which he 'added' a 'further note of darkness'. When 'we see London now,' Ackroyd argues, 'it is in part his own city still' (*D* 274–5). Our location in the urban structures of writing and mapping is the result of the echoes between texts. As Rainer Nägele puts it, '[e]ach encounter with any specific language or with any specific text is already determined by a structure of resonance' (*ET* 3).

Such resonant configuration can be traced in one example, between *Dickens* and *Dan Leno and the Limehouse Golem*. In the former, Thomas De Quincey's belated memory of his early years lost in the streets of London is cited in comparison with Dickens' own childhood experience of London around 'the thoroughfares of Oxford Street and Tottenham Street' (*D* 20). Importantly, it is the London passages of De Quincey's *Confessions of an English Opium Eater* which provide the resonating echoes for Ackroyd, rather than any historical detail. From these Ackroyd remarks in a language resonant with echoes of nineteenth-century prose, that 'it would be a foolish person indeed who did not believe that the strange mysteries and sorrows of London did not in some way pierce or move his infant breast' (*D* 20). De Quincey appears as an urban authority in *Dan Leno* also, particularly with regard to the Ratcliffe Highway murders. In the novel, reference to De Quincey's essay, 'On Murder Considered as One of the Fine Arts', is given by George Gissing, whom Ackroyd places reading an article on murder of Gissing's own, in the British Library. For Gissing, his predecessor creates a 'wonderful Romantic hero' of murderer John Williams (*DLLG* 37).

Gissing's article is at pains to connect the murders, and the recurrence of murders on the same sites, to the condition of 'sinister, crepuscular London, a haven for strange powers, a city of footsteps and flaring lights, of houses packed close together, of lachrymose alleys and false doors. London becomes a brooding presence behind, or perhaps even within, the murders themselves . . . It is not difficult to understand the force of De Quincey's obsession' (*DLLG* 38). From this, Gissing continues, to consider De Quincey's depiction of the scene in 'the great thoroughfare, Oxford Street . . . a street of sorrowful mysteries', before discussing how De Quincey's *Confessions* were believed at one time to have been written by Thomas Griffiths Wainewright, a 'critic and journalist' who championed William Blake, and who praised *Jerusalem* (*DLLG* 39–40). Wainewright, Gissing (Ackroyd) reveals, was also a murderer, who became fictionalized and 'celebrated by Charles Dickens in "Hunted Down"' (*DLLG* 40).[7] Thus, we might say: Ackroyd, recalling Gissing, recalling De Quincey, recalling Dickens, recalling De Quincey, recalling Ackroyd. It is not difficult, in this echo chamber which slips into the endless, and endlessly distorting mirroring of the *mise en abyme*, to understand the force of Ackroyd's obsession. For here, we have unfolding between novel and biography, undoing the limits and identities of both, the structure of resonance, and this occurs specifically through the obsession with London.

This is in effect what J. Hillis Miller, in defining the performative topography of Dickens' own writing, calls 'a way of doing things with words'.[8] The streets, their noise, movement and general crowded busyness, impose and translate themselves into the materiality of the text, producing what Peter Ackroyd is pleased to call in *Thomas More* 'brief but vivid intimations of London life . . .' (*LTM* 25), a phrase that we might without trouble append to *London: the Biography* as a descriptive subtitle. One key to understanding the performative element is perhaps in Ackroyd's choice of the word *intimations*, which resounds with *imitations* but neatly sidesteps the inference of mimesis in favour of a somewhat phenomenological apprehension. The words, in their frequently furious, condensed rhythms, their celerity and velocity, produce for the reader a ghostly and 'dissymmetrical experience'[9] of the London subject's experience; the dissymmetry haunts the irreversible passage from the materiality of the city to that of the letter, but in such a way that in reading it is *as if* I were that subject, that is to say, *as if I were confronted with the materiality of London*. It is not therefore a question of description. The city is not imitated or represented directly according to the devices of realist verisimilitude, for hardly is something, someone, named in its or their urban typicality, than off the passages rush again. Rather, there is a sense of dictation, to borrow Avital Ronell's term for that experience of the other's arrival, which in dictating demands a response through an act of writing appropriate to the city. Such a gesture repeatedly manages to respect the singularity of each scene according to its historical and cultural specificity while, at the same time, intimating that sense of continuity peculiar to the subject's encounter with the metropolis. Street cries for example, while being a perpetual part of the urban scene, have a historicity, a materiality of iterable recurrence and translation, the response to which offers 'another way of deciphering the chaos of the city' (*L:B* 180). However, even as the writing performs the city, there is also a ludic displacement of the intimated reality. Such displacement calls our attention to the language, to the text of the city, to recall Miller once more (*Top* 131). Thus, the 'biography' overflows its merely documentary and descriptive, recording functions. There is the suggestion of the writing escaping or exceeding the writer so rapidly do details come to sight, and so apparently without any order, except that imposed by the city on the attempted acts of inscription and memory through analogical resemblance or temporal iterability. *London: the Biography* is nothing, we might say, except this excessive flow, which is to say it is nothing other than the city.

So, in the face of such overwhelming immensity, we must return to the singular, to the figure of the Londoner. It has already been seen that this is the manner in which Ackroyd's biographies of More, Dickens, and Blake function; however, he opens his lecture on 'London Luminaries and Cockney Visionaries' by considering none of the more obvious figures but instead music hall star and pantomime dame, Dan Leno, the subject, albeit fictionalized, of Ackroyd's eighth novel. For many Londoners, Ackroyd argues, Leno was an expression of London; for the countless numbers who saw his performances and the thousands who lined the streets to witness his funeral procession, Dan Leno 'came to symbolize all the life and energy and variety of the city itself' (*TC* 341). But if Leno symbolized the city in a particular manner – and it is clear that for Ackroyd he does – then Ackroyd's writing is not simply content with illustrating the city through such an exemplary figure. It is also concerned with the demonstration of the ways in which, over long periods of time, not only are individual London subjects informed or written by their city, but also entire communities bear the iterable hallmarks of place and the effects on place of recurring events. Such dissymmetrical urban symbiosis (dissymmetrical because there is not a simple reciprocity, but rather a vertiginous dissemination, throughout the different times of the city) comes to animate the city for Ackroyd: 'sometimes it even seems to me that the city itself creates the conditions of its own growth, that it somehow plays an active part in its own development like some complex organism slowly discovering its form. Certainly, it affects the lives, the behaviour, the speech, even the gestures of the people who live within it' (*TC* 342). A popular conceit with Ackroyd, the idea is stated again in a lecture on William Blake as spiritual radical: 'there are . . . enchanted areas in London which remain visible and powerful to anyone who cares to look for them . . . The enchantment is one of place and time; it is as if an area can create patterns of interest, patterns of habitation, so that the same kinds of activity (indeed often the same kinds of people) seem to emerge in the same small territory' (*TC* 352–64; 355). Place and subject thus interanimate one another, and it is thus understood that, for the author, 'there are certain people to whom or through whom the territory – the place – the past – speaks' (*TC* 350).

III

As Ackroyd had addressed the question of the city writer's inheritance in his review of Iain Sinclair cited above, so we find the matter of inheritance inaugurating his seventh novel. *The House of Doctor Dee* begins with the words, 'I inherited the house from my father' (*HDD* 1). The sentence is the first uttered by Matthew Palmer, the narrator of one half of the novel, who, as that line tells us in part, inherits from his father a house in Clerkenwell.[10] The simple past tense of the sentence may be read as indicating a possibly endless tradition of inheritance, and thus allows for readings seeking thematic connections between this and other texts by Ackroyd, particularly those concerned with fathers and the inevitable break in filial continuity. The novel begins by recalling the past and the legacy of the past in the present, as the means by which the narrating subject seeks both to orient himself, to determine his identity in relationship to other identities, and to commence his narrative. Inheritance implicitly transforms a 'beginning' into a narrative moment *in medias res*, as the condition of self-identification. Self-awareness dawns as a condition of the recognition of temporal continuity. The first line retains an anonymity, however, despite the first-person narrative, even while it has the capacity to seduce through the mystery of as-yet-unspoken narrative threads. It seeks to inscribe a double writing: that which is both intimate and, seemingly, universal, promising the story of both Matthew Palmer and, in a certain way, Everyman.

The House of Doctor Dee is formed from two narratives, which are told for the most part in alternating chapters. This structure resembles, at least superficially, that of *Hawksmoor*, even to the point where the narratives seemingly converge. In *The House of Doctor Dee*, narrative strands are divided between Matthew Palmer and John Dee, between the twentieth and the sixteenth centuries. The dialectical interanimation between past and present destabilizes historical location and, for the reader, historical knowingness, in such a way that other Londons manifest themselves. As a result, the ontology of London is disrupted from within, thereby establishing the ground for a critical intervention in the reading and reception of the city. This is effected through the material revenance of the city's past in the form of the pastiche of period English, through the speech of John Dee and Nicholas Dyer. In both *Hawksmoor* and *Doctor Dee*, Ackroyd places London's present in crisis through its protagonists, who themselves undergo epistemological crises, leading to visions, or what Walter Benjamin calls the 'dialectical image . . . an image that emerges suddenly' (*AP* 473).[11] And it is this event for the subject of the city that 'awakens' the Londoner (to borrow Benjamin's term for the phenomenological response to vision) to the material persistence of the city, thereby inaugurating the possibility of a reading to come.

To focus though on the double structure of *The House of Doctor Dee*: Matthew Palmer's chapters are numbered, as if to give his narration only the most fundamental of structures, barely an identity at all. Dee's, on the other hand, are given titles, which are as follows: 'The Spectacle', 'The Library', The Hospital', 'The Abbey', 'The Chamber of Demonstration', 'The City', 'The Closet', 'The Garden'. In accordance with the importance given in this book to architectural structures (as suggested in the very title of the novel), each chapter title (with the exception of the first and final titles) names a formal architectural structure, whether a room or building. Arguably, even 'The Garden' may be said to name a formal structure. In the final chapter, also given a title ('The Vision'), moments of being and moments in time come together. In this last chapter there is a free flowing play between distinct temporal locations, which nonetheless are overlaid on one another in the same area of London. The more rigid imposition of formal structure is undone in the concluding chapter. At the same time, there is also a movement outside the times of Palmer's and Dee's narratives, when someone masquerading as the author steps forward to question what his responsibility is to his characters and to present his vision of London.

With regard to the idea of a structure that gradually comes to be revealed in all its interconnections, the idea of the house is itself important, as just suggested. It offers the reader an image that is simultaneously both material and spectral, inasmuch as it figures a sense of dwelling[12] across time. It is less important that it is *a* dwelling, than that it announces indirectly that which abides or dwells as one manifestation of the spirit of London, and even as its material existence writes itself into the fabric of the city, being but one figure for the otherwise unimaginable or unknowable totality. Like the name *London*, the house is one provisional signature for that which cannot be represented. In being what remains, what is inherited, the house announces the abiding sense of the preservation of the spirit of place, but because this spirit is irreducible to either direct or mimetic representation or ontology, and is only known on reflection and in response to its persistence, it can only be apprehended as a process, as a becoming rather than a being; Ackroyd's novel acknowledges the awakening of this comprehension through Matthew Palmer and through the process and time that the narrative takes to arrive at the disclosedness of spirit through Palmer's eventual vision. Significance of location only comes to be received through the processes of becoming we name time and narrative, which simultaneously unfold through difference even as they gather the traces of that double motion of deferral and differentiation, of taking place and making place. Through the singular figure of the house, we are afforded the analogical apprehension of the fact that while there may arrive the experience of the city, an experience that calls for a response through the act of writing the city faithfully, this experience is not the same as identification. Thus we are vouchsafed the idea that the city, to borrow a formula of Derrida's concerning literature, *is not*. In saying this, I should stress the fact that in offering this apparently negative formula, I am not proposing some merely formal or nihilist response. Rather, the resistance to the fixity of the ontological model implied by negation speaks to the most radical materiality of persistence, of dwelling; for, the 'historicity of its experience [which is everywhere borne witness to throughout *London* and, indeed throughout all Ackroyd's writing] . . . rests on the very thing no ontology could essentialize'. Even 'where it seems to *reside*', the very idea of the city, along with its phantomatic and phantasmatic processes, remain 'unstable function[s]'.[13]

Coming to an understanding of this, we must remark that *The House of Doctor Dee* is not particularly concerned with real buildings, except as they may be said to mark sites in London which have significant narratives to tell, so that, in Ackroyd's London, a building such as a house or library, or an area such as Clerkenwell or Limehouse, is formed through a structural resonance which is both temporal and spatial, and which therefore serves in an emblematic manner for the writer as a figure for the secret history and the spectral revenance of London as a whole, all traces of the city being interwoven. *The House of Doctor Dee* is not even concerned with the particular building in which the historical figure of John Dee had lived in Barnes. Instead this is another house and with it another Dee, an imagined figure and one of several possible Dees, as Matthew Palmer suggests, unsure of himself, when he puts it to his friend, Daniel Moore, that ' "every book has a different Doctor Dee . . . The past is difficult, you see. You think you understand a person or an event, but then you turn a corner and everything is different once again . . . It's like this house too" ' (*HDD* 136). The house, the inheritance, and, we feel, the city, is filled with inexplicable occurrences, chance encounters, possibly overheard voices, the fleeting glimpse of another reality. Matthew's acknowledgement of the ability to reinvent a historical figure also suggests that no past figure or moment of history can ever be wholly recuperated, even while it may resonate within the present. Interestingly, Palmer employs a structural, if not a topographical metaphor, when he notes how things are different once one 'turns a corner'. This metaphorical passage is given literal significance later, when Palmer, speaking of an area of London he believed he knew well, says: 'but I found myself turning down an unexpected and unfamiliar lane. That is the nature of the city, after all: in any neighbourhood you can come across a street, or a close, that seems to have been perpetually hidden away' (*HDD* 265). Whether the question concerns the city, an identity, a house, or a passage in a text, it is one concerning that which comes to light by accident, being a matter of chance illumination or concatenation rather than deliberate inquiry. Matthew's remark to Moore tries to pursue a labyrinthine thread, to create connections. Beginning with reading, interpretation, and identity, he moves through the question of time and historical narrative, to that metaphorical turn that implies the moment of wandering, to the often haunted, uncanny nature of the house. This labyrinth – which is implicitly architectural as well as formal, as are all labyrinths – is also the condition of the city itself. The connections being traced, and which effectively trace themselves, are both visible and invisible. Palmer suddenly comes to recognize the hidden course of the 'old River Soken . . . from Waltham Forest down through Bethnal Green and Shadwell' (*HDD* 179), where it will merge with the Thames. Later, Palmer thinks when looking at the flow of traffic down the Farringdon Road, that 'it seemed to me then that it would go on forever, in the various forms of various centuries, following in the direction of the old Fleet River' (*HDD* 261). Earlier in the novel, Matthew Palmer had heard running water in his house in Clerkenwell, and had imagined in that the sound of the Fleet River as heard by John Dee (*HDD* 126).

We should pause momentarily in the discussion of *The House of Doctor Dee* to consider London's rivers. Rivers are of undeniable significance to the identity of London; so much so in fact that, of the Thames Ackroyd remarks '[t]he city itself owes its character and appearance to the Thames' (*L:B* 539). Moreover, while the Thames, and its other rivers (many now vanished) flow and have flowed through the city, thereby serving to articulate London's singularity, Ackroyd has also observed how rivers flow through its inhabitants, one example being J. M. W. Turner, to whom the Thames gave 'light and movement' (*L:B* 546). The docks along the river offered to some 'spectacles of London' as 'an unnatural phantasmagoria' (*L:B* 547), and there is a 'sense of mystery – of something living and alien – that lies at the heart of the city's life' (*L:B* 546). Perhaps for this very reason the Thames is also, and has been for many centuries, 'a river of the dead' (*L:B* 551). Of the lost rivers of London, amongst which are those mentioned by Matthew Palmer, Ackroyd suggests that they are not 'wholly dead . . . and occasionally emerge into the light'; they still flow 'beneath the streets of the city, replete with their own underground ghosts and nymphs' (*L:B* 558), while, referring to an earlier study of London, it is observed that most reported sightings of ghosts take place in houses closest to waterways. Perhaps, Ackroyd surmises, 'the spirit . . . of buried waters may be asserting themselves' (*L:B* 555).

However, while London's rivers have assumed significance in the city beyond the purely commercial or topographical, Ackroyd resists making any direct assertions concerning the more enigmatic aspects of the ways in which rivers write the city, whether writing of them in *London: the Biography* or in novels such as *Doctor Dee*. In this novel, he chooses deliberately banal moments such as the flowing of water and the flow of traffic to make connections indirectly. Resisting the forcing of the mystical and hermetic, the novelist tentatively traces possible imaginative concatenations, thereby hinting at the city's identity whilst also suggestively retaining its ineffability in instances of tentative, provisional comprehension. In this way, 'a buried city had been discovered. *Something* from the past had been restored' (*HDD* 179; emphasis added). What that *something* might be remains unspoken and unspeakable, and thus all the more potent. To put this in another way, what is most important for Ackroyd is the acknowledgement of the possibility of a certain movement or 'flow', rather than the act of deciphering what the flow might mean. This is acknowledged by Daniel Moore, early in *The House of Doctor Dee*, when he tells Palmer, ' ". . . all time has flowed here, into this house" ' (*HDD* 82). If we understand the connection between identity and house, between house and city, we begin to comprehend the haunting possibilities of connection.

Such moments of illumination serve to map alternative geographies, topographies, and histories for the city, even as they make tentative topographical, temporal connections, so that, simultaneously, the city both is and is not the same. This haunting of the other within the same is intrinsic to any acknowledgement of the urban condition. Ackroyd's interest is with spiritual or spectral topographies and architectural or architextural forms, reading the possible connections of which acknowledges the haunting trace of otherness and the past within present identity, whether that identity is that of Matthew Palmer or the city of London. Indeed Palmer might well be read as one more emblematic figure of London and the connections that are made between personal identity and the urban sense of self. At one moment, Palmer remarks that ' "sometimes I feel as if I'm excavating some lost city within myself" ' (*HDD* 83). When visiting the National Archive Centre in order to pursue research in the parish records of Clerkenwell, Matthew senses the enmeshed relationship between the signatures of 'the long–dead' on the documents he handles and 'the true self' (*HDD* 89). Moreover, it is not merely a question of the signatures themselves and their ghostly traces, but also the paper on which they are written. 'I could feel the texture of the paper beneath my fingers,' remarks Matthew, 'and it was like earth baking in the heat of this modern city' (*HDD* 89). The library thus acts as the architectural form in which archives connecting the traces of London's pasts to those of the present are maintained. Importantly, the parish records determine identity through the connection of signature and place. As parish records make clear, the giving of identity through the baptismal gift of the proper name, by which one is given one's identity, is intimately bound up with the place within which one's identity arrives. One's self is authorized according to locale; the inscription of one's identity is an event that takes place within a specific area and is recorded as belonging to that area.

More generally, however, London libraries are important to Matthew, even though '[o]nce upon a time' he was afraid of them (*HDD* 129). They provide for him 'a world . . . a sweet labyrinth of learning in which I could lose myself . . .' (*HDD* 129). Libraries provide a place where, Palmer imagines, books 'are forever engaged in an act of silent communion, which, if we are fortunate, we can overhear' (*HDD* 129). This passing remark hints that nothing has been lost in the city. Begun with that invocation of the beginning of all narrative, a moment of lost origins, Matthew Palmer's discussion of the relationship between his identity and his sense of connectedness to libraries comes almost exactly at the structural middle of *The House of Doctor Dee*. It is as if Ackroyd has fashioned a textual labyrinth into the absent heart of which Palmer must probe – and the reader follow – before he can begin to emerge or awaken into an awareness of the connection between his sense of self and the city. The figure of the library provides an architectural matrix where temporal structures of resonance and spatial connections overlay one another, as archive and labyrinth overdetermine each other in a place where the present self and the texts of the other and of the past come together.

Ackroyd's description of one particular library, the English History Library, relies on the material condition of the library for its ability to hint at temporal passage and spatial significance. The library is, according to Matthew Palmer, 'of all London libraries . . . the most curious and dilapidated; the passages are narrow, the stairs circuitous, and the general atmosphere one of benign decay. The books here are often piled up on the floors, while the shelves can hardly bear the weight of the volumes which have been deposited on them over the years' (*HDD* 129). Ackroyd's writing maps out and thereby constructs the imagined space of the library, reminiscent in its inscribed delineation of Piranesi's drawn text. Like Piranesi, Ackroyd, both in his construction of the library and in his mapping of the city from various temporal moments, provides a blueprint for the urban labyrinth in that image of the decaying and dilapidated gathering of random texts. The archival crypt of the library houses the countless scripts of the city, which appear to promise to map out the city itself. Yet at the same time, to borrow from Jennifer Bloomer's discussion of Piranesi's drawings, Ackroyd's writing of the library in particular and the city in general intimates an endless reciprocity between city and text, where the library, and, in turn, the city act as markers 'of something greater' while also being 'built and ordered [or, perhaps more appropriately *disordered*] upon collective mythmaking and, most significant, . . . its palimpsestic, [PATCHWORK] like form'.[14] We come to learn even as Matthew Palmer begins to apprehend, that the city, like the self, is 'an intricate network of sites of interpretation' (*ATJP* 72). Ackroyd thus allows the city's revenants to return through the gradual awakening of Palmer and, in so doing, he weaves various strands together drawn from countless manifestations of

London, which serve in a provisional vision of the eternal city of London, from out of the secret and submerged histories of the city.

Structural resonance and palimpsest, the insistence of place, recurring events on the same location, *genius loci*: all are important in *The House of Doctor Dee*, as are recurring images, figures, and traces of light, both literal and metaphorical, and enlightenment, all of which persist throughout the text. Light, enlightenment, illumination: all are illustrative of the instant of awakening hypothesized by Walter Benjamin. Their function in the narrative is double, for they trace and enact what Benjamin terms the lightning flashes of materialist knowledge (*AP* 457, 473); in doing this, the trope of light and its cognates project the image events by which reading might begin. Matthew's father once asked his son whether he felt the light 'coming through the stone of this wonderful city' (*HDD* 7), while Matthew remarks of the house that 'the white walls seemed to be trembling with light' (*HDD* 80). Matthew, on coming to recognize something of his identity and its indebtedness to the city, remarks on the perceived connection amongst those who work with books, and who thereby travel back through the city's history as a disparate community connected to the past. He says of entering libraries that 'it is as if I were entering a place I had once known and forgotten, and in the same *light of recognition* had remembered something of myself' (*HDD* 12–13). John Dee remarks that light is 'the origin of wonders' (*HDD* 20), and that 'there must also be light within us to reflect . . . meaning' (*HDD* 74). He comments later, in an echo of Matthew's own sentiments regarding texts that 'I concluded with myself that it was only in books and histories I might find the light for which I searched' (*HDD* 33), qualifying this further still by recalling that 'I soon found myself bent towards other learning as towards a glorious light' (*HDD* 34). Indeed, while Matthew Palmer feels initially no connection to the world, to the house or the city (*HDD* 4), both men come to be connected apparently by a vision which offers to join them, not directly in occult communion but through a shared enlightenment, this being an instance of light's projection from the city:

'About a year ago I was walking by the Thames. Do you know, near Southwark? When suddenly I thought I saw a bridge of houses. A shimmering bridge, lying across the river . . . It was like a bridge of light.' (*HDD* 17)

These words, first spoken by Palmer to Daniel Moore, are heard by John Dee as he witnesses the visionary scene towards the end of the novel

(*HDD* 273). Just prior to this moment, his house having been burnt and his library destroyed, Dee walks through London to find himself presented with a city of lights, 'a holy city where time never was' (*HDD* 272), to be informed by a vagrant that ' "the spirit never dies, and this city is formed within the spiritual body of man" ' (*HDD* 273). This remark recalls Palmer's own conceit of excavating the city from within himself, already commented on above (*HDD* 83). Thus, Ackroyd traces resonant configurations throughout the structure of the text, foregrounding, often through the projection of light as the medium of enlightenment, the possibility of the revelation of connection. For Ackroyd nothing is ever lost in the city. Instead its spectres play endlessly, serving to form and inform London, time and again. Such ghostly figures occasionally project themselves in such a manner that their resonance – which Palmer describes vaguely as 'some interior life and reality which glowed within all things' (*HDD* 42) – enlightens.

The city, the dual narratives, and the text in general: all are haunted by immanence and return, therefore, in an abyssal reciprocity. A constant folding, overfolding, and unfolding takes place as if to bring to light or project the resonance of the interwoven and multiplying structures of a novel, where possible, if dissonant correspondence resounds. Conceivable correspondence is recognized by Matthew in the opening chapter, when he acknowledges that, though the house 'was only a few yards from the Farringdon Road . . . yet it was entirely quiet. I might just as well have entered a sacred room' (*HDD* 3). The correspondence is indirect, from the disturbance occasioned by the quietness, to the imagined architecture of the sacred room. He does not yet understand why the quiet disturbs and yet apprehends something about the room. The room itself is a metonymic figure for the house, and both in turn signify indirectly the city. The idea of the house itself is therefore structured as the locus of revenance, attempted communication, and the temporal persistence of a shared, if barely recognized, identity. This house therefore, and to reiterate the point, figures both the condition of London itself, and those who are 'of London'. At the same time, it is also a figure for the construction of Ackroyd's novel in particular and the resonant structures of writing as comprehended by Ackroyd: 'the eighteenth–century façade of the ground floor had been designed as a casing or shell for the sixteenth–century interior' (*HDD* 16). Layer on layer and structure within structure, the house is figured by Ackroyd as a material, architectural analogy for writing the city, as well as offering a figure for that act of writing as appropriate response to the demand of the city.

Eric Korn defines such interrelation as 'psychomorphic resonance'.[15] Although he is speaking only of the relationship between Palmer and Dee, absent from this insight is an acknowledgement that this mutual resonance belongs to the greater resonance of the city within both men, whereby one may understand the psychomorphic as also the psycho-geographic. They do not connect to one another merely; rather, both are connected by the flow of London as it courses through them, simul-taneously and across time. Clearly, Ackroyd is concerned to pursue as far as possible the interanimation between the material condition of the city and its ghostly otherness, which may be glimpsed as that which persists within the city's material being. To take one example, this is captured in the resonance and significance of street names, which are 'the visible remnants' (*L:B* 25) of earlier manifestations of the city. In this, topographical vision can be 'entwined with allegorical meaning' (Benjamin *AP* 518). As the biographies' acts of writing London show us, London returns relentlessly both through the persistence of such sig-natures, along with the ghosts they invoke for the city's readers, in the psychic and archival topography of London, as well as through more obviously material constructions, such as the incorporation of ruins into the renovation of buildings and other sites. It is as if 'the stones them-selves carried the burden of their own destiny' (*L:B* 671). To point to just a couple of textual examples of the ways in which street name proves 'ancient provenance' (*L:B* 669): London's ghostly imprimatur and 'persistent echoic effect' (*L:B* 669) arrive through the choice of place and street names in *The House of Doctor Dee*. Matthew Palmer recalls or is used to alert the reader to street names, without necessar-ily understanding their general significance himself. In remembering the area in which he grew up, he recalls a number of street names, including the Anglo–Saxon names of Wulfstan and Erconwald (*HDD* 175). There is perhaps nothing that important about these names, other than their persistence and return as the counter–signatures of another London appearing as coincidental traces within the modern city. Yet, for all that, resonance *is there*. Another example of the manifestation of the past through the remnant of the proper name occurs when Palmer crosses 'Clerkenwell Green into Jerusalem Passage' (*HDD* 40), the name of the passage recalling a twelfth–century abbey 'of the Knights Templar' (*HDD* 40) which had stood in the area until the Reformation (*AP* 522). The name clearly testifies to what remains, to the remains of an other city, even as it announces that the city is produced as much through the materiality of language as it is through the materiality of its archi-tectural and topographic structures. As Benjamin remarks, the city makes possible a 'revolution in language', through the naming of streets, whereby the city is readable as 'a linguistic cosmos' (*AP* 522), a constellation of signatures announcing multiple identities, multiple temporal moments. The street and place name thus offer fragmentary signatures returning endlessly from some other location to speak of an excess beyond what can be read.

In *The House of Doctor Dee*, the materiality of language is manifested in a number of other ways. There is of course the following admission towards the end of the novel:

> And what is the past, after all? Is it that which is created in the formal act of writing, or does it have some substantial reality? Am I discovering it, or inventing it? Or could it be that I am discovering it within myself, so that it bears both the authenticity of surviving evidence and the immediacy of present intuition? *The House of Doctor Dee* itself leads me to that conclusion: no doubt you expected it to be written by the author whose name appears on the cover and the title–page, but in fact many of the words and phrases are taken from John Dee himself. If they are not his words, they belong to his contemporaries. Just as he took a number of mechanical parts and out of them constructed a beetle that could fly, so I have taken a number of obscure texts and have fashioned a novel from their rearrangement. (*HDD* 275)

In what appears to be the voice of the author, there is the acknowledgement of the persistence of the materiality of language. The novel, it is insisted, is a patchwork construct, a constellated assemblage. The analogy between mechanical construction and writing as construction makes apparent a certain relationship between *tekhne* and *poiesis*. Neither simply a novel written in the latter part of the twentieth century nor merely a pastiche, this text is configured from multiple voices and multiple writings, from different places and different temporal instances, *making* being also a *making appear*. Dee's writing and the other inscriptions from the sixteenth century are worked into the fabric of the text, returning to make the form possible. Thus anachronistically, language marked indelibly by the traces of its own historicity returns materially, dismantling discrete temporal location, the trace of the past haunting and informing the present as a counter–signature.

Elsewhere, the ghostly materiality of language arrives to leave its mark in yet another manner. Towards the end of the novel, Matthew Palmer and his mother find some indecipherable signs scratched into the brickwork of a garage (from the bricks of which there appears to emanate a dim light), once owned by Matthew's father (*HDD* 267). Matthew has no sense of what the marks might mean, although he does wonder aloud whether the stones before him are of the present or past, or both. This question connects to Dee's assertion that ' "all that ever we were left is the London stone, which is a visible portion of the lost city" ' (*HDD* 156). Earlier, when Matthew and Daniel explore the house, they find other unreadable symbols scratched into the fabric of the building, in the basement, 'very little [of which] could now be traced' (*HDD* 14–15). Daniel speculates that the basement was never a basement at all but, originally, the ground floor, ' "and it has slowly sunk through the London clay" ' (*HDD* 15). Elsewhere, John Dee has cause to notice the marks on an inn table, which he says seemed to 'boast cabbalistical scribblings' (*HDD* 30). Signs are thus found in various places materially embedded into the very fabric of the city. However, and paradoxically, the more the materiality of the sign is made manifest – library shelves threaten to give way beneath the weight of accumulated books, stone and wood are transformed into text through the traces left upon them – and the greater the potential 'weight' or possible meaning, the harder it is to read the signs. So embedded into the material texture of place and encrypted or buried by time, the materiality of the signifier affirms its otherness and historicity by resisting any interpretative mastery. Once more, Ackroyd plays with the potential for asserting meaning and making connections, even while he never wholly gives in to the desire to make the connection explicitly. The city, like the signs inscribed in its material, is barely readable as a certain concatenation of palimpsests that are undeniably there, even while meaning and identity remain undecidable. We might suggest that we can only read the undecidable as what remains, from the remains, the ruins of the city's past inscribed into the present. All we can read is that we cannot read, and it is in this resistance that the city returns as the eternal city because it cannot be presented or represented. In this manner, Ackroyd reveals how there is always another figure within the perceived structure, which by chance may come to resonate, giving us to receive London as 'this wonderful city' (*HDD* 29), 'the entire mystical city', and 'the most wonderful city on the face of the globe, a mystical city eternal' (*HDD* 167, 168).

The phrase 'the mystical city eternal' concludes *The House of Doctor Dee*, as though the reiteration of the phrase itself were somehow able to announce the condition of London, or as though, in the absence or impossibility of definition, the phrase itself would speak of the city, albeit indirectly. If language and text, stone and structure leave their trace, what of the countless Londoners? Perhaps most poignantly in the act of writing the city, in striving to return via language the sense of the eternal city, Ackroyd seeks to recall those whom he calls the 'forgotten inhabitants of London' (*HDD* 276). Towards the end of the final chapter, an anonymous voice once more appears, speaking of shining his light in the 'dark streets of London' (*HDD* 276), this illumination falling on the faces of the forgotten. These are not only the tramps or itinerant street vendors who appear, across the centuries and across the biographies in Ackroyd; they are also 'the Moravians of Arrow Lane, the Ranters, the followers of Jakob Boehme', the Swedenborgians, the Huguenots, and other dissenting groups. In this attempt to bring to light so many anonymous figures, we read an act of responsibility. The ethical gesture is sought in the effort to allow the other London voices to speak for themselves (often through the mediumistic act of pastiche), rather than to speak for them. It is perhaps as part of this gambit on Ackroyd's part that he only ever traces the possibility of connection, rather than forcing connections on his readers. It is in this way that we come to comprehend how, for the novelist, these forgotten inhabitants, 'and so many others, all of them still living within the city' (*HDD* 276) are 'all those with whom we dwell – living or dead' (*HDD* 277). In comprehending this, we come to understand how we, like all the others, 'will become the mystical city eternal' (*HDD* 277).

IV

Dan Leno and the Limehouse Golem produces London as a resonant configuration of textual grafts, trace upon trace, fold upon fold. It chooses to make little if any apparent distinction between the 'evidence' of so-called 'real' or 'imagined' texts. Texts thus compose and construct the urban space as much as the pages from the Bible pasted to the walls construct in a certain manner the room in which Elizabeth Cree lives as a child: 'Our two rooms were bare enough, except for the pages of the Bible which she had pasted to the walls. There was hardly an inch of paper to be made out between them, and from my earliest childhood I could see nothing but words. I even taught myself to read from them . . .' (*DLLG* 12). In this instance, pages cover, obscuring, copying, and assuming architectural form. This single domestic instance provides the reader with a performative textual and synecdochic figure, for the comprehension of the city that the novel advances. At stake are the ways in which particular texts belong to a greater textual network or structure, and the uses to which textual evidence is put in searching for meaning or framing the definition. To recall the novel's title in the USA (*The Trial of Elizabeth Cree*), 'on trial' before the reader as witness is the reliability of the city's texts, none of which is allowed any especial precedence or validity in Ackroyd's performative and playful structure. Formed from endless replications and palimpsests,[16] London is performed as a transformed series of texts, having always already become, in Carol Bernstein's words, 'the scene of writing' (*CS* 45) where there are enacted equally endless 'correspondences between urban and verbal creation [in] a city now conceived of as text' (*CS* 45), into and through which Ackroyd weaves his own act of urban inscription, as yet one more turn in the performance of London. 'Here we are again', the phrase uttered on various occasions by Elizabeth Cree, Dan Leno, and John Cree, is readable as the city's own performative epigraph (*DLLG* 2, 191, 279, 280).

The novel is divided into four principal narrative strands: the journal of John Cree, Elizabeth Cree's 'autobiography' or 'monologue', pastiched contemporary documentary sources, including journalism of the period (Ch. 37), court transcripts, and third–person narrative, which occasionally assumes a somewhat pedantic historical-critical tone. *Dan Leno* raises questions concerning authenticity and masquerade, circulating its numerous texts around the condition of the city, which, Ackroyd makes us aware is excessive – concerned with performativity, performance, iterability, transformation, and translation. Among the four principal narrative structures, composing a four–fold London narrative structure, there are many more voices and texts at work. There are citations, and citations within citations. Ackroyd cites, or otherwise alludes to, Marx. He cites Gissing. The novelist cites Gissing citing De Quincey or Babbage, while Gissing is said to compare Babbage's understanding of London to that of Dickens (*DLLG* 117). In the discussion of Babbage's vision, William Blake is commented on, via a critical study of Swinburne's from the *Westminster Review*, which Gissing had been reading, allegedly, prior to his visit to the site of Babbage's experiments with the 'Difference Engine' and the 'Analytical Engine' in Limehouse (*DLLG* 118). Ackroyd comments that Gissing is struck by the possible correspondence between Babbage and Blake, in that both men conceive of designs, the significance of which is obscure to all but themselves. Commentary within commentary, text enfolding text, the significance of location in its historical continuity and resonance cannot escape Ackroyd's readers. We can suggest that the phrase 'Difference Engine' names not only Babbage's invention. It identifies also the complex layering of coincidences, of textual and historical events within the city and the differential structure, the temporal and spatial construct which is London.

Elsewhere in Gissing's musings, the texts of the city are cited and coincide, bringing together topographical and architectural concerns. Gissing's article, 'Romanticism and Crime',[17] tells how Thomas De Quincey and Ann

> would meet in order to console each other among 'the mighty labyrinths of London'. That is why the city and his suffering within it became – if we may borrow a phrase from that great modern poet Charles Baudelaire – the landscape of his imagination . . . it could be said that the old highway led him directly to those nightmares and fantasies which turned London into some mighty vision akin to that of Piranesi, a labyrinth of stone, a wilderness of blank walls and floors. These were the visions, at least, which he recounted many years later when he lodged in York Street off Covent Garden. (*DLLG* 39)

Ackroyd draws together writers for whom the urban and imaginary structures present similar possibilities of poetic imagination in this passage. He thereby appears to promise forms of connection, linked not merely thematically but, more importantly, structurally or temporally. The urban imaginary is mapped through the occurrence of the proper name, which itself stands in for other texts in an implied, potentially endless *architexture*. Furthermore, Ackroyd implies that the city, its streets and buildings, its localities and details, can only be known through the trace, the ruin, and analogical reverberation. Moreover, the city can only be given form through the textual act, an act which is a response that recognizes the already textual condition of the city. The city can never be recovered except as the labyrinthine archive of anamnesis. Endless replications and palimpsests are the only true forms of the city; there is no originary or single identity or ontology for London, which can then be represented faithfully and unequivocally.

The second chapter adopts the historical–critical discourse, to introduce the story of the 'Limehouse Golem', detailing the myth and the meaning of the word 'Golem', which we are assured 'literally means "thing without form"' (*DLLG* 4) (another possible translation could be 'matter without form'). As with both narrative and the city, the creature only comes to have shape as it is 'filled', so to speak, with details, descriptions, and actions. Form is the result of narrative, and each narrative will take on a different structure, as we come to understand through the multiple layerings of *Dan Leno and the Limehouse Golem*. The Golem is compared to that other mythological creature, the homunculus, before the reader is told that the secret of the 'revival' of the Golem is 'to be found within *the annals of London's past*' (*DLLG* 4; emphasis added). Once more, there is that sense of cautious, calm critical delineation in process. The reader is then directed to the description of the first of a series of murders, vaguely reminiscent of those of Jack the Ripper:

> The first killing occurred on the 10th September, 1880, along Lime-house Reach: this, as the name implies, was an ancient lane which led from a small thoroughfare of mean houses to a flight of stone steps just above the bank of the Thames. It had been used by porters over many centuries for convenient if somewhat cramped access to the cargo of smaller boats which anchored here, but the dock redevelopments of the 1830s had left it marooned on the edge of the mud banks. It reeked of dampness and old stone, but it also possessed a stranger and more fugitive odour which was aptly described by one of the residents of the neighbourhood as that of 'dead feet'. (*DLLG* 5)

Once more, the discursive 'source' or 'tone' appears easily identifiable and assumed. The documentary detail, the use of date, the reflection on name, all point to an historical–critical 'voice'. The reader is thus expected to partake in a performance of a particular kind, being expected implicitly to accept the verisimilitude of the performance. Ackroyd sets up a structural resonance with a critical discourse, here as throughout the text, especially when speaking of supposedly factual and historical matters relating to London. However, what gives the reader pause is that final definition of the 'strange and more fugitive odour'. The tone, and, with it, the identity of the passage is unsettled through the attributed definition. Moreover, what is interesting about this playful effect is that it works in a number of ways. The phrase, 'dead feet', is caught between a kind of gothic cliché or the intimation of a sense of the uncanny which often haunts texts of terror in the 1870s, 1880s, and 1890s (this novel is set in the 1880s), such as *Dracula, The Picture of Dorian Gray, The Strange Case of Doctor Jekyll and Mr Hyde,* or *The Beetle,* and a comic, farcical effect more immediately reminiscent of Charles Dickens. Furthermore, the phrase arrives as the punctuating and defining moment from outside the critical–historical discourse being mimicked here. An other London emerges from within, exceeding as it does the limits of fin de siècle representations of London. And, as we are told, the phrase belongs to an unidentified Londoner. A disembodied East End voice, a voice belonging to and returning from Walter Besant's 'immense, neglected, forgotten great city' (see Chapter 1) displaces the authority of the assumed discourse, bringing back the urban scene and its community. A certain authority is subverted, and this takes place, importantly, in the form of a return, a certain haunting which, in each case, is given a specific London identity. In effect, the text is disjointed by the return of the urban trace, a trace always connected, however obliquely, to the city, and pertaining to irreverence, to performative and dissonant, even dissident identities. It is as though the city haunts any normalizing or homogenizing narrative which seeks to maintain distance from it, as the others rise through any moment of stability, as if to remind us that 'here we are again'.

Hence the 'return' of violent acts, of serial killing and mass murder, as particularly violent traces or echoes of the city's disturbing identity (of which more below); for 'London has always possessed a reputation for violence', Ackroyd remarks in *London*, 'it stretches back as far as the written records' (*L:B* 477).[18] The historicity of violence is paralleled then, by the act of narrating such brutality. Such traces are both indelible and spectral, and given particular, exemplary 'form' in the imagined shape of the Golem. As already suggested, the Golem never exists as such. It is only a textual trace, a shared, communal memory, given life only through the articulation of its possibility. This possibility of resonance extends from the novel to the murders identified as those committed by Jack the Ripper. The resonance between Ackroyd's novel and the Ripper murders is enough to seduce certain readers into seeking further correspondences, even though these are not necessarily there. Indeed, given that the prostitutes, a Jewish scholar, Solomon Weil, and a family are murdered, it is as true to say that the scene of Ackroyd's novel in no way resembles the Ripper murders, other than in the coincidence that this 'scene' is staged in the East End of London. The Ripper murders occurred in Whitechapel, the victims being exclusively prostitutes, as is well known. Ackroyd's 'murders' have little in common with the events in Whitechapel, unless we take John Cree's word that he has committed them. The murders of the novel are all particularly staged, bloodily violent and melodramatic. Indeed, Cree persistently connects the murders to theatrical performance, seeing London as his stage. At one point, one of those moments in Ackroyd's writing where 'tone' doubles itself being, in this example both horrific and crassly comic, Cree recalls of one of his victims that, 'her head lay upon the upper step, just as if it were the prompter's head seen from the pit of the theatre' (*DLLG* 62).

However, beyond this, there is no connecting meaning for the murders, unless it goes by the mystical and mystifying name 'Golem', which in itself tells us little about the identity of the murderer but is merely a journalistic means for creating and constructing a narrative pattern pertinent to the East End of London in general and to Limehouse in particular. While John Cree 'admits' to the murders of the prostitutes, Weil, and the family who occupy a house on the Ratcliffe Highway, the site of the Marr murders (those discussed by Thomas De Quincey) in his journal, there is no conclusive evidence in the novel that Cree did commit the murders. All the reader has to go on is textual evidence without any access to authenticity or any authenticating trace. Whether or not Cree did kill and butcher the various victims of the so–called Golem, the suggestion is never made that he is the Golem. Indeed, the Golem only 'exists' in writing, in the form of words on the page, at least as far as *Dan Leno and the Limehouse Golem* is concerned.

This is in itself appropriate both to the mythology of the Golem and to the narration of London. As mentioned before, 'Golem' can mean thing or matter without form. The *Oxford English Dictionary* renders the term from the Hebrew as 'shapeless mass'. The Golem can only appear by its being given form, so that, every time the Golem is made, it necessarily must assume a singular identity. Part of the formation of the Golem is the inscription on the Golem of the Hebrew word *emet*, meaning *true*. The word must be inscribed on the Golem's hand, in order that it come to life (at the same time, however, if the first character of the Hebrew word is erased, what remains is not 'true' but the Hebrew for 'death'). Each Golem is therefore the true Golem, given identity by the inscription of the word. The 'truth' of the Golem is only found in its singular manifestation, its truth embodied in itself. Writing thus gives the Golem its being. Writing determines form, while simultaneously enacting it. The shapeless mass is effaced even as it is transformed in the act of inscription made upon it, which changes its shape with every textual act. For these reasons, there is no Golem in Ackroyd's novel, even though there, *there*, is Golem – Golem written or whispered everywhere, the effect of the revenant trace, without presence but only ever witnessed apophatically, read partially.

We may suggest therefore, albeit provisionally, that Ackroyd implicitly acknowledges the truth of Golem's truth, in his writing about the Golem without representing it. The act of writing the novel gives the Golem shape. Or rather, shapes. For the Golem of the novel is multiple, assuming as many shapes as there are narrative and textual formulations in the novel, which is, moreover, a novel always acknowledging its indebtedness and the possibility of its form to prior acts of writing which allow it to take shape, and without which it would be a shapeless mass, matter without form. Indeed, the novel is itself Golem–like, formed in its various true shapes according to the forms of inscription. Furthermore, the Golem is, in a certain sense, London, though never restricted to this, anymore than London is restricted to a single definition. When Ackroyd, in critical–historical voice, suggests that the secret of the 'revival' of the Golem is 'to be found within the annals of London's past' (*DLLG* 4), he effectively dismisses the possibility of any pure or single origin for the Golem, by contriving its revival as an iterable effect of place and what takes place. The city determines the identity of the Golem, but, more than this, the city assumes a form determining the condition of the location throughout time, even though it becomes transformed. What this is remains undecidable, London having no form, no shape, unless it takes place performatively through the constellation of traces in an image event.

Elie Wiesel, in his version of the Golem legend, suggests that the 'whole picture' of the Golem was only obtained by piecing together various 'visions and memories . . . everyone possessed a fragment of a tale; they had to be brought together to create a legend'.[19] Inscription is not a solitary act, an original act of invention or genius, but a response to countless texts. The act of creating and narrating the Golem relies upon numerous voices, a community of voices. Once again as Ackroyd shows us, the city, like the Golem, only comes into being through the multiplicity of enunciations and inscriptions, while never remaining the thing itself. These narrations, like the city itself, rely on previous narrations, previous structures and architectural forms, out of which both the narrations and the city grow. Thus, London is both performative and transformative. Having no particular meaning as such, it must always be redefined, even though in this the city will always have escaped definition. Such escape is in part because the haunted layering of location and citation shapes the writer's response. *Dan Leno and the Limehouse Golem* is, like both city and Golem, an act of multiple, heterogeneous swirling voices, constantly reinventing itselves. In this, the novel enters into, even as it responds and opens itself to the condition of London. Golem–like, the novel is determined from countless other places, others' texts, both real and imagined. (The novel is the city is the golem is the novel . . . we find ourselves always already underway, on the drift, by analogy, in analogy.)

This persistent Babelian resonance is a favourite conceit of Ackroyd's, not only in his writing in general, as he militates against notions of originality, invention and solitary genius, in favour of pastiche and palimpsest, textual grafting and weaving, but specifically, in *Dan Leno*, where no voice is authentic or original. Indeed, even as the phrase 'here we are again' is reiterated, so too is a comment of Charles Babbage's, which, repeated and remembered by George Gissing in the novel, defines the Ackroydian conceit: 'The air itself is one vast library, on whose pages are forever written all that man has ever said or woman whispered' (*DLLG* 117). Gissing later repeats this line to himself, 'as he walked through the damp and misty streets of London', until he becomes lost in a labyrinth of streets that are thoroughly unfamiliar, even though they lay only 'a mile or so from his own lodgings' (*DLLG* 243). Encountering a number of poverty-stricken Londoners in the 'maze of streets', Gissing comes to realize that 'if the air indeed were one vast library, one great vessel in which all the noises of the city were preserved, then nothing need be lost' (*DLLG* 246). The idea is manifested earlier in Gissing's thoughts. When temporarily apprehended by the police for questioning over the murders, Gissing considers the stones of the cell in which he is held. He 'had read in a recent copy of the *Weekly Digest* that part of the ancient city of London had been found during the building of certain warehouses by Shadwell Reach. Some stone walls had been uncovered, and it occurred to Gissing that this cell might have been constructed from the remnants of them' (*DLLG* 146–7). Though not connected to Babbage's text, Gissing's thought hints at how nothing is ever lost, how the city is reinvented within itself, so that, even in the most basic architectural manifestations the city's past leaves its trace.

Gissing is thus employed by Ackroyd as a medium for the city, for its traces and its textual reconfigurations. From Babbage's general comment, Gissing hypothesizes about the condition of London itself. Indeed, the partial reiteration and paraphrase of Babbage's conceit is performative in that it becomes part of the babble of London voices in the text, filtered via Gissing through Ackroyd's urban imagination. However, as if to resist a desire to attribute the phrase to either Babbage or Gissing alone, Ackroyd denies that the image of the babble belongs to any one figure. The image of the vast library of textual traces and voices as a possible figure for the constant refiguring of the city is offered as a continuous anonymous generative and performative process in this description of the British Library. 'They were lost in their books,' we are told, 'as the murmuring of all the inhabitants of the Reading Room rose towards the vast dome and set up a whispering echo like that of voices in the fog of London' (*DLLG* 140). If the figure of Gissing is suggestively delineated as a kind of medium, he is not alone, for Ackroyd intimates that the process of communal articulation enfolds countless readers.

Ackroyd therefore establishes an endless reciprocity, a process of folding and unfolding, whereby any distinction between 'reality' and 'writing' becomes erased. This is seen in one passage where the scene is set in an apparently conventional manner. We read that 'the notorious pea–soupers of the period, so ably memorialised by Robert Louis Stevenson and Arthur Conan Doyle, were quite as dark, as their literary reputation would suggest' (*DLLG* 45). The line reads ambiguously, or appears to, at any rate. Beginning with a literary cliché, it moves to indirect citation of two London authors whose work is largely responsible for generating stock images of the late Victorian city. In that 'ably' there is readable a possible suggestion of these writers being damned with faint praise, as is perhaps appropriate when referring to such a cliché. The comic play in the passage in question mocks the very fin de siècle representations of London it acknowledges, and in so doing, exceeds the limits of such modes of representation. The sentence plays between the reality of the London smogs and fog and their literary representations, the curiosity of the line being in that hint that one turns to the 'literary reputation' primarily for verification. The 'reality' of the city is, it would seem, dictated by stock literary devices for staging the *Grand Guignol* urban experience. It is as if we cannot know London, without prior access to its canonical texts.

Another example of the city's history mediated through textual filters occurs in the citation of Gissing's article 'Romanticism and Crime': 'the house which had witnessed the immortal Ratcliffe Highway murders of 1812 . . . [had been] preserved forever in the pages of Thomas De Quincey' (*DLLG* 117). De Quincey's text, returning to us through a textual detour of nearly two hundred years, becomes the form by which one aspect of the city is given shape. This aspect or persona of the city is a particularly violent one, as already suggested above. The historical reiteration of violence violently marks a locale such as Limehouse, which in turn becomes the focus of writers through the centuries who retrace the bloody scene of the location, thereby mapping the urban event both temporally as well as spatially. As Ackroyd remarks of the Ripper murders, these have proven to be 'an enduring aspect of London myth' and it is through such brutal phenomena that the 'essential paganism of London . . . reasserts itself' (*L:B* 273). It is as if the history of the city is written in the blood of its victims. Violence is part of any city and leaves its trace in a particularly indelible fashion on urban experience or memory. The legend of the Golem is of course a narrative response to acts of violence, and Ackroyd draws upon the urban legend as a means of approaching, or bearing witness to, that which is unrepresentable in any city's history, while admitting in *London* that 'the element of mystery remains perhaps the most interesting and suggestive aspect of the London murder, as if the city itself might have taken part in the crime' (*L:B* 272). Violence is of course in certain respects theatrical, while theatricality is 'entirely characteristic of London itself', being 'heterogeneous and egalitarian' (*L:B* 149). To turn this analogy around, one aspect of the city is obviously its theatricality, as Ackroyd repeatedly suggests (recall that in the sixteenth and nineteenth centuries even silence is theatrical). However, that theatricality is frequently of a dark and often destructive kind. Theatricality is not an escape from the darkness of the urban spirit, but a grotesque manifestation of that spectre. It is this thought that leads the novelist, in his own masquerade as the critical voice of the text, to remark that, 'it would not be going too far to suggest, in fact, that there was some link between the murder of the prostitutes in Limehouse and the ritual humiliation of women in pantomime' (*DLLG* 171).

Whether or not we are to take this remark at face value is undecidable. The reciprocity of which we have already spoken is not discernible in terms of an originating point, for the textual configurations of resonant structures suggest the *mise en abyme* rather than the *mise en scène* of the gothic fictions of Stevenson, Wilde, Conan Doyle, Morrison, Richard Marsh, or even Joseph Conrad. Any sense of authenticity collapses due to the perpetual cross–contamination between supposedly distinct identities such as 'art' or 'life', 'history' or 'fiction', 'world' or 'word'. What remains, however, is a somewhat ineffable sense of the power of the city, of its violent, haunting trace, a trace that remains resistant to identification, as the following two passages imply.

> It was almost as if [Londoners] had been waiting impatiently for these murders to happen – as if the new conditions of the metropolis required some vivid identification, some flagrant confirmation of its status as the largest and darkest city of the world. This probably accounted for the eagerness with which the term 'golem' was taken up . . . It was an emblem for the city which surrounded them as the search for the Limehouse Golem became, curiously enough, a search for the secret of London itself. (*DLLG* 88)

> Some dark spirit had been released, or so it seemed, and certain religious leaders began to suggest that London itself – this vast

urban creation which was the first of its kind upon the globe – was somehow responsible for the evil.

Even as there appears an effort to strain towards comprehension of the spirit of place, any advance towards understanding is undercut through phrases and words such as *as if, probably, or so it seemed, somehow responsible.* What London is remains a secret; that there *is* a secret is apprehended, but this recognition does nothing to resolve the enigma. Ackroyd plays with the question of the secret, the condition of the city being that it is undecidable. Size seems to matter, for in part it is size that makes definition or identification impossible, even as it is a question of massiveness related to formlessness that dictates the desire to determine meaning. Tellingly, Ackroyd defines attempted definition as 'flagrant confirmation', as though those who rush to give the city meaning and therefore make it knowable are in breach of the laws of the city's structure, which are as secret as the city itself. The city comes to be blamed as though it were, if not living exactly, then some manifestation of the undead or otherwise haunted by its own spectre, the spectres of all its violated and oppressed inhabitants, reaching back over the centuries.

That which Peter Ackroyd strives to make us familiar with is London's ineffability and undecidability. We cannot speak of the city with any certainty, and where we believe we can, there we come to find ourselves confronted with the undecidable. London resists definition, in part through being recognizable and available only by the voices, the texts, the traces that are of it, endlessly reconfigured and performed, time and time again. Ackroyd toys with the idea of the city as a golem–form, even as, finally, he rejects this too facile a definition. For, to name the city 'golem' and to come to rest on that identification, albeit one shrouded in mystery, legend and obscure cabbalism, as the *only* identity for the city is to mark the narrative with a relapse into fin de siècle staging. The play in which Ackroyd partakes is risky, to say the least. He engages playfully, time and again, with the very meaning he refuses to assign, even though he tempts his readers into slipping into the act of easy assignation, assuming the wrong kind of familiarity. For Ackroyd, the idea of the Golem, its narrative potential, is more important than any cheap trick stage illusion of an urban monster. Playing with the suggestive possibility of a haunting return is but one way in which to approximate through indirection the condition of infinite London. The idea of the Golem provides just one more textual trace. It is merely one more text, itself composed of numerous voices and inscriptions, put together piecemeal by the heterogeneous community of urban dwellers, who come to define the city as much as its architecture. We read this in the final paragraph of the novel:

> The audience filed out into the dark night after the performance was over, the young and old, the rich and the poor, the famous and the infamous, the charitable and the mean, all back into the cold mist and smoke of the teeming streets. They left the theatre in Limehouse and went their separate ways, to Lambeth or to Brixton, to Bayswater or to Whitechapel, to Hoxton or to Clerkenwell, all of them returning to the uproar of the eternal city. And even as they travelled homeward, many of them remembered that wonderful moment when Dan Leno had risen from the trapdoor and appeared in front of them. 'Ladies and gentlemen,' he had announced in his best mammoth comique manner, 'here we are *again!*' (*DLLG* 282)

Once more, there is that implicit familiarity in the play of proper names, as the map of the city is reconfigured through the writer's toponymic gambit. At the same time, the play between the polar opposites of the audience is echoed in the play between the immateriality and materiality of the streets, alive with the movement of insubstantial vapours and nameless millions. The performance gathers its community, only to release them to the various areas of the city, to become themselves urban performers, traced through by the endless return of Leno's words. This final paragraph plays through a series of reiterated rhetorical and syntactical structures, even as it performs the movement away from the theatre, a movement in which the reader is caught up, as s/he prepares to leave behind the performances, the stagings, the dressings up, of *Dan Leno and the Limehouse Golem*. This serial play is itself one more variation on both the novel's construction and the comprehension of the city which we read in the textual performance. Yet nothing is ever quite left behind completely, as the phrase 'eternal city' suggests. For, even as each member of the audience recalls Leno's words, so the past moment returns to the present moment of memory, caught in the present tense of the comedian's words, and oscillating through this structure as its own anticipated future return, where the eternal city will therefore have brought us together – *again*.

5
Sites of resistance, sites of memory: Iain Sinclair's 'delirious fictions' of London

> Today, we seem to suffer from a hypertrophy of memory . . .
>
> Andreas Huyssen

> 'I want to make tracings of unseen acts . . . I want erasures . . . I want the acts to repeat . . . To erase time and to bend its direction of flow.'
>
> Joblard, *White Chappell Scarlett Tracings*

> We only plunge deeper into our own confusions: turn away and the maze unravels. It is a ghost trap.
>
> Iain Sinclair

I

This chapter will therefore have failed.

It will have done so because inasmuch as it seeks to be faithful to the movements of the writing of Iain Sinclair, it must perforce fall into habits of reiteration that, in their excessiveness, are doomed merely to express what Sinclair has already expressed, and by which process he has already forestalled and resisted any act of critical appropriation, however sympathetic to his project of creating a London that is, itself, in its excessive play of memory's traces, a site of resistance.

My aim in the present chapter therefore is to explain rather than interpret essayist, novelist, poet, and polemicist Iain Sinclair's strategic use of particular techniques that he brings to bear in his acts of writing and remembering London. I am tempted to argue that no reading of

Sinclair is possible, if by reading the idea of a more or less coherent translation is implied. Put another way: Iain Sinclair's texts cannot be read, they are unreadable in a very real way, which has nothing to do with the language, the syntax, the grammar or any other formal element. They are unreadable inasmuch as everything that is to be said already finds itself on the surface of the text. Informed by a belief that *poiesis* is also, always, a praxis, and that writing is always capable of engaging in acts of affirmative resistance when opening itself to the multiple voicings of the city's historical and cultural others, Sinclair's modes of presentation, urban staging, and mapping interrupt normative models of urban representation, engaging, it might be added, in a kind of terrorist warfare with all representations of the city.

Sinclair's publications engage with particular Londons through mapping, affirming, and bearing witness to the singularity of specific urban spaces and their multiple temporal traces, which have no other connection than the fact that particular events or types of events have occurred in the same location. Such tracing on Sinclair's part is also performative; for in its wayward delineation, generated as so many responses to what is encountered in the city in the process of walking its streets endlessly as a means of compositional preparation, writing and research offer irrational, heterodox narratives of place; and these re-enact that which takes place in the urban site. The materiality of history thus becomes translated as the materiality of the letter. Through such transformations, Sinclair's texts aim at an ideological intervention in the political and historical stakes of that representation and who lays claim to it. The first part of this chapter therefore traces briefly possible inflections of Sinclair's writing through particular critical models, while the remainder of the chapter turns to particular examples drawn from a number of Sinclair's publications.

II

This section of the chapter offers the reader a highly adumbrated schematic of possible epistemological figures and theoretical discourses by which to imagine, if not comprehend, *what Iain Sinclair does*, for want of any better phrase. Thus I am proposing here what to some will seem a highly improbable theoretical fictional key to gain one possible, precarious access to Sinclair's London, the image of which is inaccessible – even though everywhere in plain sight – because Sinclair's text can be understood as tracing an originary doubling of the image, wherein the image is only apprehended, if at all, as the image of a certain efface-ment of an image.

To begin with Guy Debord: through his engagement with Debord's and the Situationist International's notion of psychogeography, partic-ularly those tactics of repetition and stoppage, of the *dérive*, the act of drifting through the streets, and *detournement*, the appropriation and often polemical gathering of otherwise unconnected phenomena belonging to a particular urban place, Sinclair generates a London con-stituted as so many heterogeneous sites: of singularity, collectivity, resis-tance, and counter-memory. Appropriation, gathering, and drifting are significant inasmuch as, through the constant employment of such ges-tures, Sinclair claims access to the alterity of London while resisting any rationalization of polemical activity. To put it simply, Sinclair's text resists by effecting maximum irritation. His writing is an allergen. In order to provoke and frustrate, it works with afterimages of the city of a kind similar to those with which Walter Benjamin works in *The Arcades Project*, and which are defined by Jonathan Crary as being 'those of collective historical memory'. These are 'haunting images of the out-of-date that had the capacity for a social reawakening'.[1] What social awakening that might be is never spelt out in Sinclair's writing, for the purpose of the text is, I would argue, not to articulate or prescribe the form taken by any social awakening but to provide the possibility for such coming to consciousness on the part of each reader as, itself, a chance occurence. Sinclair's text is thus produced as a performative *mnemotechnic* that both affirms and produces particular hyperbolic urban identities, the nature of which always run the risk of being mis-understood, not received, not read at all.

Such textual archiving is therefore not simply an act of historical reg-istration. Instead, it enacts 'a fluctuation between spatial and temporal registers', the purpose of which is, in part, to 'resist the reifying ten-dency'[2] in much conventional urban observation and history, whereby the past has no purpose other than as museum exhibit, installed to remind us how much we've 'progressed', and how much 'better' things are now, or otherwise to provide us with entry into a knowable past through the control of representation. If the reader finds in him- or herself a sense of irritation or rage at Sinclair's hyperbolic celerity, that over-the-top, speed-freak aphoristic annotation of London's material condition and the signs of its occluded pasts, then it is arguable that Sinclair's text is successful in its agitprop forays into the city's rhizomic being.

The London pasts on which Sinclair draws are multiple, a powerful network of forces operative in, and yet irreducible to, any given present moment. Sinclair's purpose, I wish to argue, is to maintain other traces of the city as so many imaginary resonances through acts of archiving and memory that counter the hegemonic imperative of globalization by which particular urban identities are being erased. With its enforced erasure of the specificity of place through architectural projects and town planning, with the displacement of local communities, and with the implicit or explicit denial or non-recognition of temporal continuities, the globalizing urban refit seeks to enforce a politics of forgetting. Responding to this, Sinclair's work is thus not merely an attempt to document that which disappears or has disappeared, that which is in the process of being forgotten or which has been forgotten in various processes of urban renewal; it is also, I would aver, a significant intervention in, and disruption of the 'globalization of memory',[3] wherein forgetting also implies the imposition of invented false-memory. In examining this process, I will suggest that Sinclair extends the play of the Situationists, while acknowledging the necessity of maintaining other modalities of production that are excessive in order to counter the work of normative histories and documentary accounts of urban space.

What is at stake specifically in Sinclair's tactics is the construction of a London through a constellation of sites mapped by what he calls '[d]elirious fictions' (*SM* 10): narratives of violence, irrationality, vision and hallucination, along with other excessive tropes and events of rebellion, all of which are irrecuperable, either by any domesticating neoliberal, humanist discourse of class, race, or gender experience (to which I would add any gesture on the part of academic criticism), or by any anodyne, universalizing, or transhistorical appeals to nebulous notions of culture or heritage, as with the building of the Globe Theatre or the Millennium Dome. Sinclair's mapping of the city involves itself in the affirmative resistance troped though impersonal urban memory as so many traces of the materiality of history become the materiality of the letter, in a prose that is itself performative in its polemical eruptive violence. Such violence – of language, of representation, of the events presented – halts the reader in his or her tracks; there is thus an act of writing as ideological caesura, the intervention or stoppage favoured by Debord, which, in its 'power to interrupt', figures for Giorgio Agamben, 'the "revolutionary interruption" of which Benjamin spoke'.[4] In this, Sinclair's text assumes both a resemblance to the psychogeographic work of Guy Debord and others of the SI (as already suggested), to the historical afterimage conceived of by Benjamin, and also to that definition of messianic history provided by Agamben. Messianic history, writes Agamben, 'is defined by two major characteristics. First it is a history of salvation: something must be saved. But it is also a final history, an eschatological history, in which something must be completed, judged . . . it must leave chronology behind, but without entering some other world' (DR 314). Given Agamben's insistence on the eschatological termination, it might perhaps be more appropriate to speak of Sinclair's text as embodying a quasi-messianic history of London, for his vision of the city is one always in the act of becoming, always overflowing the limits of representation and teleological or ontological delimitation. Sinclair's is thus a bastard-messianism, where, in his words, 'time itself is on the drift' (*SM* 7); this, in itself, is a response to the unending sense of constant becoming that London as other imposes on the writer sensitive to its alternative histories, its occluded memories, and to what Sinclair terms 'spectral traces' (*SM* 8). From the critical perspectives on the city that we are considering here, the motif of the spectral is no mere conceit, for as Benjamin reminds us, the city, as location and topography, 'bears witness to the dead, shows itself full of the dead'.[5] As the final part of this chapter will show, the spectral is fully at work in Sinclair's *Lights Out for the Territory: 9 Excursions in the Secret History of London*.

In their mapping of the city's forgotten sites, Sinclair's texts extend the work of place in the city, through their collective function as so many *lieux de mémoire*, sites of memory, a concept for an alternative historical praxis addressing the relation of memory to particular locations, conceived by Pierre Nora. Now while Nora writes of memory in relation to historical sites rather than of literature, when he remarks that 'there are sites, *lieux de mémoire*, in which a residual sense of continuity remains',[6] surely one such constellation of sites, at least by analogy, is the book, as a recursive, untimely gesture seeking to gather together the fraying edges of some irrevocable rupture. The very idea of the book can, in principle, fulfil the three criteria established by Nora for a *lieu de mémoire*. The *lieu*, the site or place, is defined according to its being 'material, symbolic, and functional' (*GI* 14). The book is the material place of imaginative investment; it is functional in that it exists to be received, to be read; and it is symbolic in Nora's sense, in that, disrupting time, it concentrates memories, those of its ideas and intertexts, of its authors, and its readers, all of which supposes an 'interaction

resulting in a mutual overdetermination' (GI 14), always already immanent in the idea of the book, and in every material experience of the
book.

Thus, I am addressing the *lieux de mémoire* as so many double figurations, for in effect each of the sites of London becomes reiterated, even
as it is mapped, in Sinclair's writing. There is at work here a doubling
which is also a rhizomic extension of material locations. Where various
areas of London have been radically emptied of collective memory,
through extensive rebuilding, commercial development, and gentrifica-
tion, alongside projects of community relocation, it becomes the
writer's responsibility as the conduit for the mnemotechnic, producing
the palimpsest-topography of that which would otherwise be obliterated. In this manner, the psychogeographical historian contests what
Andreas Huyssen describes as 'the myth of cyber-capitalism and globalization and the denial of time, space, and place' (*PPUP* 28) through
the articulation of the 'register of imaginaries' (*PPUP* 4). Inscribing the
temporal dimension of urban place in such textual production is
significant, argues Huyssen, in two principal ways: it brings out of
the present location 'memories of what was there before', while, often
simultaneously, it projects 'imagined alternatives to what there is' (*PPUP*
4). In lieu of living communities of collective memory, as the material
taking-place of immaterial memory, the book is therefore in this sense
an analogical manifestation, one possible apparition that takes place,
taking the place of some otherwise unpresentable other. Sinclair's text
exemplifies the experience of the city as hybrid place, which as *lieu* is,
to paraphrase Nora, 'compounded of life and death, of the temporal and
the eternal'. London read as so many *lieux de mémoire*, is available to us
in Sinclair's writing as 'endless rounds of the collective and the individual . . . the immutable and the fleeting. For, although it is true that
the fundamental purpose of a *lieu de mémoire*'

> is to stop time, to inhibit forgetting, to fix a state of things, to immor-
> talize death and to materialize the immaterial . . . it is also clear that
> *lieux de mémoire* thrive only because of their capacity for change, their
> ability to resurrect old meanings and generate new ones along with
> new and unforeseeable connections. (GI 15)

Thus, language gives place to the taking place of the urban, albeit in
unexpected ways despite all efforts to programme or control the
outcome. As a singular locus engaged in resurrection and generation
responding to the articulations of alternative London sites, the book

proffers both the staging and the performance of excessive encounters and reactions.

III

Repetitive excess and excessive repetition – repetition *is* excessive – produce an abyssal text where all is on a surface that forestalls any possibility of representation implying depth perception. The production of an impenetrable surface network only ever reiterating itself produces a performative text that situates a politics of resistance in Sinclair's city poetics. Such chiasmatic frustration is to be found everywhere in the writing of Iain Sinclair, where local topographic, social, cultural, and political groundings 'are being renegotiated in the clash between globalizing forces and new productions and practices of local cultures' (*PPUP* 4). So much so in fact, that when Sinclair writes, 'We're moving on now, exchanging the odd unconnected anecdote or random fact' (*SM* 60), one could easily be forgiven for taking this statement of Sinclair's as both a statement on the experience of random drifting through London on the part of the psychogeographical tour guide, as well as being a reflexive, if not performative commentary on the constitution of Sinclair's own texts. As one reads Sinclair, whether the early poetry (*Lud Heat* on which we will focus, below) or the most recent raging polemic against the drab excesses of New Labour (the fiasco of the Millennium Dome exploded in *Sorry Meniscus*), reading becomes the experience of exactly this: seemingly aleatory motion, fuelled equally by rage, obsession, memory and history. In short, the endless exchange of odd unconnected anecdotes (on Sinclair's part and on the part of those he encounters) and random facts. Simultaneously however, this writing/reading process is also an imaginative act of alternative mapping, a mapping which undoes the very coordinates on which the presumption of knowable, finite topography relies. It relies on resistance to finite instances of comprehension or absolute accessibility, in Sinclair's constant, obsessive drive to disinter the phantom effects of the city's familiar sites.

Take, for example, an essay on New Labour's attempted sanitized reworking of a peninsula of land in Greenwich, through the building of the Dome. Such a process, Sinclair reads as '[c]lap sores revamped as beauty spots . . . while the dark history of Greenwich marshes, a decayed industrial wilderness is brutally elided'. However, it is Sinclair's project to return to us the proper name of that which has been erased from nineteenth-century maps, 'a pre-amputation stump known as Bugsby's Marshes'.[7] This resurrected name provides the potential for an alternative counter-narrative, haunting the present authorized revivification with its distinctly Dickensian sonorities; pushing against received wisdom, official histories, it provides Sinclair, and the reader, access to an alternative history of

> the manufacture of ordnance, brewing, confectionary, black smoke palls and sickly sweet perfumes. The cloacal mud of low tide mingled deliriously with sulphurous residues trapped in savage greenery . . . Terrible ghosts were trapped in the ground . . . Executions and bloated bodies washed over by three tides. (AC 211)

The unconnected and the random succumb of course to chance gatherings through Sinclair's edgy conjuration. This is, though, in a way, the very point: for an other London emerges, as traces interweave in a disparate seriality of vengeful spectres through such concatenations, undoing in the process the organized and official images of Greenwich – a location which appears as constellated image, instances in the nineteenth and twentieth century enfolding one another in Sinclair's *Downriver* (*D* 19–20) – as the location of the prime meridian, erstwhile centre of the British Empire, the Royal Naval College, and what the writer names archly '[a]cceptable glories' (AC 211).

Moreover, such mediation of urban revenance that traces certain returns *of* rather than *to* other Londons resonates in memory of other instances of textual dissidence. The 'black smoke palls' echo or, at least, gesture towards William Blake's 'London', a poem which, as is well known, also invokes terrible ghosts juxtaposed to the 'charter'd Thames'. Through such recognizable conjunctions, Sinclair weaves the random and chance through relationships at once esoteric and mythopoetic, while also factual and historical. He produces a similar effect in the title of one of the many sections of *Lud Heat*, 'From Camberwell to Golgotha'. There is in this a doubleness, projecting London in the act of undoing any finite, knowable identity. Sinclair thus engages in a paradoxical poetics of the city, working through an excessive, fragmentary inscription which both speaks of the city and speaks to the city's ineffability.

If Sinclair appears to owe more than a little to T. S. Eliot in *The Waste Land* in his quasi-modernist bricolage drawn from the sensual experience of life and mythological, arcane knowledge, there is also a sense in which he owes as much to Dickens, if not Blake, in the apocalyptic, idiosyncratically visionary quality of his writing, which cuts past Eliot's studied (self-)reflection and despair over the absence of mastery, to unfold for the reader with sensuous immediacy the spirit of the city, a spirit at once protean, labyrinthine, and Babelian. Sinclair impresses on the reader the conditions of the metropolis in all its paradoxes, so that, '[w]hen we understand the condition it no longer exists' (*LHSB* 69). When we believe we comprehend London it ceases to be, for perception, sensuous communion with the city, precedes and escapes understanding.

Command of comprehension founded on representation is thus avoided, ahead of the settling of any representation by the very condition of London, which Sinclair would have us know is not to be understood if we are to be true to any thinking or writing of the city. Such a challenge to conventional epistemological frameworks with regard to the production of urban images is at the heart of Sinclair's writing while at the same time conveying imperfectly the sense of perceiving the city. We are forced to read the city's fragments in *Lud Heat* as we receive London itself: imperfectly, semi-consciously, sensuously, without analytical distance, disinterested overview or comforting sense of tradition or history. Revealing this, Sinclair's poetry fails to apprehend the city; yet its failure is not a limit so much as it is an indirect acknowledgement that this is one of the few appropriate modes of *poiesis* for the writing of the city, in the faithful translation from the materiality of the city to that of the letter, however fraught this may be with the very risk of its own failure. Reading *Lud Heat*, we share in the very condition of the city even as we fail to capture finally its nature. As readers, we may recognize the signs which constitute London, but translation is always left in ruins. Identifying all the figures, tropes, images employed in *Lud Heat* will do no more than offer us an entertaining intellectual jigsaw puzzle.

Lud Heat is composed of one book, 'The Muck Rake', which in turn is divided into sixteen sections, including 'Nicholas Hawksmoor, His Churches', 'Closed Field, the Dogs of the Moon' ('Field' is within a closed field, framed by a rectangle), and 'The Immigrant, The Sentimental Butcher'. 'The Muck Rake' is also named Book One, leading you to believe, perhaps, that there might be a book two or three, although (so far, at least) this has not proved to be the case. (Though, then again, it might be argued that Sinclair's novels, *White Chappell, Scarlet Tracings, Radon Daughters*, or *Downriver* are continuations of the London project.) Thus, what the reader is confronted with is what seems to be an unfinished work – not that we can be sure – or, at least, a work with no ending, which is quite a different thing. The poem opens itself onto a futurity without horizon, much like the city itself. Some of the sections assume the form of rambling reflections on, amongst other things, the cabbalistic pattern allegedly mapped onto central and East London by the churches of Nicholas Hawksmoor (a conceit developed by Peter Ackroyd in his novel *Hawksmoor*). The sections break off and start up abruptly, as indeed do sentences within sections, and as do the areas of London and the streets traced therein; some seem ordered, some appear shabby. Thus the structure of *Lud Heat*, at once open-ended and wilfully fragmentary, appears to be motivated or governed by no clear plan, other than that which London imposes as an extension – rather than being merely a copying – of the structure of the city itself.

The text is marked throughout by a particular Egyptian hieroglyph, in what is apparently a form of sectional punctuation and division, while the literary, historical, sociological, cultural, and mythopoetic references are as diverse and random as the city's own histories and memories. Thus we proceed as we would according to Sinclair's proposition for passage through London: by exchanging the odd unconnected anecdote or random fact. Street names appear, as do area names, while place names can be equally contemporary/real or mythical/biblical, as with the Blakean 'Camberwell to Golgotha', where the map translates itself, from one place to another, from one order of place, and also in the same place, a phantom effect or ghostly event, oscillating within supposedly knowable or locatable topography.

Such work is taken further. We encounter street names which are also the names of authors, for example Ben Jonson Road (*LHSB* 43). Material places, locations and names frequently serve doubled, doubling, disorganizing functions, functions which are governed by both fact *and* mythology or textuality. Lambeth, for instance, is not simply Lambeth but also Blake's Lambeth (*LHSB* 17), which in turn jostles for attention in the text with Cleopatra's needle, situated on the Chelsea side of the Thames across from Lambeth. Furthermore, we read a quotation taken from Pepys' diary, delivered in the passage through London, while we are informed elsewhere and in passing of a location where Dickens once stayed. De Quincey, Newton, and many others rub shoulders in this London, regardless of the specificity of temporal location. This is a place where the Mile End Road, Ratcliff Highway, Limehouse, and Lambeth cohabit quite happily with Cardinal Heenan and the Gods of Ancient Egypt or the Temple of Mithras. Hawksmoor's churches occupy sites in real urban space – Bloomsbury, Limehouse – as well as being transcribed as the structures and places focusing metaphysical, arcane dark powers. The occult and the criminal inhabit the same passages as the cultured and powerful. Ryvita and Greek epic share space in the same lunch box.

Why mention all this detail? The city, thus conceived as so many found objects in relation to recovered or occluded memory, demands an activity of responsive, endless performative commentary or transformative critique as a necessary task. We are obliged to apprehend this, even if this task cannot help but be haunted by the potential for its own failure; a failure that is caught in the need to maintain the unfolding of the endless seriality of supplementary analogy in the mapping of a surface network, from which there is no access to any possible meaning other than the acknowledgement of the increasingly complex and irregular planar arrangement. If we don't begin by *sensing, feeling,* the teeming excess of London's being, throughout all the discontinuous interrelations, along all the chance diachronic and synchronic axes, we can begin nowhere legitimately in Sinclair's text. And yet, following the contours of this text only reinforces the sense that there is no absolutely justifiable starting point as such. The city, and the poem which responds to London, are always already events of constant becoming, without origin, without centre, without absolute truth, except that truth which is London itself. The architectures of both *Lud Heat* and London are always on the way to becoming because neither can be read as complete; neither are finite or closed systems but have to be acknowledged as radically rhizomic in condition. Instead, the text of the poem and that of the city always remain ahead, before us, awaiting traversal and translation but, equally never offering any promise of completion and always remarked through processes of renewal, return, reiteration. To draw on Sinclair's poem again, 'These are rhythms to recognise, to accept or oppose' (*LHSB* 68).

Sinclair also installs into his text certain prescriptions and caveats, pertinent both to the city and his poetry:

What you suffer is the place you choose to live. Do not remain victim to a solitary level of discourse . . . avoid the static condition. (*LHSB* 69)

Such a direction arguably presents the reader with the conditions for imagining the provisional, open-ended interaction with both Sinclair and London. As *Lud Heat* is always composed of multiple discourses, so too is London at particular levels. Similarly, both text and city are events, always taking place, dismantling in the process any static condition, identity, or meaning. If we are urged to avoid the condition of the solitary – perhaps the architectural or architectonic level of discourse – whereby all is ordered in the projection/comprehension of unity and uniformity, so too are we given examples of such avoidances on a textual, metropolitan and historical/mythical scale.

To conclude with Sinclair's poetry before turning to *Liquid City* (a text shared by Sinclair with Marc Atkins' photographs), one brief passage, where landscape *is* passage, where it is staged through intervallic and irregularly rhythmic mapping. The passage is taken from 'The Immigrant, the Sentimental Butcher', addressing the East End:

> We all adjust: over the stadium, the missing spire, the half-circle of border ditch around Limehouse keeping out the histories of Mile End, Ratcliffe, Poplar. Laneways weighed under different glasses.
>
>   The encroaching fen. The
> speed of time of the place
> changes. Now I am frighted
> in retrospect by a glimpse
> of the original wood:
> Hawksmoor's staircase
> rising from the recently
> sealed porch. Unvarnished
> grain of parallel universe.
> There is also Hablot Browne's
> etching. Strong ground.
> To be here is wide enough. (*LHSB* 123)

We begin with incompletion, the city undone through that which is absent ('the missing spire'), and that which remains to be closed or finished ('the half-circle'). Structure in ruins, in fragments, remaining to be completed, and haunted by the ghosts of structure to come, while also disturbed through the spectral possibility of that which might once have been there. The time of the city is every moment, though never present as a finished architecture, or totalizable in the present as such. Names sketch a skeletal map, the points awaiting connection, while the prose passage ends in its announcement of an alternative modality of urban spectatorship. Later in this section, we will read references to tabloid newspapers, the *Mirror* and the *Sun*, nylon stockings (*LHSB* 125), and Virgil's *Aeneid*, along with 'cheese rivita tomato Homer' (*LHSB* 126). What we witness, what arrives, is the gathering of ungovernable elements, having no discernible taxonomic economy, randomly brought together, and this by the merest of coincidences, in text and place (as the textual ruins of place, the taking place of place). Food, newspapers, clothing, books: found and recorded, dislocated from place, without specific connectedness. Where we are is almost as uncertain as *when* we are; memories and echoes of endless voices merge without coalescing, the seventeenth-century architect's design jostling for attention with the etching of Dickens' illustrator. Sinclair creates an experience of the landscape which is not grounded, and which, in fact, inaugurates what Ulrich Baer has called (with regard to the relation between subject position and landscape in Baudelaire's 'Landscape'), the 'deconstruction of position' (*RSTE* 101). The landscape, released, as Baer has it, 'from contingency . . . is neither confined nor free' (*RSTE* 100).

In the light of Baer's commentary, the problem here – a problem that is the problematizing of representation through a mapping of location's ruins as polemical gesture resistant to reading and recuperation – in Sinclair's writing is that London is always nowhere, merely the contingent play of substitutive tropes all tending to the same perception, and thus ineffable, unavailable to any registration, and yet simultaneously suggestive of a universality that runs the risk of making London merely one more city: nowhere and yet everywhere, nothing of which one can speak and yet, in being spoken of, only available to general representation, remaining hidden within and as other than the absence of grounding. Thus Sinclair's poetry situates the experience of the city as the constant event of the aporetic, and also as 'the freedom of poetic speech', which speech runs the risk of effacing London's singularity (*RSTE* 102). It is the encounter with the experience of the aporetic that opens one to this freedom in one's response. Yet, conversely – and here we find ourselves caught within the experience of the aporetic which haunts every effort on Sinclair's part to write what he knows cannot be written – if poetic speech is to be free, it must not be caught up in the very historicity of London's singular traces. And so London escapes once more from Sinclair's obsessive, repetitive gestures of apprehension, and which themselves are repeated in my own writing, in the effort to be faithful to Sinclair's response.

If London is thought as a series of events, as that which is not so much a place but that which takes place (to use a formula expressed at the beginning of my *Writing London*), it has to be acknowledged that the apparently chance temporal and spatial conjunctions and juxtapositions which inform the urban condition, and which, subsequently, when registered in textual form, assume this uncanny force we name the experience of the aporetic. This force appears in the most supposedly familiar locations, in those places where we might believe we no longer have to read. Indeed, it may be said that the textual form as

urban locution is precisely that which traces the dislocation within location, unveiling invisible confluence within any given site, and thereby
opening to us the necessity *and* the impossibility of reading. We are
confronted, perhaps taunted by, our frustrated desire to read, reminded
irritatingly of our inability to do so.

In *Liquid City*, the problematic of reading in relation to representation of urban phenomena and the city text is always before us. The tone
is set, from before the first page. There are shadows, echoes, irrecuperable debts. In the place of the epigraph, that liminal and improper location in any text, which gestures towards giving everything away while
simultaneously pausing on the threshold and intimating an impossible,
unfathomable reserve, a citation from James Thomson's *The City of
Dreadful Night* appears, alongside a photograph. This is how Marc
Atkins' and Iain Sinclair's *Liquid City* begins (*LC* 5), with a pairing, a
double act: that of the photographer and writer, and that also of writing
and reading London. We find ourselves in pursuit and yet also with the
sensation of being haunted, in the midst of something that is already
underway and yet which will never come to a halt. An impossible quest,
therefore, one driven by the name of the city, in the name of which
photograph and inscription are generated, and which, in turn, generate all the frustrating figures of unspeakable desires by which that city,
as other, appeals, calling to us as its subjects.

The photograph, its angle slightly askew, that which is represented
being somewhat out of focus, shows a passageway projected onto which
is a shadow, the absence of light in an otherwise penumbral place, the
shape of which it is tempting to anthropomorphize. Possibly, we think,
the photographer – a projection from the margin of the image, across
its threshold in fact, imprinting a material mark, and yet, for all that,
being without substance. Indeed, elsewhere in *Liquid City*, Marc Atkins
is reported as telling Iain Sinclair that the solution to the problem of
photographing absence is addressed in part by allowing his shadow, a
phantasm of the self, to appear in the image (*LC* 122). The shadow –
the first we witness, reading the image from left to right, our eye
arguably drawn to this shadow because the most clearly defined *and* the
most temptingly human – wraps itself up the wall, elongated and
deformed, while its positioning intimates it – or, rather positioning at
least invites us to read it – as extending from each and every person
looking at the photograph, as well as at that which the photograph presents. Ours is the gaze, emanating from an invisible locale, a non-place,
not exactly *of* the image – we know that the gaze is ours, yet where
exactly are 'we', where is this pronominal position? – and yet making

possible its presentation. The phantom-human projection falls similarly to other shadowy striations, from right to left, from bottom to top, a series of diagonal motions, rhythmic striations each reiterating every other. We follow their material traces, which, like the unknown figure being followed in Thomson's poem, are 'shadowlike and frail' and which, again like the motion of the extract, 'unswervingly though slowly onward went'. There is therefore, once again, an element of performative transport at work within and yet exceeding any merely constative or simply mimetic functionalism. The photograph complements in its composition the motifs of motion that the lines chosen as the epigraph convey. The reader, of both the photograph and the passage from Thomson's text, are enjoined to travel 'many a long dim silent street'.

The choice of lines for the epigraph is telling in the context of many of Iain Sinclair's other publications. It announces his interest in the darker aspects of London history, literature, and culture. It returns to us Sinclair's obsession with the city at the fin de siècle, the city not only of Thomson, but also Arthur Machen, Arthur Conan Doyle, Wilde's *Dorian Gray*, and, of course, Jack the Ripper. And, arguably, the photograph echoes also with such literary resonances or, to be more precise, it is available to be read in this way. (For, of course, one can only orient oneself if one already has a sense of the topography.) The blurry, crepuscular scene, with its shining brickwork and paving, belongs to or, perhaps, cites any number of textual representations of a certain London from any point in the last one hundred and thirty or so years. While precise location is unreadable, something else arrives, given to us to apprehend here so that the photograph becomes an instance of analogical synecdoche: it stands in for various histories of the city, bearing witness through the most circuitous apperception to urban horrors, urban monstrosity, those otherwise unspeakable phenomena that arise from the phenomenon that is the Babylonian megalopolis. It is *as if* the photograph could encompass and so attest to the innumerable traces of the city's darkness. It also attests to a fundamental relationship between the photographic image and the materiality of its marks, and the materiality of history: 'The possibility of history', writes Eduardo Cadava, 'is bound to the survival of the traces of what is past and to our ability to read these traces as traces'.[8] Thus the image is haunted and history returns as the articulation of a legibility in the instant not of its happening but in its readability in what Walter Benjamin terms *Jetztzeit* – 'now time'.[9] More than itself, the image overflows itself as mere mimetic copy or representation of reality, as already suggested, in order to convey via the indirection of the spectral relation between non-relation, what might best, yet haphazardly, be described as the truth of London. As an image it is already remarked by more than it represents, traced by an excess that is not simply of the city, but also *is* the city of London or, at least, a significant aspect of the city's *hauntology*; for, as Atkins' pictures make apparent, photography is always a matter of 'photographing absence', as Sinclair has it at one point in the book (*LC* 122). The photograph is suggestive of various scenarios that are never there, never re-presentable as such, scenarios which it has been Sinclair's abiding obsession to explore, in fiction, poetry, and non-fiction prose, and all of which leave their indelible mark on London's 'now-time'. Thus, like *Liquid City*, we begin before the beginning, finding ourselves *in medias res*, enfolded in an abyssal reciprocity between word and image, and lost in the heart of darkness that is named London. It is as if we are reminded that, in Joseph Conrad's words, 'this also has been one of the dark places of the earth'.[10]

Furthermore, as if to accommodate the otherwise unassimilable darkness, in order not to reduce its events and phenomena to the work of a methodological or formulaic riff, *Liquid City* is available to the good reader as having no particular order or, for that matter, justifiable organization. Photographs accompany essays, essays accompany photographs. However, whatever order might be discerned is always and solely of the reader's making, as there is no place from which to start that is any more legitimate than any other. The book spills over itself therefore, much like the city it encounters, comprised as it is (again, like London) of any number of possible departure points or, equally, being composed by moments of gathered intensity that momentarily suspend innumerable flows. (To insist on the point yet again, the book's formal organizations and disjunctions are thus so many singular, potentially undending instances of iterable analogy in serial, supplementary relation with one another, in excess of mimesis.[11]) Such intensities are not simply interruptive or suspensive, however, even though they are precisely that. For each essay and its photographs, each photograph and its contrapuntal prose accompaniment, constitutes the record of flow, of drifting, of a certain responsive situational transport, each of which belongs like so many tributaries to the liquid conceit around which the text is organized (even as London is organized around, and according to the passage of the Thames) – and by which, equally, it remains disorganized.

It is crucial at this juncture that we register the transformative relationship between photograph and word, as the two are so proximally and intimately bound up with one another, without either succumbing to the other in some kind of hierarchical ordering. Indeed, it is arguable that the reciprocity between one form and the other, in being connected through their own singular mediations of the figural, as well as through their acts of figural intervention, share in processes of endless disordering and abyssal unveiling. Such disjunctive work amounts to a strategic gesture that refuses repeatedly any greater semantic organization other than what may, by chance, be gathered as a series of responses – perhaps this is what is implied by the title of one of the pieces, 'a serious of photographs' (*LC* 24) – to, and in the name of, London. What does take place as the condition of textual destabilization that *Liquid City* presents is a simultaneity of reciprocally transformative strata, a desedimented performance of what Gilles Deleuze describes with reference to the work of Raymond Roussell as an act of 'speaking and seeing *at the same time* . . . although we do not speak of what we see, or see that of which we speak. But the two comprise the stratum, and from one stratum to the next are transformed at the same time (although not according to the same rules).'[12] Photograph and word inform and deform one another, in a discontinuous serial tension, whereby both address and respond to the city, even though neither is merely subordinate to or supportive of the other. Indeed, it should be said that the relationship between photography and writing functions analogically, a formal reciprocity already noted in other ways. Photography and writing both serve to respond to particular heterogeneous instances, events, singularities that may be inflected through or intimate indirectly aspects of what goes by the name of London; moreover both on occasion are keyed by the same events or happenings, and this is of course inevitable, given that Sinclair and Atkins travel together in their acts of intervention, interruption, and what might be termed 'guerrilla documentary'. However, both media open to the reader specific city traces, signs, revenants in ways that stress repeatedly that each medium is irreducible to the other. Neither can stand in the place of the other, as one always addresses that in the city for which the other cannot account. Thus, to return to the figure of analogy, Sinclair's essays speak of scenes *as if* a representation in words could take place, while Atkins' photographs figure scenes *as if* they implied readings that, as far as the photograph can present them, are immanent, not manifest. Each medium therefore acknowledges what is absent in different ways.

How can we show or, indeed, speak of this? Perhaps the beginning of the very first essay, 'Elective Anonymity' and photograph of the ghostly nude preceding it offer us a significant example. Sinclair's essay opens with an exposure of the arbitrariness of biography, that element in this mode of writing that equates with a certain algebraic calculation: 'Marc Atkins lives in X, sharing his life with Y (and Z and P, Q, R, S). He bases his philosophy and work practice on a thorough knowledge of O. "What I want," he told me are '******of******'." What he also wants is to exist in his art. Nothing else . . . It goes without saying that he is not and never was, "Marc Atkins"' (*LC* 7). All choices in biography are arbitrary, selective, and exclusive. Inasmuch as they are not all the facts, they comprise and stage a fiction of the self, and that fiction has little or nothing to do with the person whose name is appended to such fragments. Atkins, as he appears in another of Sinclair's books, *Lights Out for the Territory*, is, says Sinclair, 'a fictional construct. An *analogue* of what he ought to be' (*LC* 7; emphasis added). This is true equally of a city as it is of a person. London is nothing more than a figure constantly undergoing construction, performance, revision, invention, as Sinclair admits in the same essay, where he states that what he wants to deliver, through techniques of caricature and exaggeration, is the 'city as a darker self, a theatre of possibilities' (*LC* 7). Each in their own way, the photographs and text aim for the figuring or the performative staging of London as such a theatre of possibilities, as so many stages for the potentiality of its becoming.

Sinclair's pyrotechnic hyperbole and stuttering pronominal disorientations thus map the possibilities of London with a frustrating suggestiveness. In 'Elective anonymity', one reads of 'a figure on Vauxhall Bridge, the fantastic Tradescant tomb, rainwater on a skull-and-crossbones monument, the vegetative head of Bunyan in Bunhill Fields' (*LC* 7). Such topographical and architectural listing sketches in quicksilver fashion the urban traces that articulate a provisional city identity. But they do more than this. For, even as this is a sketch, it is also a performative moment, a double text redrawing London according to an unavailable and disquieting logic and grammar. Memento mori, burial grounds, tombs, bridges, and anonymous figures vie for our attention, without justification. 'If an image is too complacent, if it fails to disturb' (*LC* 7), writes Sinclair, then the performative dimension does not adequately register. And, while speaking of Atkins when he says that the photographer 'interrogates a random documentary impulse until it archives a pre-fictional state of flux: agitated light, ambiguity, significance', Sinclair could be describing as easily his own technique, designed to 'locate the single, pre-existent and eternal mark on the wall' (*LC* 8) without offering any possibility of that mark's translation.

What comes to be revealed through such remarks is also that which the photographs give up: that response and registration have to do with apprehending the pre-phenomenal materiality of the mark, chronicling and cataloguing the urban trace in all its material efficacy, its 'austere poetic' (*LC* 9), without succumbing to acts of translation into some coherent semantic content. Here again we sense the frustration of the encrypted surface. London in ruins is received through *Liquid City*, the city in disarray, encrypted and telegraphically stuttered as a series of iterative absences, supplements, and spectral revenants, so many 'vanished writers, demolished buildings, unique epiphanies of light that can be re-imagined but never experienced for the first time. 'You can't', Sinclair reminds us, 'rebuild London from this formidable catalogue, but you are free to work your own combinations. You can conjure up the grid-patterns of a shining city from these loud particulars . . . this dreadful library of memory' (*LC* 11). The city never exists as such, nor do its traces operate as so many signs of an intelligible, discernible reality. London is discernible, if at all, as merely the effect, produced in a reiterated fashion, from the remainders of incalculable and excessive phantasms, which, though immaterial, leave their material trace on the urban subject. This subject, given a locus through the eye of the camera and the 'I' of Sinclair remaps the city from its traces through so many peripatetic forays around and through London and neighbouring locales bordering the Thames.

'Walking the tidal Thames' is the second prose occasion, sequentially that is, its principal motif a series of 'strategic walks', none of which amounts to anything. Each is given a provisional definition, however: portrait, prophecy, rage, seduction, language-provocation, working out the plot, chemical release. As Sinclair remarks, 'there was no ulterior motive', he and Atkins are simply 'on the drift' (*LC* 15). This last phrase is the alternative title for this particular essay. It appears on the page as neither title nor subtitle. Strictly speaking it is impossible to assign it a proper place. Appearing in grey, rather than black lettering, in a larger font size yet partially overlayed by the other title ('Walking the tidal Thames'), it contests with that title for attention, thereby offering the reader a graphic approximation of the reported tension between photographer and writer, as well as that between image and text.

Barely a page, Sinclair's comments end with a remark about the shore-line of the Thames' power to resist metaphor. Writing stops, then, as photographs take over, seeking to chart deserted post-industrial locations along the 'length of the tidal Thames' (*LC* 15). The only sign of human life amongst the photographs between pages 12 and 37 are a pair of sneakered feet, standing at the top of the frame on a gravel track before a discarded reel of film. Stationary except for the fluttering of

Union Jacks in the breeze, the photographs give nothing away. The image of each site, not of London but belonging to the banks of the Thames, plays on an impression of impersonal, inhuman desolation, resisting any act of witness that the camera strives to present. As the brevity of Sinclair's piece makes clear, no metaphor is sufficient to the task, no narrative equal to the brute materiality of place, or what Sinclair, in 'A serious of photographs' (a poem interrupting the photographic sequence-without-sequence being considered), calls 'obscenery'.

While it may be the case that metaphor is insufficient in one sense, Sinclair's insistence on random drift signifies a level at which all attempts at representation or staging are always, irrevocably, ineluctably metaphorical in the motion that occurs without end. If meaning for the city is exhausted, we as readers find ourselves exhausted by Sinclair's writing, and by a city only ever fleetingly perceived, always vanishing even at the moment that apprehension appears close. Thus, *walking*: as both itself and not itself, as the metaphor for metaphoricity's elusiveness, for writing's endless movement. As the various walks already mentioned make plain, walking is a becoming: every walk differs from every other walk, its function or meaning transported in every case. Walking is always something other than walking and walking as such can never be represented nor made to seem significant when given direct attention. If we turn back to that photograph from the series in which a pair of feet are featured, the feet are arrested. There is no indication of motion, only the static, truncated human form signified synecdochally and juxtaposed to the discarded film. Is there metaphor here? And, if so, for what, precisely, could such a metaphor be said to stand? Perhaps, one may read this image as a metaphorical attestation of the limits of any purely mimetic representational modality. When confronted directly, everything comes to a halt, nothing functions as it should. Such a supposition holds true for the images of the landscape to which we are witness. Electric pylons, oil refineries and power stations stand mute and stark in a dishevelled, unpopulated landscape, the various images suggestive of a potential for energy and the absence of any energy: representation as the zero-limit of entropy, while words appear desirous of a certain displacement onto other words, as if to acknowledge simultaneously their own exhaustion and the exhausting desire to drift elsewhere. Is this how one is prepared to enter London? And from such erased locations, how does one find the city?

This question provides the occasion for the next essay, 'Is this London?' As well being the title of the essay, it is also a question allegedly asked of Sinclair and Atkins by a French tourist (*LC* 38). Location is everything, but place remains obscure, difficult to approach and comprehend. London is a place of absent figures, whether buildings or poets, its history being a 'deleted history' (*LC* 38). The city offers nothing other than the occasion to 'wander', an act defined by Sinclair as 'vagrancy with a slate roof over its head and the price of an egg roll jangling in the pockets' (*LC* 38). The city thus exists through both that which has been erased and, at the same time, as an open-ended architectural structure for the nomadic, itinerant, and peripatetic thinker, a barely visible phenomenologist of urban ephemera collecting by chance the city's random elements. Sinclair's statement, just quoted, indicates a minimal, reciprocal relationship between self and sky, all other relation emptied out. Such erasure is echoed momentarily in the writer's commentary on the architecture of the 'scoured hulk of Hawksmoor's St Anne', which 'has been restored to anonymity' by steam cleaning. The church imposes discomfort on the photographer, who is recorded in Sinclair's writing as contorting himself to find the most appropriate position from which to photograph Hawksmoor's structure. Sinclair, however, gives little away. The city's histories and literary inhabitants are rendered as inaccessible unless already familiar. Proper names – 'Eric Mottram . . . Allen Fisher, Bill Griffiths, Barry MacSweeney' (*LC* 38) – function as little more than metaphorical markers of or coordinates insinuating the possibility of alternative narratives '(Hawksmoor's St Anne . . . a Masonic resource for apron-wearers who have long since decamped)', though without the possibility of some shibboleth that grants access.

It is not that the narratives are absolutely secret, for if they were no commentary would be possible. Rather, it is the case that this is London encrypted, its signs surfacing to entice and frustrate with the already reneged promise of comprehension and explanation. Location or identity thus dislocates and disorients even as it appears to show signs of opening itself to its readers. Sinclair and Atkins know this, and push such disjointing work in different ways, so that, far from explaining any of the narrative possibilities in mimetic images or prose guaranteed to fulfil any representational contract in a calm, constative statement, their texts enact the city performatively. Without filling in the detail – and, indeed, admitting that such completion is always already forestalled by the ruinous condition of London itself – the photographs and prose respond to the singularity of the city's sites by reiterating London performatively – so many sites of memory translated into so many sites of resistance. Sinclair records seemingly chance observations, their documentary registration serving to estrange and disorient further, through the flat concatenation of disparate, heterogeneous images and objects otherwise inassimilable into any coherent totality:

> Llamas are grazing on Mudchute in the demesne of Canary Wharf. Spectral orchards around the fringe, fringing the ditches. White blossom on black skeletons. Marc doesn't like the look of the cows. Nor they him; the shapes are not complementary. They don't belong in the same landscape. (*LC* 39)

Much takes place here, as language makes manifest the irresolvable incongruity of the observed moment. As in the poetry, fragments stage minimal detail, implying in their frequency all the while the impossibility of recuperating such ruins into a mimetic whole. Representation is only available as the ruins of representation. It is not simply that the content is incongruous and any representation of such serves performatively to heighten such oddity. The passage is also performative to the extent that the language itself is marked by different modalities of discourse, different and differing registers of articulation, timbre, style, and so on. Comedy and gothic intermingle and contaminate one another, even as what might catch the eye materially as poetic effect or diction ('demesne') intrudes as a kind of counter-discourse to the work of slightly off-kilter and dyspeptic documentary description. For example, orchards are spectral, their image given stark contrast of tonal absolutes (white on black) and via the catachresis of blossom on skeletons. There is also to be noticed the reliance, already caught in the spareness of the representation of the orchard, on minimal geometries of representation, where shapes that are not complementary to one another are noted as being inappropriate in the 'same landscape'. And of course, that which is inappropriate is everywhere: llamas inhabit, along with cows, a quasi-Dickensian location, the Mudchute, in the shadow of late twentieth-century corporate architecture. Sinclair's text, haunted possibly by both a Bach cantata ('Sheep may safely graze') and an image from Patrick Keiller's film *London* – that of grazing cows (Keiller's image is equally disorienting, its cows grazing in a field in the background of which is the eighteenth-century architectural splendour of Richmond, while the soundtrack offers the accompaniment of Peruvian pan pipes) – takes its force from its situational occasion, even as it stages an anti-landscape, a pastiche mockery of mimetic cohesion and representational hierarchical decorum typical of landscape painting. Sinclair thus produces what might be termed a counter-picturesque aesthetic.

In 'Watching the Watchman' from *Liquid City* (*LC* 83–5), the Elizabethan Magus, John Dee, becomes one privileged figure in the mapping of London. Sinclair defines the act of walking as a narration, in which there occurs the tracing of the journey 'onto the skin of the Northampton visionary' (*LC* 83). The walk, taken with Alan Moore and Eddie Campbell, gets underway in its prose restaging by recalling Peter Ackroyd's reinvention of the life of architect Nicholas Hawksmoor, in *Hawksmoor*. From this, it is announced that the walk amounts to articulation of an obsession shared by Sinclair and Moore with 'gothic mystification in Whitechapel, surveillance and sculptural coding in the City . . . and the paranoid poetic of Lambeth and Vauxhall' (*LC* 84). Proper names and locations serve equally in the figuring of the city, as space is charted through the temporal oscillation that echoes through the proper name, whether that of location of person. In the first two pages, Sinclair interrupts himself, the narrative, and the reader repeatedly in parentheses. Ackroyd and his text are as much figures in the visionary and imaginary register of the city, as are Dee, Hawksmoor, and of course Sinclair himself. Even Blake is present here, albeit in the most shadowy, spectral manner, given the passing reference to Lambeth. Space, place, and time interanimate one another in the motion of a prose that interrupts, drifts, appropriates, and reiterates, in the manner of psychogeographical method. In this process there is to be glimpsed writing as archival, ghostly palimpsesting; for the palimpsest, it should be acknowledged, while being a trope intimately associated with writing and the literary, can also 'be fruitfully used to discuss configurations of urban space and their unfolding in time' (*PPUP* 7). We read the troping operation in the accretion of otherwise disassociated detail, each element of which is tied to locale and therefore becomes available as a place is crossed or entered, even as that motion – a double motion of both walking and writing – conjures the phenomena of past histories – in the gesture of mapping a route for which only the most cryptic and minimal coordinates are given. But of course, coordinates are all but impossible, because we are south of the River Thames, moving from Putney to Mortlake, Dee's home, and Richmond.

The south is always dangerous, as Sinclair acknowledges in most of his texts. It is this irrational force perhaps that makes Peter Ackroyd relocate John Dee, away from his home in Mortlake in the novel *The House of Doctor Dee*, to Clerkenwell, a 'zone that had a peculiar resonance for him' as Sinclair hints in one of those erupting, interruptive parentheses (*LC* 83), north of the river and nearer the City of London, with its own dark power. It is almost as if the south is too wayward, too much its own force to be governed in a fiction. South London is where time drifts, in Greenwich, near to the Millennium Dome. Crossing the river to the southside, to Lambeth, the 'Lamb of the River' (*SCA* 88), is to bring about 'a kind of death', as Sinclair remarks in 'The Griffin's Egg' (*SCA* 89), a graphic text that interrupts the prose narrative of *Slow Chocolate Autopsy*. In its material embrace of *detournement*, 'The Griffin's Egg' – a collaboration and contest between Sinclair, the photographs of Marc Atkins, and the artwork of Dave McKean – reveals London as a chaos of traces. It is described as an 'autopsy catalogue', and referred to also as the 'unedited city' (*SCA* 90, 84), a phrase which resurfaces in *Lights Out for the Territory*, in which we read of the 'unedited book of the city ... filled with a cacophony of quotations' (*LOT* 232). 'The Griffin's Egg' names the memorial ornament at St Mary's Church, Lambeth (mentioned again below). The photographs and drawn images of the pages bleed into and ghost one another, while Sinclair's text strains to compete with its own ghosts, chiefly Axel Turner, a fictional photojournalist and haunting double of Marc Atkins, belonging to Sinclair's tale but resistant to the narrator's desire to write or edit the city. The graphic text, with its combination of photograph, drawing, and writing, disorders all readerly orientation or possible priority. Lambeth, south of the river, is the home coincidentally of both William Blake and Jeffrey Archer (*SCA* 88). This momentary concatenation, a small constellated image that speaks not only to matters of the literary but also of the political, pulls one up in one's tracks, projecting as it does that which chance makes possible in urban place, providing in the process a spatial and temporal coordinate that is otherwise unmappable.

IV

Which brings me to *Lights Out for the Territory: 9 Excursions in the Secret History of London*. *Lights Out* is a loose collection of essays, the shared excessive subject of which is a series of Londons. *Lights Out* explores in aleatory fashion the various energy flows and lines of flight of the city, as Sinclair maps out the psychogeography of London. This psychogeographical act belongs to a poetics of raising the dead and responding to the spectral traces, which, always already there, are so many revenants of London, returning and endlessly recalled, presented for our fleeting view. The essays move from a consideration of randomly observed graffiti, through the observation of Ronnie Kray's funeral, some caustic critique of Thatcherite policy, to the possibility – or otherwise – of filming London. From anonymous writing, we might say, to the lyricism and poetics of the image – this is the trajectory of the book as Sinclair moves with furious energy through the streets.

As with Sinclair's other writings, the nine essays comprising the volume offer often cryptic, occasionally journalistic, often polemical considerations of various aspects of London culture, as well as its history, its textuality, and its spectral condition. Drawing on the various histories and narratives of gnomic mysticism and urban violence that haunt the structure, history, and cultural identities of the city – from the Temple of Mithras and the alchemical works of John Dee and Elias Ashmole; through William Blake, Charles Dickens; from Jack the Ripper to Jack 'the Hat' McVitie – Sinclair seeks to be faithful in his responses to the psychic forces of the city as he comprehends their role in the fashioning of London, revealing what Peter Ackroyd has called 'a shadowy and merciless city' (*TC* 342). The looseness of structure, the rapid-fire, seemingly scatter-gun approach to subject, is deliberate, allowing for the full play of various resonances and oscillations between otherwise unrelated images and figures. The body of the city is thus unveiled as a babble of languages and graphic marks, belonging to a pattern of echoes, so that one encounters 'the paradoxical side-by-side and interlacing of rational construction and phantasmagoric quality . . . The site of construction is also the site of allegory . . . What is lost is lost. The allegorical construction does not recover' (*ET* 28–9) histories of London, but instead produces and illuminates the subject of the city through the simultaneous projection and disruption of the self that is open to receiving London. Disturbance is inherent in the structure itself, and the very act of writing the city always involves its own dislocation, thereby displacing, disorientating, and translating all who bear witness to it from within themselves.

Thus, London can be read as imposing its odd axiomatic inscriptions on its subjects. Acts of writing are present everywhere as surface signs that bear encrypted witness to the phantom memories which any reader of the city may find, and to which she or he is called upon to respond when walking through London. This is witnessed in example of the 'cosmic egg' entwined by a 'dentated snake' from the Sealy Tomb in St Mary's Church, Lambeth (*LOT* 193–4). Beneath the verse which appears on the egg, Sinclair notices, there is another writing: 'on closer examination . . . the ghost of another another poem, or earlier version of this one . . . hidden beneath; the letters filled in and partially obliterated' (*LOT* 194). So, the trace of London: palimpsest and haunting or, in Sinclair's own words when describing the work of sculptor, performance artist, and poet Brian Catling: 'iteration, transformation, erasure' (*LOT* 261). All such items figure the disorienting occasions of anamnesis, to the origins of which we have no direct access, being in a certain manner belonging to what Sinclair describes as 'the unedited book of the city . . . filled with a cacophony of quotations . . .' (*LOT* 232). And, as Sinclair remarks in *Radon Daughters*, these found traces belong to, return from 'our unconscious. Somewhere in that drifting unfocused world the link was to be found' (*LOT* 1).

One possible revelation of the nature of this link comes into view in the relationship between writing and walking. While I will have more to say on these figures below, it has to be remarked that, for Sinclair, there can be no doubt that writing is the phantom double of walking, even as the act of writing returns the peripatetic revenant. In this fashion writing doubles and divides, producing the same effects of differentiation and deferral within any supposedly stable image or ontology of the city. Writing generates images, the ruins of which appear as the signs of an inaccessible encryption, a hieratic discourse for which there is no key. Sinclair recognizes this, insisting in the process that walking and writing are analogous, though dissimilar: 'I had developed this curious conceit while working on my novel *Radon Daughters*: that the physical movements of the characters across their territory might spell out the letters of a secret alphabet. Dynamic shapes, with ambitions to achieve a life of their own, quite independent of their supposed author' (*LOT* 1). London is thus acknowledged as a cryptic space, and one which is also a spacing. What takes place produces another crypt, an encryption of the cryptic. There is the movement of difference which, in spacing, in taking place and becoming, also encrypts and occludes all the more densely in a constant vertiginous motion between the word and world. Writing London thus challenges and resists the supposed plenitude of any mimetic representation through the projection of what Jodey Castricano describes as a 'cryptic spacing that is the result of violence [not simply the 'representation' of violence but language as violence], contradiction, and pleasure'.[13] What is clear is that mapping, as opposed to representation or interpretation, disjoints and erases any simple opposition such as walking/writing or observing /remembering. Such disjointing movement is clearly spectral. For, as Jacques Derrida points out, the logic of the spectre disrupts all oppositions, between the sensible and the insensible, the visible and the invisible.[14]

Lights Out begins with a consideration of acts of anonymous, spectral writing – graffiti. The ostensible purpose of the first essay from *Lights*

Out – 'Skating on Thin Eyes: The First Walk' – is to serve as a record of Sinclair and Marc Atkins' walk, which traces a V-shaped route from Abney Park, Hackney, south-east to Greenwich, to return north along the line of the River Lea to Chingford Mount, 'recording and retrieving the messages on walls, lampposts, doorjambs' (*LOT* 1). Everything is surface, without source, without context other than London. Graffiti is spectral to the extent that it is always the sign of a return, a trace of revenance without origin. And if the sign no longer functions as an access code, if it is a ruin lacking the 'proper' identity or context, then in its disruption of the field of vision (a rupture surely implied in the force and rapidity of the very idea of the epiphany) it also is excessive. Thus graffiti is perceived as ' "open field" semiological excesses on the wall . . . [looming] like the back projection of a middle-period Godard film' (*LOT* 18). Reading graffiti as cinematic projection is merely an acknowledgement of the way in which, while the phantom or phantasm may be visible, it remains intangible (Derrida 'Sp' 129). The semiological precedes and exceeds the semantic and the very distinction between the opposition is disrupted by graffiti. Graffiti is also defined as 'reproduced words [which] join the rest of the trumpeting exotica of in the encyclopaedia of the city' (*LOT* 16). The telegraphed metonymy of the phrase, 'walls, lampposts, doorjambs', recalls and is haunted by numerous Dickensian accounts of the details of urban architecture in all their arbitrary chaos.

Moreover, graffiti also belongs to an act of exorcism for Sinclair: words reiterated on different walls, in different streets and neighbourhoods, suggest a constant apparitional revenance, which transforms one place into the partial image of another, while turning the walker into a ghost to be exorcised in the act of reading (*LOT* 16). Sinclair's perception arises out of his conviction that '[f]ragments of London are perceived [in the act of walking] as Polaroid epiphanies; signed and abandoned' (*LOT* 2). The partial, sudden image event that is the instantaneity of the photographic revelation is suggestive of the arrival and retreat of ghosts, which 'always pass quickly . . . in an instant without duration, presence without presence of a present, which, coming back, only *haunts*'.[15] The 'infinite speed of the furtive apparition' spoken of in the same passage by Derrida as just cited is that of the Polaroid revenant haunting Sinclair; this is also what is captured briefly in coming to pass through his appreciation of graffiti. There is in the suggestion of the epiphanic nature of unveiling the idea of a momentary appearance, which, in returning retreats again into invisibility, thereby consigning writer and reader to 'uncertainty and indirection'.[16]

The precarious liminal passage of spectrality is implied once again when Sinclair observes of the graffiti that '[s]prayed messages are meaningless, having no programme beyond the announcement of a non-presence' (*LOT* 3). Given the encounter with the disembodied status of the trace, its ruinous condition, the very act of walking is, itself, threatened, turning all too easily into a 'phantom-biopsy' (*LOT* 4). Sinclair's response to London is readable not so much as an interpretation as it is a performative mapping that opens new realities. The distinction is made clear by Tamsin Lorraine, who, writing on Deleuze and Guattari, remarks that 'interpretations trace already established patterns of meaning; maps pursue connections, or . . . "lines of flight", not readily perceptible to the normative subjects of dominant reality'.[17] Sinclair's act of walking–mapping–writing produces the city as a 'collective assemblage of enunciation' (Lorraine 'Sch' 269). This is marked at the very level of the image in Sinclair's writing, as it figures itself as the remainder that ruins identity. For it is not simply a question of observing chance concatenations. Instead, the chance and random – both the encounter with graffiti and every instance of graffito itself – contaminates the language of representation itself. London is thus revealed as a complex textual affair caught up in drifting and transference, enmeshed within the snares of an encrypted archive.

To recall my earlier comment on the profoundly intimate relationship in Sinclair's text between writing and walking: we should remember that walking for Sinclair is not simply a matter of raising ghosts or responding to them, even if it is this. It is also a profoundly spectral process in its own, often furious acts of writing the city, as well as in its mediation of random inscriptions, projections, and the marks of irrecuperable witness and memory. Sinclair signals the restless energy of urban movement in his writing by describing his movement throughout *Lights Out* as *stalking* the city. In Sinclair's text, *stalking* and *haunting* may be read as being on occasions non-synonymous supplementary reconfigurations of one another. Indeed, haunting is a figure in Sinclair's writing for a certain kind of obsessive act of walking and often mediumistic communion: poets must 'haunt a particular territory, tune themselves up to notice everything, every irregularity in the brickwork, every dip in the temperature' (*LOT* 145). An anonymous 'junkman' is a 'stalker of the margins. He haunted market stalls, gallery openings, theatres' (*LOT* 253). Poet Brian Catling 'moves across the city, haunting it like one of Wim Wenders' terrestrial angels' (*LOT* 268). There is also a strong temporal tension in the relationship between *stalking* and *haunting* that undoes both the notion of stable location and meaning in Sinclair's text.

While *stalking* appears orientated towards a future purpose or goal, *haunting* offers a figure of return, leading to the temporal tension. However, stalking the spectral means moving towards a trace that is always already the sign of that which has retreated, always ahead of us, and always from a past to which we have no access. Stalking also intimates a form of drive or desire. What brings such a drive to manifest itself is nothing other than the haunting, haunted condition of the city. The act of writing redoubles the drive, so that the walker is figured and translated again as the trace of a movement, through the process of inscription and memory, neither of which are originary but responses themselves to already displaced phantasmic figures. The spectral condition of the city is thus returned, though never as such, through an irreversible, abyssal troping – abyssal because taken up, immanently implied in the act of reading, which remains always to come. In this manner the walking/writing/reading subject is transformed into both stalker and ghost.

Stalking – which the author opposes consciously to *flânerie* – is movement with a purpose but, in the singular instance of *Lights Out for the Territory*, without a goal, dictated as it is by the city despite any planned expedition. It is also an act that Sinclair admits is intrinsic to those writers and artists who most faithfully respond to, and are driven or haunted by, the phantomatic revenance of London: artists such as Brian Catling, Gavin Jones, Rachel Lichtenstein, Rachel Whiteread, Aidan Andrew Dun, Marc Atkins, Alan Moore, Chris Jenks, Arthur Machen, Angela Carter, Allan Fisher, and Richard Makin. Makin offers a definition of graffiti cited by Sinclair – 'a transparent and resonant superimposition of word and place' (*LOT* 6) – which remark offers us an appropriate aphorism for the haunted topography of London. Stalking is this forceful motion. Doubled as other than itself in the action of the pen or keyboard, *stalking* makes appear what Sinclair terms 'multiple cartographies' (*LOT* 145) of the city, serving (to borrow from Sinclair's citation of Chris Jenks) to 'delineate fragmented localities and senses of placement and identity' against what had been described earlier as the globalization of memory.[18] It generates and performs the 'assemblage' – whether as city or book – 'that opens and multiplies connections' through the 'virtual relations of events' (Lorraine 'Sch' 273), whether by this last phrase one understands the relation between walker and place, writing and memory, text and the city, reader and text, or any matrix of these provisional locations. Stalking is a singular, ghostly rhythm imposed by the city and thus marked by the city's revenant traces; it is always already available, to borrow a remark of Andrzej

Warminski's, as a 'repetition' of some irrecuperable 'inaugural act that put[s] the tropological system in place'.[19] And stalking as haunted motion puts in place a furious displacement of presence, plenitude, and the promise of any stable ontology.

Walking clearly then facilitates acts of displacement and disorientation. It is also one means of opening oneself to the resonances of London's collective memory, which openness makes it possible to respond to the ghosts of memory that are archived and encrypted in any particular location. In Sinclair's text the phantasmic force of anamnesis serves to disrupt the acts of cultural amnesia that urban redevelopment often seeks to enforce. Most frequently in Sinclair's text, writing in doubling walking becomes the medium of anamnesis, as Sinclair's prose becomes the bearer and translator of other texts of the city, texts which are themselves the memories of others, whether one understands such figures and traces as either 'historical' or 'literary' in any narrowly defined sense. Consider, for example, the following two passages:

> And yet, outside the City, beyond the influence of the walls, this millennial fear persists, the flood at the end of time. There is a decayed Unitarian chapel at 49 Balls Pond Road, a ghost with an interesting history, hidden behind corrugated sheeting. Once this was the headquarters of Oswald Moseley's legions – from which they ventured out for acts of provocation in defiance of Dalston's long-established aliens: a skirmish in Ridley Road market. The kind of affair that was witnessed by the young Harold Pinter. (*LOT* 98)

> Piecing a walk together along the craggy remnants of the London Wall – ragstone blocks, brick bonding courses – is like retrieving a false memory, the visual evidence for truths we prefer to forget. The Wall defines the limits of the imagination of Roman London – and is, in this, an act of modesty. To try to get a sense of the original shape by tapping its accredited ruins, following the designated route, is futile. You are contradicted, misinformed, fenced out, overseen for every inch of your journey. But the perversity of that desire, to pick up on the energy field, is as strong as ever. I am haunted by a mythology of gates: as metaphors and as facts. (*LOT* 102–3)

Both passages put to work a play within and between architectural, topographic, mystical, and historical fields. Both also suggest a certain apparitional disturbance that rewrites perception of the past through the agency of collective memory. Both passages serve Sinclair as *lieux de mémoire*, in that they embody and enact 'material, symbolic, and functional' purposes, to recall Nora's words. Here we read the politics and poetics of mnemotechnicity in full force as Sinclair's text assembles 'against the truths we prefer to forget' the traces of what Jonathan Crary describes, near the beginning of this chapter as 'collective historical memory, haunting images of the out-of-date that had the capacity for a social reawakening'. There is a spectral logic at work here, which is at once political and deconstructive.[20] We come to comprehend from such passages that, in Jacques Derrida's words, 'to be haunted by a phantom is to remember something you've never lived through; for memory is the past which has taken the form of presence'.[21]

V

Writing the city is for Sinclair always a process of being open and responding to the traces of the spectral, as already implied. The subject who engages in such encounters with revenance conjures 'a spectre [in order] to conduct an indissoluble marriage with place' (*LOT* 214). Writing London involves acts of fidelity to memories which are not our own. Sinclair's comprehension of this engagement with the city's others is expressed in *Lights Out* in the following manner: '[f]urious displacements of energy are capable of damaging the membrane of what we call "the past". The past is an optional landscape. We are gifted with unearned memories, memories on which we have no moral purchase' (*LOT* 214). Sinclair's analysis is telling in its language. The past is not merely a temporal location, sealed off from the present; it has a dermis and yet is also a topography, a space with possible coordinates, which, once we are in conjunction with it, will not depart. That the marriage of subject and spectral event is indissoluble speaks of the irreversible transformation of the city in the present when viewed through the translation effected by the gift of the other. Such displacement – described by Derrida as 'ghostly disjunction' (*AM* 81) whereby the arrival of the other displaces the illusory solidity of the present – means that for Sinclair '[w]e are [written as] the fiction of vanished lives and buildings . . . misremembered and ineradicable' (*LOT* 237). The power of any London narrative is in its haunting force, its spectral ability to leave an indelible mark and thereby transform the subject of the city, even while any perception concerning the city is only ever the result of the most precarious assemblage of ruins. London is thus a site of multiple flows and, simultaneously, multiple interruptions, provisional, haphazard organizations and disorganizations.

Flow and interruption, appearance and retreat: writing of course allows ghosts, which have left an indelible or 'ineradicable' mark (*LOT* 145) on the structure of the city, to return, to stalk or haunt Sinclair's text, even as he stalks the city streets. Moreover, Sinclair's text is informed not only by the multiplicity of London's traces, but also by a singular density of reference and allusion to other London texts. Such a strategy serves to express faithfully the always haunted architecture and structure of London, whereby texts arrive in Sinclair's writing to transform the perception and image of place. In this manner, he demonstrates how, in the words of Matt Matsuda, 'no history can be pure event, pure evolution; each is rather a repetition, a return to a story which must be retold, distinguished from its previous tellings'. In the sense of history as repetition, the belated arrival of endless iterability figured through narrative ruin without access to originary event, London's traces announce the trauma of the city's constant becoming, a trauma, the violence of which resonates in Sinclair's prose, often at the levels of both form and content, in the structure of sentences and in the narratives of murder, violence, obsessive movement.

The purpose of such obsession, such fury, is explained in Matsuda's discussion of the reading of the past and the work of anamnesis. He continues:

> The past is not the truth upon which to build, but a truth sought, a re-memorializing over which to struggle. The fragmentary, disputatious, self-reflexive nature of such a past makes a series of 'memories' – ever imperfect, imprecise, and charged with personal questions – the appropriate means for rendering the 'history' of the present.[22]

Fragmentary, disputatious, self-reflexive. Ever imperfect, imprecise, charged with personal questions. Here we might read appropriate summaries of Sinclair's prose. That Sinclair brings together multiple diverse elements and texts; that he mingles without apparently discernible architectonic preference fiction, poetry, found objects and occluded historical narratives. Such gestures of montage and bricolage serve to illustrate how the history of the city is only receivable in the present as so many ruins, erupting from and dismantling any possible ontology of the city, as I have insisted throughout this chapter, with an iterable insistence intended to parallel Sinclair's own. In unveiling the city's projections in this manner, Sinclair demonstrates how the image is more powerful than identity, or how the image is always the ruin of being (*LOT* 130). Sinclair's writing is a fictive monument to the otherwise unnameable, in which various citations, events, authors' names, and other iterable replays perform in each and every phrase and page of a kind of originary revenance, which strikes out the efficacy of representation in its return. There is in effect in this writing a certain recirculating flow, a cyclical rhythm and structure. Therefore, what Matsuda calls the 'history' of the present becomes irreversibly translated, and the act of drawing on poetic and fictional texts serves in producing the 'fragmentary, disputatious, self-reflexive nature' of the city's pasts. The city becomes all the more haunted, all the more spectral, because Sinclair refuses to privilege one kind of text or type of event over another; neither does he privilege the materiality of history over the materiality of the letter, insisting that what is received as so many revenant traces are all of equal force potentially.

It is perhaps in and through such traces as that to which Sinclair directs us, that the otherwise unheard and anonymous, the 'ghosts of labour' for example (*LOT* 91), arrive awaiting our witness, demanding a response. Such spectres are everywhere and London, which has no centre as Sinclair rightly insists, is only apprehended, if at all, when it reveals itself as 'an erasure, an absence' (*LOT* 130). At most, London is, throughout Sinclair's writing, the 'unheard voice that is always present in the darkness' (*LOT* 162), resisting appropriation through the demand to be remembered. In such a city, the writer who is open to such revenance is one of the most disruptive of figures,

an involuntary shaman ... [who] develops strategies of derangement, activat[ing] some small part of the map ... (*LOT* 269)

V. Punctuations

VI. Constellations

6
A coincidence of disparate incidents: London undone or, seven artists in search of the city

> Kew holds even more attractions, if only bitter-sweet ones, memories of prewar lust.
>
> Michael Moorcock, *Mother London*

> [. . .] – or as [if] noon and night
> Had clapped together and utterly struck out
> The intermediate, undoing themselves
> In the act. Your city poets see such things . . .
>
> Elizabeth Barrett Browning, *Aurora Leigh*

> She's certainly a great World, there are so many little worlds in Her; She is the great Bee-hive of Christendome . . .
>
> Donald Lupton, *London and the Countrey Carbonadoed*

I

'London', writes Iain Sinclair, 'is begging to be rewritten' (*LOT* 141). Such rewriting is of course already underway, not only in the texts of Iain Sinclair, in those of Peter Ackroyd, Maureen Duffy, and Elizabeth Bowen, as we have seen in the previous chapters, but also in the work of a number of other artists and writers. Such writers and artists acknowledge the modernity of the city, a modernity as old as London itself; for in their articulation of urban modernity in art they recognize and so respond to 'the preservation of all the temporalities of place, the ones that are located in space and in words' (Augé *N–P* 77). Even as the city is always in the process of recycling and reiterating the traces of its otherwise occluded memories, so too are those who respond to London, a place read by Sinclair not as an identity, but as a 'network of coincidences and cyclic collisions' (*LOT* 141). Allen Fisher's London is, for Sinclair, a 'fragmentary, multivoiced schizo – only invaded by a consciousness of "the other" ' (*LOT* 154). As such, Fisher's work produces a topography rather than a representation of the city; it 'fosters connections between fields',[1] unfolding 'in dynamic thought movements, mutating as they go' (Lorraine 'Sch' 276). Such haunting echolalia is also at work for Sinclair in the verse of Richard Makin, whose poetry is composed of 'revenant diction geistraum' (*LOT* 238), so that the writer's response is understood also as a telepathic channelling of the city's traces of alterity. In such texts, and through such ineluctable processes of anamnesis, channelling and bearing witness to the other in which such texts engage, we read an opening to that which is beyond interpretation. Through this opening there is available the return of the impossible as that which arrives, and which may otherwise be named undecidability. The city engenders and encourages alternative modes of writing that make the identity of the city as 'a determination of fixed boundaries impossible',[2] through the temporal flux of the spectral trace within and across particular locations.

The relationship between the artist, spectrality, and the responsibility of memory is therefore undeniably important. The artist and writer are possible spirit mediums, attuned to the energy fields and memories of London. Rachel Lichtenstein, for example, is 'an artist who specialized in not-forgetting, the recovery of "discernible traces" . . . Without the hard evidence of a past life, she . . . would be an unjustified survivor, a ghost with no substance . . .' (*LOT* 238). Gavin Jones paints 'in negative', conjuring spectres in his reverse-field images (*LOT* 254). Brian Catling understands London not as an actual city but as a 'shape-shifting place'; he also admits to conjuring spectres, while his poetry is described as so many 'acts of mediumship' (*LOT* 263). Aidan Andrew Dun's *Vale Royal* is one of the most significant of late twentieth-century London texts. According to Sinclair, Dun 'wills himself to disappear into his text. He recovers it, rather than inventing it . . . [*Vale Royal*] was the present articulation of an ineradicable benediction; an incarnation of the numinous on the ground of the city' (*LOT* 144–5). It is *Vale Royal's* cast of London characters – William Blake, William Stukeley, Chatterton – who were to become Peter Ackroyd's own ghosts (*LOT* 141). And Rachel Whiteread's Turner prize-winning *House* is described by Sinclair as a 'solitary representation of all that . . . [Hackney] had once been. It mocked the destruction of so many hectares of East London; this self-elected survivor, ugly ghost' (*LOT* 226).

Given the undeniably disturbing force that acts of writing London force us to confront, let's start once more.

II

When seeking to address the modalities of urban mapping and representation (terms concerning which the good reader should be cautious) in much recent London textuality, myriad questions and problems arrive to impose themselves with an iterable insistence, as we have seen in the introduction to the present volume, and indeed throughout its chapters. *Writing London – Volume 2: Materiality, Memory, Spectrality* has sought to unravel the intricacies of such questions rather than proposing anything except the most provisional answers. What might be recognized here can be formulated in the following way: beyond any boundary, convention, or merely thematic concern, the insistence of such queries, with their frequency and resonance, announces nothing other than London's illimitable condition (to recall Ford Madox Ford's definition), and with that the experience of, and response to, this condition. Amongst such questions raised by writers and artists through the 1990s, one might consider the following: are we spectators to the empirical coercion of the individual response due to the overwhelming nature of the subject? Or are we witness to some phenomenological registration of what might be called appropriately an intimate (and, perhaps, therefore partially inaccessible) psycho-topographical reconstitution? Can we tell or, even more fundamentally, separate the one from the other?

The texts of Iain Sinclair (already discussed in the previous chapter), Patrick Keiller, or Allen Fisher, for example, propose such conditions of undecidability, albeit in highly different ways. Such writers and other artists appear to disturb simultaneously the limits of the urban condition objectively rendered on the one hand and any purely individual, idiomatic translation on the other, so that everything oscillates, everything figures as and in an endless analogical, fractured series of non-synonymous correspondences. In comprehending this, it must be suggested that there is in operation a certain passage between modes or locations, a shuttling or weaving between supposedly external and the internal locations (or vice versa), in which all boundaries either begin to be dissolved or are otherwise always already under erasure. This is, in effect, what comes to be traced by Elizabeth Bowen in *The Heat of the Day*, in the interplay between the psyches of characters such as Stella Rodney and 'that particular psychic London' as Bowen has it. The very nature of London's appresentation with which we have been concerned, figured by the phantasmagoria of so many hitherto occluded traces returning in ruins as the signs of the work of involuntary memory, brings repeatedly to light the complication and, concomitantly, the destabilization of the very idea of representation. This is the case especially where the mode of representation relies implicitly on supposedly stable dialectical locations, as well as on a certain mimetic fidelity that eschews or distrusts exaggeration or amplification.[3] In an effort to comprehend what is taking place, this may be termed, provisionally, urban *dis-identification*, if by this we might indicate an *auto-disidentification*. What is past does not remain past but is all the more dissonant for being registered in an ever-present tense that has no presence, and which therefore is never quite of the present but only ever accessible through a seriality of 'now-times' as 'now-being'.

Clearly, the questions which the city text foregrounds come to articulate themselves within spatial and temporal matrices, which in turn interface through an engagement between the poetics of topography and that of subjectivity. It is possible to read through the texts of Keiller, Michael Moorcock, Lavinia Greenlaw, and others, a concern with a comprehension of urban time that differs from a purely linear, progressive historical understanding. In the works in which we are interested, there is registered a sense that the past is transformed but has never disappeared (even though, obviously, it is never there as such). Recognizing both the psycho-topographical nature of London and, with that, understanding the experience the city imposes on us amounts to the recognition of a materiality – as I have already insisted in the introduction – distinct from any simply or purely phenomenological modality or aesthetic intervention. Such materiality of the city persists as a constant articulation of a threshold of becoming throughout history, maintaining itself in ruins through ineluctable processes of translation, 'transformation, passage, wave action' (Benjamin *AP* 494). Comprehending in this manner is perhaps a question of seeing 'as the poets do it' (*wie die Dichter es tun*), to borrow from Kant on the material sublime.[4] Such an act of seeing, 'merely in terms of what manifests itself to the eye', to cite Kant once more (*CJ* 130), registers that striking out of the intermediate peculiar to the response to London, as Barrett Browning has it ('Your city poets see such things'). Such registration involves a chronicling and revelation of temporalities expressed through the enfolding and unfolding of material and spectral phenomena onto the present experience of both the city and the text, and, it has to be argued, in the re-marking of the text as city, a topography comprising and comprised of so many encrypted and overt citations. The artists to which this concluding chapter turns explore temporal paradox in relation to the experience of London, as this paradox is best expressed by F. W. J. Schelling: 'For different times . . . are necessarily at the same time. Past time is not sublimated time. What has past certainly cannot be as something present, but it must be as something past at the same time with the present . . . And it is equally inconsistent to think of past being, as well as future being, as utterly without being.'[5] The city, articulated through text, photography, film, and installation comes to be revealed as having that 'materiality without matter' announced by Jacques Derrida. This recognition of temporal and material aspects of London in turn makes the city available (to borrow Patrick Keiller's liner notes from the video of his 1993 film, *London*) 'as it is and, at the same time', as it can be reconstructed and reimagined. Thus, with this implicit comprehension at work, the writers and artists in question interrogate the interstices that emerge and open as the imagined coordinates of such concerns.

In such openings, questions similar to those which had announced themselves in the introduction to *Writing London – Volume 2* reappear: in what sense for many London artists is the past always with us, though never as such, never being reducible to an overall homogeneous, idealized or romanticized space? As we have witnessed, the past figures as so many haunting traces, disjointing the fields of vision and registration. It therefore has to be asked once more: in what ways do alternative chronicles and catalogues of the city come to be figured in flows through both the individual figures of writer, artist, or narrator, and technological media such as the still, cinematic, or video camera? And is it the case that we might read these fluxes or pulsions as challenging the classical efficacy of mimetic, hegemonic representations, thereby demanding in turn a response, and a responsibility, first on the part of the artist and subsequently on that of the reader, spectator or audience, to the persistent experience of the city? Risking all, perhaps, in that knowing conjuration of nostalgia is the call of the past where, paradoxically, one gives up the illusion of any possible possession as one gives oneself over to becoming possessed. The city becomes available as so many ungovernable events of revenance, regeneration, and acts of affirmative resistance to the authority of, on the one hand, the city planners, and on the other, any grand narrative. Such excess, ironically appropriate to the condition of London, informs and generates this final chapter in its consideration of novelists, essayists, film makers, poets, sculptors, photographers, and artists of the last decade of the twentieth century. It is impossible to pretend to anything like a 'reading' of these artists in so short a space as single chapter. However, I hope, in concluding *Writing London – Volume 2: Materiality, Memory, Spectrality*, to avoid conclusions while indicating in however telegraphed or adumbrated a fashion certain shared interests and obsessions amongst particular urban artists and the singular manner in which such obsessions are encrypted within their work.

II

Starting with the first epigraph of this chapter, from Michael Moorcock's, *Mother London*, a novel in which outpatients – Mary Gasalee, Josef Kiss, David Mummery – from a clinic treating the mentally ill wander through the city, 'overhearing', 'voicing', or otherwise being the conduits for the involuntary revenants of the city's memories, the alternative, marginalized and forgotten London voices. At first glance, Moorcock's apparently whimsical phrase (*ML* 274) might be taken as somewhat Betjemanesque: the ambivalence intrinsic to nostalgia, the encrypted resonance of personal memory (appealing *because* exclusive), the nod towards secreted impropriety, as predictable in its own way as the banal security of the suburbs.

By extension, the suburban location, Kew, furthers the passing resemblance between Moorcock and Betjeman on initial acquaintance, being one of those untimely places which persist around the peripheries of London, belonging simultaneously to London and to one of the home counties also (in Kew's case, Surrey). Kew, typically of so many of the capital's liminal sites, is recognizable architecturally: there are the mid-to-late Victorian and Edwardian houses and, less frequently, purpose-built apartment buildings which are, in Moorcock's words, 'scarcely touched by the War' (*ML* 273). There is just enough of the past, then, materially visible in the present to disturb temporal stability, to suggest the passage between external, material form and the internal, mutable structures of attempted *rememorization* (to adapt Toni Morrison's term). Moreover, Moorcock's play between material persistence and immaterial memory arguably effects the 'striking out of the intermediate', to borrow Elizabeth Barrett Browning's definition of temporal confusion and the concomitant erasure of knowable specificity.

At the same time, however, in the instance of recall, and despite the 'striking out', there is, nonetheless, the unveiled perception – perception as urban sensibility – in the act of memory as afterthought, a reconstitution which is also the trace of incommensurable identities, drifting, disinterring, within one place, yet taking place and returning from different times. Layered one over the other, each thread woven into every other, that which returns involuntarily in present memory undoes identity's stability through a gesture akin to the Freudian concept of *Nachträglichkeit*, the work of mourning as the negotiation between the subject's recall and the belated arrival of the haunting trace. There is thus mapped out as the work of memory in response to a particular aspect of London, in the words of Nicola King on the Freudian concept, 'an exploration and an enactment of the interplay between social structures and the structures of the psyche'.[6] This is witnessed repeatedly, as here in David Mummery's vision: 'Frequently Mummery imagines the city streets to be dry riverbeds ready to be filled from subterranean sources. From behind the glass he watches his Londoners . . . They come from Undergrounds and subways . . . flowing over pavements . . . A cold sun now brightens this eruption of souls . . . Momentarily Mummery feels as if London's population has been transformed into music, so sublime is his vision' (*ML* 7). From this individual mediation comes a greater apprehension and image of the city:

> the city's inhabitants create an exquisitely complex geometry, a geography passing beyond the natural to become metaphysical, only describable in terms of music or abstract physics: nothing else makes sense of relationships between roads, rails, waterways, subways, sewers, tunnels, bridges, viaducts, aqueducts, cables, between every possible kind of intersection. (*ML* 7)

Thus David Mummery's visionary reconstitution: initially this is his vision, his response, and yet it is also comprehensible momentarily beyond Mummery's response to London. Here the city is mapped through the fractal motion of the city's eight million subjects, unimaginable except as they belong to London; it is traced too by their movements, and the various forms of communication comprising an innumerable and otherwise unimaginable network of relationships that reveals the city's topography in the excess of surface motion, the very meaning of which is in itself. Moorcock's focus on the mnemotechnic processes of projection that take place in and through his outpatients (as we see above) might be taken initially as a reading of psychoanalytic effect grounded in the individual subject. However, that the novel works with several principal characters suggests a broader historical or material structure of revenance and resonance akin to Benjamin's notion of the constellated image. Something is shared between Kiss, Gasalee, and

Mummery that cannot be described through the identification of any particular mental illness; avoiding any pathological, forensic, or essentialist reading that grounds affect in character, the presumption of a psychoanalytic dimension is perhaps more accurately recognizable as the psychogeographic. The latter inhabits, offering itself as counterpoint to, the former, even as, in resonating across and through the characters, the psychogeographic discourse of the city exceeds the limits inscribed by the identification of any individual symptomatics.

When David Mummery acknowledges in his writing therefore that any city only survives through the persistence of its mythopoetic elements, through those traces which, in surviving *make* the city, affirmation of this assertion arrives for the reader through his first 'voiced' words, which are not his but William Blake's: 'Bring me my bow of burning gold . . .' (*ML* 5). Blake's vision of the New Jerusalem within and other than London introduces an other London from the very beginning of the novel, and confirms the affirmative, ghostly arrival of mythical London which endures. Importantly, while Mummery's first statement is written – 'By means of certain myths which cannot easily be damaged or debased the majority of us survive . . . Amongst London's in recent years is the story of the Blitz, of our endurance' (*ML* 5) – the first words from his mouth are those from another temporal moment, a fragment of millennial vision. A vision of the city arrives, confirming and supplementing that image of the written statement, which is comprised of the very first words of *Mother London*. Moorcock produces a constellated image through the concatenation of Blake's text and his own citation, a mythical citation from an imagined text concerning the mythologization of London's survival during the bombing of the Second World War. Writing meets writing across time, while still retaining and being maintained by the difference of discrete temporal instances. The city, then, endures and is apprehended indirectly through the location of several temporal moments – that of Blake's writing, that of Mummery's own act of writing (further displaced through reference to his antique pen, used in conjunction with his '19th-century clerical desk' [*ML* 5]) – in the now of reading the beginning of *Mother London*. To stress a point already implied throughout the volume, this *now* is not a privileged present but is simply one more moment of now-time analogous with Benjamin's now-being. Furthermore, that 'Mummery' first appears through a surviving ruin of his own text, indicates that he himself is written, part of the city's psychogeography, a figure through which the city has the possibility of arriving, rather than being a source. Writing before voice, textual rhizome prior to originary source: here is what we are given to read from the beginning of Moorcock's novel; and as one more double graft onto the rhizomatic network that traces and is comprised of so many traces of London here is both *Mother London* and the name of the author *Michael Moorcock*.

In effect, the novel gets underway (if it is not in fact always already in motion, being merely the visible nexus of hitherto invisible flows, those of the city), neither from an originating moment nor a single voice, but instead through multiple 'lines of articulation or segmentarity, strata and territories; but also lines of flight, movements of deterritorialization and destratification . . . All this, lines and measurable speeds, constitutes an *assemblage*. A book is an assemblage of this kind [and so, too, is a city, as is also a representation of the city through a book which does not attempt a reductive mimetic figuration], and as such is unattributable (*TPCS* 2–3). Thus, Deleuze and Guattari, whose notion of the assemblage allows us an apprehension not dissimilar to Benjamin's conception of the image, and, through this, access to an acknowledgement of how the city writes and is written. More than this, the true city text, the true act of writing the city, allows for the production of the text that, in its formation is analogous with the city, and is thus a performative text inasmuch as it never merely represents or speaks of the city, but enacts the city's assemblage through the assemblage of traces, ruins and remainders that write the city in ruins, though never as such. For the city – and this is what manifests itself through Moorcock's singular textual strategy – 'is a multiplicity . . . a machinic assemblage . . . a kind of organism . . . *a body without organs*' (*TPCS* 3); and it is also apprehensible, in Walter Benjamin's words as a 'nexus of meanings . . . akin to that of the fibres of spun yarn' (*AP* 272).

Thus we see how there arrives the image of the city that 'attain[s] to legibility only at a particular time', and that this 'time' cannot be affixed to a date or final temporal location. It is instead always the time of reading, which is itself always untimely in that it is not the instance that is made to appear through the act of reading. Through the critical and untimely moment haunting manifests itself, as the ghosts of the city disturb the page and disrupt the narrative with the material force of italics, as one more example shows: '*trying different drums well you can't have them clapping four four to the bloody tabla I said and he said he was a Huguenot journalist what's your paper I asked him Dutch treats in old Soho put an urban freeway straight through . . . we feel no city lacks some pleasing sight hammering at it till it assumes a manageable shape barking in Essex barking Babylon*' (*ML* 381). This passage, which, following Deleuze and Guattari, we can identify in its form-without-form as one of many '*collective assemblages of enunciation*' (*TPCS* 7) is typical of the violent interruptions and suspensions in the narrative of Gasalee, Mummery, and Kiss, through so many often unattributable inscriptions. With its sudden break with coherent narrative, beginning in mid-sentence and shifting subjects without diacritical or grammatical warning, this passage and the many others, similar in form though not in content, throughout *Mother London* disorders coherence and any single recuperable temporal instance, as different historical moments interweave with one another in performative acts of narrative montage. Through 'principles of connection and heterogeneity' (*TPCS* 7), passages undo the work of representation and any stable relationship between book and world. For, far from being simply an image of the world, Moorcock's ruined text, this text of traces 'forms a rhizome with the world' (*TPCS* 11) of the city, and thus apophatically implies London, thereby giving place to the possibility for recognizing the truth in London's writing. In this recognition and reception of the city initially projected through and yet exceeding endlessly the already destabilized subject, Benjamin's 'now of recognizability' flashes upon the reader; there is, in Benjamin's words, 'the moment of awakening' (*AP* 486), that poetic unveiling through involuntary memory the knowledge of the city's singularity 'available only in lightning flashes' (*AP* 457).

III

' "How many fucks, do you reckon, in the history of Soho?" ' Thus Robinson, the eponymous protagonist from Chris Petit's 1993 novel of Soho and the sex industry, particularly porn films (*R* 10). If, as Samuel Weber suggests of Walter Benjamin's *Arcades Project*, the burden of the writer is to expose 'the *allegorical cast* of apparently material reality'; and if such exposure 'takes responsibility for the unknowable that sits at the heart of all efforts to decipher and decode, interpret and communicate', taking responsibility as Weber has it 'for something that cannot be controlled, but that nevertheless calls insistently for a response' (*SST* 19); then such a burden is caught here. And capture takes place, if not in the ostensibly glib, crudely direct question spoken by Petit's Harry Lime-like entrepreneur, then at least in the question's registration of an erased history, a material reality belonging to one aspect of London that flashes upon us, remaining all the while inaccessible as such. We become aware of the insistent and yet unavailable ghosts of the city, caught in this one line, in the historicity of its image, yet to which that image is irreducible nonetheless because 'what the image intends is the irretrievability of the present [of any present as presence] itself'.[7] What comes through the directness of the language is the Benjaminian simultaneity of intimate proximity *and* distance, so that historically, materially, past and present collapse in the double moment of the question's articulation and the response that is recognition or awareness. What comes to be produced is, again in Weber's words, a 'different sort of space' and, we might add, a different sort of image of the city's history: one 'which does not result in a simple identity' (SST 20). Thus in this one line – which finds itself returning parenthetically, edited slightly later in the novel ['("How many fucks in the history of Soho?")' (*R* 173)] – there is to be read the convergence of the 'lightning flash . . . and the *constellation*' (Weber SST 20).

The convergence of lightning flash and constellation is caught in the following brief example from *Robinson*. Pulled by some indefinable urge, the narrator recalls that 'sometimes I drove myself out to wander the city'. He continues:

> I walked through the centre of the city, those parts that were still negotiable. The bookshop was half-gone . . . I saw myself caught in some kind of time slip – an invisible crevice . . . I saw cracks in the pavement of Meard Street; I watched Humphrey Bogart dying in *High Sierra*; saw a hand clutching a number eight bus ticket . . . I saw a woman swinging out her right arm. William Blake walking down Poland Street, shadowed by a dog . . . Blind Borges wrote: *I saw a tattered labyrinth (it was London)*. (*R* 198–9)

The motion of the narrator, his movement and identity nothing other than a series of 'nows', is everything here in its fleeting moments of perception, putting to work the poetics of the city, even as the city comes into being in and through the spectral machinery. The very image, through its performative collage or bricolage, intimates that irretrievability of any present through the performativity of narrative's serial *nows* (and *now* and *now* . . .). The city and the subject are intimately and reciprocally constituted through the unending pulse of what Walter Benjamin terms the 'concretion of now-being ⟨*Jetztsein*⟩ (waking being!)' (*AP* 391). The narrator comes into being – is awakened, if you will – through the 'concretion' or making material of the self that occurs through the revenance of London's disparate traces. At the same time, however, the subject *is* the screen onto and through which the singularity of collective anamnesis takes place. The responses to the arrival of material fragments and ruins comprise and acknowledge so many unassimilable phantasms and traces of memory. Without any order, except that imposed by the double time of walking and writing, the city comes to be mapped in ruinous fashion. This double time is abyssal in its complexity: for walking is remembered even as it is an act of writing and reading, which is then returned as shadow to and echo of itself, writing as memory being the trace of the reading within walking. And still there is no coherent image, no bounded representation other than what takes place between the 'I' and the city, where *between* is the measuring out of what takes place in the afterthought of memory's filmic montage of what has occurred in the unfolding of the dimension between the eye and the materiality of the city. Through its remains, through remnants that are figured not simply in the clausal play of memories and phantasms but also in the recognition and motifs of cracks, disappearances, absences, deaths, body parts, and motions, the city remains concealed in its self-disclosure, its performative gesture of unveiling. This is a performative passage precisely because the narrative prose does not simply report or observe; in its fictive bricolage given place through the conceit of 'I' the city is disclosed, disclosing itself, even as 'it' remains unavailable, and ultimately unknowable. Everything about London is in transition, even as the labyrinth of streets is translated, time giving way to multiple moments in the times of traversal (effectively we read an immanence of 'I', a montage of self-multiplying, disseminating selves). One arrives at the paradoxical 'image' of Blind Borges' vision, the materiality of the city becoming translated into what it always already is, which is the materiality without matter (TR 281) of textual and tropological work, in the unravelling of (and by) a tropology which is also a topology.

The topology of *Robinson* always maps what the narrator calls a 'fine tuning of the social itinerary' (R 8), involving as it does the endless substitution of 'half a dozen public places' (R 8), the names of public houses, and the briefest and vaguest of map coordinates: 'north of Oxford Street . . . the border of Soho's Chinatown . . . the corner of Manette Street . . . Greek Street under the archway . . .' (R 9) There is a hieratic power to such signification, a power recognized in the narrator's comment on the Greek Street archway: 'it was like a border post, the crossing point where obligations could be left behind' (R 9). The topography of this particular London is invoked through the resonance of proper name allied to the power of the threshold or border, which, even though they may be substituted by one another, are not of course synonymous, as Walter Benjamin urges us to recall (AP 494). As Petit's sketch of the narrator-flâneur's habits shows us, the motion of the city's subject inscribes the map in gestures of rhizomic flight. The relation of subject to city is caught later in the novel, when Soho, the haunt of De Quincey in his *Confessions of an English Opium Eater* (a text which is of significance to Petit's narrator, thereby situating him as belonging to a constellated textual image apropos the city), is described as 'a state of mind, that crumbling time zone built up of absenteeism, dereliction, vagrancy, and atheism (I had sought out the irresponsible heart of the city)'. He continues, '[f]or a long time I stared, helpless, at the church [St Anne's] with its bombed-out body and surviving steeple. It was an appropriate landmark and symbol . . . for this other, less tangible realm' (*R* 40).

Thus all at once, this particular district of the city is both material *and* psychic, allegorical and historical; it offers the image of a temporal as well as a spatial threshold, which in recalling to the subject those traces and ruins of anamnesis, figured appropriately in the material architectural ruins of Wren's St Anne's Church, Dean Street, performs the London subject's relation to that which flows through any present moment, thereby dismantling it: from the Great Fire of 1666, through De Quincey's opium-induced visions and memories, from the Blitz of the Second World War, to the phantom focus of the narrator's gaze. The gaze registers what it sees, and a certain vision, in excess of the visible, is promised, through the other of the empirical gaze 'in which the magic of distance is extinguished' (Benjamin *AP* 314). Here, Petit's narrator serves as one example of Benjamin's urban allegorist, in that 'he dislodges things from their context' (*AP* 211); the allegorist is the one 'for whom objects represent only keywords in a secret dictionary' (*AP* 211) as the text itself maps and is mapped by 'a sort of productive disorder', which is, as Benjamin reminds us, 'the canon of the *mémoire involuntaire*' (*AP* 211).

IV

The exploration and enactment of the subject's relation to the past is also at work in particularly intimate fashion in Rachel Lichtenstein's installations involving images of a room inhabited by David Rodinsky. As with Petit's text, Lichtenstein's work operates allegorically, viewing singular reality 'under the sign of fragmentation and ruin . . .' (*AP* 33), and it is this allegorical vision that is captured for Lichtenstein in Rodinsky's lodging room in East London.

David Rodinsky lived above a synagogue in the East End of London, in Princelet Street, traditionally a location synonymous with the settlement of immigrants over several centuries, whether Huguenot, Chinese, Jewish, Kurdish, Kashmiri, or Bangladeshi, as well as being the place associated with dissenting religious proletarian groups. Such associations have, perhaps inevitably, produced an area which, while vital to the life of London, has, nonetheless, come to be associated with an identity 'as somehow alien and mysterious', as Peter Ackroyd puts it.[8] It is on such identities that Lichtenstein draws, as she traces a much more personal identity, enfolding as she does fragments of her own family history (Polish Jews who fled from Poland to England in the 1930s). Simultaneously, she focuses on the fact that Rodinsky, otherwise unknown and unremarkable, disappeared mysteriously in the mid-1960s, leaving only his room and, particularly, its countless fragments of writings, books and notebooks covered in annotations, all of which are concerned with matters of language, encryption, cabbalistic scribblings, 'strange indecipherable symbols' (*RR* 27). Even Rodinsky's *London A–Z* had been written over with scrawled fragments, installing it as simultaneously a textual access to London *and* an implicit acknowledgement that any area of the city is traced, haunted, by an ineffable, forgotten, and frequently resurrected otherness.

As part of the preparation for the installations, and in order to place herself in a particular relationship to Rodinsky, Lichtenstein walked the streets highlighted by Rodinsky in his *A–Z* (*RR* 286). Such acts, and the subsequent rewriting of the events as a record of Lichtenstein's processes of rememorization arguably brings back in discontinuous moments a London past which always belongs to the imaginative reconstitution of the urban site. Thus, Lichtenstein works with what Iain Sinclair has described '[n]umerous fragments that composed an unreliable biography . . . before memories became memorial plaques' (*RR* 4). Such fragments are put to work reassembling, as he puts it, the mementoes of a 'missing text' through 'sympathetic marriage', whereby the installations refigure what the room always already was: a 'structure in abeyance' (*RR* 5). Rodinsky's room thus becomes a 'theatre of ghosts' passing 'beyond reconstruction and authenticity' (*RR* 9). Lichtenstein's installations take on a performative role as acts of resistant rememorization. Resisting official memorialization, situating in particular relationships personal and impersonal memories after the event, the installations maintain the fragment as that in which is focused revenance and responsibility beyond the immediate life of either David Rodinsky or Rachel Lichtenstein, to speak, in encrypted, archival fashion of the East End's alternative histories. Arguably, what comes to be maintained is the necessity of bearing witness, to maintain relationships of witnessing, as if there is a recognition on Lichtenstein's part that '[w]hen there are no longer any witnesses, there is no longer any memory', as Paul Virilio has suggested.[9]

In this, I would contend, we read the negotiation between the limits of the empirical, the question of ineffability, and a certain return, not *to* but *of* the urban fragment – London as so many fragments, London in ruins, and writing the experience of an urban mnemotechnic. London is perceived and conceptualized in much recent writing as exactly *just* this recognition of ruinous revenance, of which Moorcock's commentary and the various pieces of Rodinsky's room are exemplary, but to which Lavinia Greenlaw also gives articulation in her poem, 'Love from a Foreign City': 'There are parts of the new *A to Z* marked simply/ "under development". Even street names have been demolished.'[10] Here, the city trembles through specifically, always already dismembered textual-topographical traces and coordinates, already erased, momentarily suspended, awaiting inscription, the memories of a particular site no longer accessible except as the potential ebb and flow of the fragment. When Greenlaw writes 'The one-way system keeps changing direction, / I get lost a hundred yards from home' (L 44), she provides access to London's ineluctable discontinuitiés, its bit-stream processing of constantly changing flows which render the familiar uncanny.

There is a sense of the ineffable which the fragmentary writing of the city perpetuates, an ineffability which is also marked as the experience of urban iterability. Greenlaw's narrator getting lost so close to home appears to recall those figures from Dickens' *Martin Chuzzlewit* who can never find Todgers' boarding house. It is as though, in seeking to measure memory against place in response to the city, one finds oneself left with what Ken Smith in *The London Poems* describes as the experience of 'the phrase book / for yesterday's language'[11] (Smith 1986 53). Yet, there is also in such writing and other textual forms a comprehension of the significance of the fragment for the resurrection of the other histories of London, as well as an endlessness, a sense of Londons to come. If what we read is what is supposedly lost or disappearing, it is also, in being read, in being remembered after the event, a sense of memory's haunting persistence. Writers such as Iain Sinclair or Aidan Andrew Dun, and artists such as Rachel Whiteread and Rachel Lichtenstein, all comprehend the necessity, of what Hans-Jost Frey calls the 'depiction of several fragmentary states'[12] as appropriate to the description of the city. Instead of reading the various fragments as objects to be defined and placed in a determinate context, responding to the fragmentary states of the capital's places, inhabitants, events, and temporalities announces an 'anonymous, posthumous endlessness' (*SPD* 48) to the condition of London. This is, I would suggest, precisely the gesture of 'undoing' readable in the processes of a revenant writing residing within, acting as the countersignature to, those Betjemanesque resemblances, noticeable for example in the epigraph taken from Moor-cock. In large part, it is the work of such undoing and the play between the spectral and the material that this implies, which touches and illuminates so much London textuality of recent years, as already intimated, whilst also acknowledging the irreducible singularity of the experience and memory of the ruin. The apparent organization of the seemingly familiar and habitually assumed is dislocated through the conjuration of the forgotten or otherwise occluded, returning to be dis-quietingly traced in, and as, the unfixing of the present. Reading and writing London in the instances in question *just is* the experience of the ruined text; this experience does not stop at the limit of the fragment, but rather, as Frey suggests, outlasts it (*SPD* 49).

V

Allen Fisher's poetry is very much a discourse of fragments and ruins, particularly his sequence, *Brixton Fractals*. Since the 1980s at least, Fisher has concerned himself with alternative poetic modes for the represen-tations of local London history. At the same time however, as *Brixton Fractals* shows (and as its name intimates), phrases, 'facts', details, and other fragments resist any coalescence into a homogeneous meaning, and indeed the fractal offers itself as a possible non-synonymous substitution for the Benjaminian constellated image or the rhizome of Deleuze and Guattari. Instead, the lines we read amount to nothing other than the inscribed translation effects of response to the material-ity of the city, or what Fisher calls, in the prose poem, 'The Mathemat-ics of Rimbaud', a series formed from 'generalised, unformalizable changing topologies – the poetries of the inventive memory', otherwise called in the same poem, 'the multiplicity of attentions' (*FE* 42–9; 49). Clearly, in the announcement of attention and memory there is the acknowledgement of a subject, however dimly apprehended. This is, though the most meagre of personae, opening onto and as the conduit for, the various, irreducible fluxes of the city. The attention to the generalized and unformalizable, along with the announcement of transformation, translation, and mutability points to Fisher's apprehen-sion of both fractal action and rhizomic form, which 'fosters connec-tions between fields . . . [and] the maximum opening of bodies without organs onto a plane of consistency' (*TPCS* 12). This discussion of the map from *A Thousand Plateaus* will be immediately recognizable as an appropriate definition of Fisher's text and the act of mapping London without reducing it to an image, which such expressions of 'a radical *poiesis* produce. Like Fisher's text, the map (and, by extension, the city in all its serial figures and 'changing topologies') 'is open and connectable in all of is dimensions' (*TPCS* 12). In the condition of its construction, *Brixton Fractals* can be read as a performative rhizome connected to the rhizome of the city itself, in that it allows for multiple entryways, without resolving itself into a homogeneous and single, simple image or representation.

How can this be seen beyond the suggestiveness of Fisher's title? *Brixton Fractals* compiles detail, it records and catalogues fragments of its South London location, as the poems, in their irregularity, their unpredictability of motion, rhythm, form or focus remain resistant to analysis, maintaining themselves in their irreducible complexity, as well as in the endless possibilities of fostering connections. Archetypal figures – Painter, Bellman, Informer, Photographer – appear, disappear, and reappear, modern urban types or, perhaps more accurately, tropes, impossible to describe, traversing the city, as so many nomadic cursors along the city's rhizomic lines. Seemingly anonymous, each 'character' (if we can use this term) is less a figure than one facet of a composite, yet heterogeneous, always changing structure, through which to perceive – and through which is projected – a particular aspect *of* or moment *in* Brixton. For example, 'The burglar leans out of someone's window', while the Painter 'follows a path to a simple hut' (*FE* 65–104; 94). Each archetype inscribes himself into, onto, the topography of Brixton, becoming an echo of himself, which resonance is subsequently caught, in making itself manifest, in the act of reading by 'A reader [who] follows the marks up the path/occasionally losing balance/ . . . /stopped short by the figure of Blake' (*FE* 96). Following the mark, tracing a path, we might say, an other trace emerges or arrives; calling a violent halt to the acts of reading/writing/walking already performed in the rhizomatic layers of the lines. In this, the reader does not simply trace, in order to produce an image, but instead marks one more moment in a relay, another re-marking of the already existent and hitherto phantasmatic trace, which in turn is displaced onto another reader. This loss of balance, its figural disorientation, at once announces the reading experience, which can equally be considered as gesturing towards the experience of the city and/or the experience of our encounter with the text. The invocation of Blake provides a form of

reference, though any potential meaning which such a moment of signification might produce is inevitably poor and limited, as the occasional enunciation of an anonymous first-person narrator makes plain:
'I respond to the stimuli realised / as alien to my nature' (1992, 96).
Atypical events disinter the reader from any formalizable relationship
to both the text and the city, for there is little here which one can
connect to Brixton in any comforting manner. We might point out, for
instance, that Blake lived at one time in adjacent Lambeth, but this gets
us nowhere. We are in a 'landscape of events', to borrow Paul Virilio's
phrase, a landscape, which, according to Virilio, 'has no fixed meaning,
no privileged vantage point', least of all in the location or locution
known as 'I' (*LE* xi). To cite Virilio further, what we encounter in reading
Fisher is a sense that 'it is no longer the big events that make up the
fabric of the landscape . . . but myriad incidents, minute facts either
overlooked or deliberately ignored. Here, *the landscape is a passage*'
(*LE* xi).

The idea of landscape as passage rather than fixed site with determinable coordinates available to reproduction and representation is
crucial in the textual imagination of London as here considered,
whether by *passage* one understands the movement through particular
places or that which returns through the temporal passage implied in
the conjuration of multiple resonances and oscillations of alternative
pasts. In 'Birdland' (from *Brixton Fractals*) it is 'endless destruction' that
makes Brixton, along with the simultaneity of prohibition and transgression, the play of 'carnival' and 'jouissance', as these connect to children's games, a busker, Brixton High Road, figures of dance and dream,
and, once again, the revenant of London *par excellence* William Blake
(*FE* 101–4; 102).[13] Irreducible to a technique or a method for producing
the image or enacting stable representation precisely because that which
haunts and returns determines the mnemotechnicity of the London
text, there is nonetheless to be comprehended what Bernard Cache calls
the event of seizing,[14] a process of sampling wherein is acknowledged
the excess which always escapes apprehension. Such apprehension or
perception 'places us immediately within memory' (*EMFT* 143), where
memory comes to name, beyond the immediately personal, acts of overfolding and unfolding the inscriptions of place, in the course of which,
the 'entire past [at least by implication] becomes concentrated in the
present of an excessive reaction' (*EMFT* 17). And in this fashion, in
the movement of its now-being, 'Brixton abandoned / challenges the
closure of meaning / so far removed . . .'; and here we read '. . . a riant
spaciousness become temporal' (*FE* 103, 104). Fisher's Brixton is one

such excessive reaction to what is always excessive, the rhizome of the city. Rhizome-text and rhizome-city: neither has beginning nor end. Both are what Deleuze and Guattari call interbeings (*TPCS* 25), topographies the very fabric of which is woven in the unending conjunction of the non-synonymous. The idea and motif of interbeing 'carries enough force to shake and uproot the verb "to be"', and, it has be added, any effort to articulate the ontology of London.

VI

Such excessive reaction is to be found everywhere in Patrick Keiller's film *London*. The film searches obsessively for the unhomely and the unfamiliar, within the recognizable, bringing back the excess of trace that is invisible within visible form, structure or place. This is readable whether, by the 'invisible', one is acknowledging an alternative past, a forgotten fact, a submerged detail, or, more simply, an otherwise overlooked coincidence of disparate elements that return, and which, in the resurfacing and imagined construction of anamnesis, affirm excess erupting from within: a Heraclitean divergence within the ontological, the telos of representation's attempted closure, or, as in the example of film, the imagined unity of the viewing (and narrating) subject. The film is neither simply factual nor fictional, neither wholly documentary *reportage* nor narrative *invention*, neither solely 'historically accurate' nor entirely an imaginary assemblage. Constellated images of London are presented, a static camera recording the movements in a given place, such as a bus stop, the forecourt of a pub, the checkout isles of a supermarket, or the window front of a driving school. And within every frame, various traces offer themselves to the viewer. In such work – and, it has to be said, in the work of each London artist to which we are attending – and the singularity of witnessing that is presented, the question of attuning oneself to the invisible within the visible is of the most urgent necessity. (As Keiller makes perhaps most immediately clear the imperative obligation attendant on 'seeing' London is, and has been, political in nature.) For the invisible bears the vision of the city, distinct from what is merely visible, even as what is visible serves to structure an act of *poiesis* that is simultaneously an act of *tekhne* (to use a formula already announced in this volume), whereby the ontology of London is undone, and London's alterity has the chance of arriving. There is then a demand, always already made by the city, by the invisible traces of its alterity, which is figured in Keiller's text, as the demand for a true act of witnessing and response. And what 'genuine witnessing requires', to cite Veronique Fóti, 'and what empowers eyes and ears, is an attunement to the logos that is held in common [in this case the phantom logos *London*, as subject without identity, identity undone in its very name] and articulates the fundamental patterns according to which all things come to pass . . . the key issue is how to understand the counterplay of separation and unification within this logos . . .'[15]

Counterpoised to, creating tensions with, and supplementing the generation of images, from within which vision might be witnessed, is a first-person narrative involving an anonymous narrator, a cruise ship's photographer, who, on visiting London, spends time with an old friend, Robinson, a part-time university lecturer, who, in the words of the narrator, 'was searching for the location of a memory'. The question of the invisible countersignature to a visible reality is most clearly foregrounded through the persistence of the narrative – the voice of a figure never seen, speaking of another character also never present, yet all the while commenting directly or otherwise on that to which the audience is witness. In the light of the invisible Robinson's remark, the tension revealed and the space opened by this should serve to remind us of Henri Bergson's caution that 'to *picture* is not to *remember*' (*MM* 135). Thus, we see, in effect, through the eyes of ghosts, our perceptions conditioned through the doubling spectral mediation which narrative and imagined character makes possible. Yet, what is visible and what may or may not be seen are incommensurable. Whether one finds the location of a memory is undecidable. When we are told that Robinson listens to the stone gateposts of a municipal garden in Vauxhall, we comprehend, albeit dimly, certain ghostly histories invoked by location, and yet, while we see the material reality of the gateposts, whatever may or may not be heard, and which may therefore come to vision is never known or knowable.

Robinson's narrative is woven into historical events including the General Election won by John Major in 1992 and various IRA bomb attacks on central London. Robinson's narrative involves the unearthing of a series of alternative London moments, such as the temporary residence in the capital of Rimbaud, or the possibility that Montaigne had once visited the city. The function of narrative perception is, then, within Keiller's film, to place us 'within memory, where the present is determined by the past. For memory', Bernard Cache remarks, 'has two aspects: inscription on the one hand, and contraction on the other' (*EMFT* 144). Contraction and inscription occupy many of the film's scenes, even as the scenes are themselves inscriptions of imaginative contraction. A brief exploration of two such scenes should suffice to illustrate this, as acts of what Keiller's narrator calls 'psychic landscaping, drifting, and free association'.

The first shot in question is a street corner in Soho, the corner of Wardour Street to be precise. We see pressboard hoardings covering a building, into which is let a temporary door. The door and hoarding announce the 'Montaigne School of English'. Robinson, we are told, reads Montaigne. A citation surfaces: 'It is good to be born in depraved times for, by comparison with others, you are reckoned virtuous at little cost.' A policeman walks in front of the hoarding, and the narrator offers the following commentary: 'it is not generally agreed that Montaigne lived for a time in London, in a house in Wardour Street, the first of a number of French writers exiled in London'. These include, significantly for Robinson, Mallarmé, Rimbaud, and Verlaine. We are told that though Baudelaire never lived in London, his mother was born there and spoke English as a child.

The second shot brings back Baudelaire, this time through a quotation given the narrator by Robinson concerning romanticism: ' "Romanticism", wrote Baudelaire, "is precisely situated neither in choices of subjects, nor in exact truth, but in a mode of feeling". For Robinson, the essence of the romantic life is in the ability to get outside oneself, to see oneself as if from outside.' The image accompanying this citation is of a McDonald's restaurant, on the roof of which an inflatable Ronald McDonald bobs about in the breeze, while, nearby, a large Union Jack flutters.

The city is clearly figured, in these as in other scenes, through the chance and random concatenation of 'found objects', where it is the eye of the camera which obviously locates and transforms through the act of filming. Possible significations are transformed in the process of recording material reality, while the invisibility of the narrator and his words, those of Robinson relayed through him, and the layers of already translated quotation from Montaigne to Baudelaire, further affect experience and reception. Particularly intriguing in both these scenes is the play between visible and invisible: not only is there the translation within the visible – Montaigne becomes the signature for a language school, the Union Jack and Ronald McDonald in proximity are suggestive of various genealogies of colonial and corporate expansion – but, against what is visibly there, there is, whether through citation or narration, an emphasis on negation which it would be easy to overlook. Thus the very possibility of representation is transformed, tensions between the voices of the city and the city's images serving to undo and fragment the experience of London; which experience is itself the experience of fragments, there being only the possible ghostly trace of Baudelaire to bring together Ronald McDonald and Soho.

Each image demolishes as much as it reinvents, making any episte-mological assumption about place suspect, any interpretive activity impoverished. Moreover, the relatively static condition of each shot is solicited in a fascinating manner by the act of narration as a certain temporal otherness mediates against the constant present and presence of the image. Which is not, of course, to suggest that the image, what it represents, is simply undifferentiated within the frame or field of vision. As the 'signature' of Montaigne juxtaposed with the policeman on the beat, or the flag and the fast food restaurant suggest in a manner perhaps indebted to Henri Cartier-Bresson's dictum concerning pho-tography that one records whatever is there, seeking to leave nothing out: *this just is the city*. What gives the lie to any possible documen-tary verisimilitude, of course, is that, in being framed, captured, the moment is translated irrevocably. Chance elements are made to operate rhetorically and tropologically, confusing, blurring, and disintegrating: topographics becomes *tropographics*. And what we come to understand from Keiller, as from Moorcock and others, is that (to cite Stephen Barber) 'the transformation of the city is a restless process of negation . . . The city is perpetually invested with a dynamic jarring and upheaval of its configuration.'[16] While this is arguably the case, if one were to speak from certain perspectives concerning local government acts of demolition and rebuilding, of the relocation of the city's inhabitants and the political justifications accompanying such acts, what is inter-esting is that the writers and artists in question take on the what appear to be similar processes of transformation, yet with wholly different ends in mind. The imaginative and perhaps dissonant processes of imagina-tive undoing and demolition come from within the very same struc-tures of urban reconstruction as the most politically motivated and cynical of acts. Yet, as the risk entailed in the aesthetic-epistemological acts with which I am here concerned, what the various texts maintain in the face of the politicians' makeovers in the name of uniformity and homogeneous identity, and the attendant obliteration of memory which such makeovers desire, is the maintenance of memory, of alter-native memories occluded by history and ideological 'necessity'. It is thus possible to read negation differently, to see, again to quote Barber, '[d]emolition of the city's elements [in the poetics of various recent texts as that which] strengthens what remains and [which] also strengthens the sense of vital damaging through which the city takes its respiration' (*FEC* 29). There can be no doubt that what *strengthens* for Barber is the sign of a certain violence, a double inscription, which simultaneously is also the sign of ruination: the ruins that remain articulate all the more forcefully the sense of place, while, through the violent, perhaps necessary demolition, the city survives.

Keiller's film thus makes explicit the formal condition of fraught epistemological and material contest as intrinsic to that registration of the nature of London shared by the writers and artists considered here; although, it has to be stressed, such representation and response is always singular even within a particular text, as the example of Keiller's film makes clear. This shared response to the city, which allows for the inscription of London as so many heterogeneous texts along with, constituted from, the resonances on which such texts, textures and architectures rely, acknowledges London as what Kojin Karatani terms 'the self-differential differential system as a formal precedent'[17] (1995, 83). The formal radicality of difference, beyond or before any absolute, formalizable law of difference is, for Karatani, that which the city makes possible. Karatani's 'self-differential differential system' is an invaluable quasi-concept, acknowledging as it does how difference is excessive, irreducible to any recuperation into an economy of the self-same or the programme which the term *system* implies. Difference is thus 'other than itself', so to speak, the trace of the non-ontologizable other within any *itself*. It is not an *it*, but is plural or, more accurately, excessive beyond plurality. Nor is it simply inscribed through reference to a multiplicity belonging to a single determinable or delimitable order. Differences differ and defer, differing and differentiating itselves from within itselves (as the good reader of Derrida will doubtless know). Coming to terms with Karatani's formula, a formula that allows for the experience of the aporetic within the logic or the very idea as system, we may provisionally and with caution take up the idea of the 'self-differential differential system' as an unruly, ungovernable figure or historical and spatio-topographical precept. By this very idea, the city maps and remaps itself, and, in its process of becoming, comes to govern Keiller's formal praxis. Thus, we can suggest, the response of Keiller to London is an act of letting the city write itselves onto his text, however improbable his various figural, historial, and topographical contrapuntal moments might appear, however irreconcilable with a merely historical narrative. In short, there is a radical disorientation of vision and the visual, apropos temporality: what we see, and what we come to see we have not seen, that which comes back while remaining unseen, is nothing other than so many Londons taking place, undoing London in the process. What Keiller's film gives us to see as a countersignature to the ideologies of representational unanimity, is that the 'visual arena of the city *must* move through concurrent acts of construction and obliteration, extrusion and intrusion' (*FEC* 29) in the name of memory itself.

VII

The double process of transformation and negation particular to an alternative perception of urban identity through time, within and yet distinct from dominant representations of the city, is captured in my final example, the work of Rachel Whiteread. Whiteread has responded in a number of places to acts of demolition, as area after area of what were once working-class neighbourhoods undergo transformation. A series of photographs, included in the Tate Gallery's 'Century City' exhibition at the beginning of 2001, capture the instance of destruction. *Demolished: a Clapton Park Estate, Mandeville Street, London E5; Ambergate Court; Norbury Court, October 1993* offers the viewer the precise moment at which tower blocks begin to collapse, immediately following the controlled detonation, attested to in the suspension that photography enacts by clouds of smoke. Paradoxically, the event and its experience are rendered permanent, transformed by the camera into an impossible experience of immutability: the city, always already fixed in the act of passing away, and fixity punctuated further through the chronicling effected in that ghostly trace, the title whereby topography, location, coordinates and naming become irrevocably translated. No longer the signifiers of location, they have been reinvested as the inscribed memories of that which is no longer there as such – hauntological tropes figuring invisible maps. The *punctum* of the image estranges the viewer's relationship to the event. Even as it captures the historicity of the image, it exceeds that moment in envisioning a memory at the border, in the passage, between the picture and the memory. Indeed, we are witness to that which we cannot see in the moment of its taking place, but which has now assumed, if not an afterlife then, at least, an afterimage. The photographic event speaks beyond the singular instance of demolition to a paradoxical ghostly permanence as well as the fleeting transience of the material. At the same time, it also brings into view through the artifice of aesthetic permanence manifested in the materiality of the photograph the invisibility of the city's constant processes of passing beyond the immediacy of any perceivable present. Demolition, the politically driven instant of obliteration, is transformed through photography into the memory of one aspect of an otherwise invisible urban experience. Such experience is translated into an other form, which calls for witness.

At the same time as Whiteread was photographing the demolition of the council estate, she began what in retrospect has become her most visible project, *House* (1993–4), a concrete cast of the interior space of an East End house. Whiteread had transformed an abandoned house in London's East End into a ghostly palimpsest of itself, first using the house as a shell or mould into and over which concrete was poured; then the house was removed, brick by brick, to leave its simulacrum in its place, which double was entitled *House*. When torn down *House* remained only as a series of concrete ruins, remainders and reminders of its other self. It was described appositely by Iain Sinclair as a 'white ghost . . . seen in negative' (*LOT* 232). It was an 'absence, a brick outline in the grass . . . a removed structure' (*LOT* 237), available and apparent only by remaining at the margins, the extreme limits, between visibility and invisibility, between presence and absence. The brick outline called by Sinclair 'Whiteread's revenant' (*LOT* 227), undoing either presence or absence, being neither and yet both, effectively figured as a footstep if you will, a sign announcing itself as the spectral crossing of borders.[18] In this, it also figured a temporal step, as a ruined rem(a)inder, but also as a material revenant, tracing not only what had disappeared from the location but what had been erased, what threatened to be forgotten, and yet what was part of the collective memory, otherwise demolished or moved elsewhere, of all who had lived in Hackney before successive acts of renewal, rebuilding, and 'regeneration' on the part of developers and government.

Once again as with the photograph already described, *House* demonstrates how the transformation of place, the destruction of domestic space, operates through both translation and ghostly survival and, simultaneously, memorial. In this re-invention of 'the nineteenth-century *realist* house into an abstract composition'[19] we witness how 'the traces of former patterns of life [are] now rendered dead but preserved' (*WS* 146). The effect is curious, estranging, and, once again, paradoxical. While place becomes memorial, what is also preserved – or, perhaps more accurately, suspended, hovering between past and present, the visible and invisible and blurring, in the process, all such distinctions – is not the past as such, as is usually the work of the memorial-effect, but instead an act of bearing witness, of testimony. We witness or, at least, are encouraged to witness a negotiation or tension between visibility and invisibility, between that which art can represent and the unrepresentable, the hidden, forgotten lives of working-class and immigrant inhabitants of the East End. This is perhaps all the more poignantly made apparent by the fact that the cast is of course that of the hitherto invisible domestic space, the architecture of the house displaced by the reinvented, materialized location of 'home', idea made concrete as it were. (A brief parenthesis: interestingly, shortly after the completion of the casting and the demolition of the house, an act of ghost writing, an instance of graffito took place, appearing on one side, proclaiming 'Homes for all Black + White'.[20]) Thus, the ghosts return, as Whiteread renders habitation permanent and simultaneously uncanny or 'unhomely', as Anthony Vidler correctly suggests (*WS* 147). The 'temporary act or event' (*WS* 147) of the cast resonates with all it cannot represent directly, thereby constituting itself 'as a memory trace of former occupation and a traditional notion of dwelling' (*WS* 148). Whether in the case of photographs or sculpture, Whiteread transforms urban architecture and topography into nothing less than belated memory otherwise articulated.

VIII

To return to where we began then, in conclusion: the city as spectral machine. The condition of reading, writing, representing London introduced in this final chapter amounts, in Peter Nicholls' words, to 'a forgotten history [which] has the power to shake the social and metaphysical forms against which it breaks . . . the idea of history as a violent intrusion from somewhere else'.[21] The acknowledgement and incorporation of the chance and the random, the various acts of listing, the creative chaos of colliding between disparate images and events: all resurrect and engage in the archival exhumation of what was always there, yet, seemingly, forgotten, with regard to London. What comes to light are only phantoms, (a)material forces, so that one comes to comprehend writing London as a series of singular acts where 'the contested sites of historical memory'[22] come to be mapped through an urban *poiesis* that 'precludes a definition of the urban phenomenon in terms of a system or as a system'.[23] In such acts the 'fluctuating contexts of languages and desires pierce the logic of cartography and spill over the borders of its tabular, taxonomic space' (*MCI* 92).

There is to be read in these overflowing acts or narrative and making, of writing and making-appear, a constant tension between the wilfully aleatory as a mode of being-open, and the desire for intervening in the conjuration of specific ghost stories of the city. As the narrator of Patrick Keiller's *London* remarks, towards the end of the film, 'the true identity of London is in its absence'; such absence gives place to phantasmic play, and thus London may be read, if at all, as a place, which is not a place but which is not *anywhere*. But this 'identity' is, if anything at all (and to borrow a formula of Derrida's on Los Angeles), 'the singular organisation of the experience of *"anywhere"'*.[24] Thus there must take place the play between the necessity of response to the call of the city, to the injunctions that London's others articulate, and the recognition, in the very act of responding, that response arrives late and cannot respond adequately to the excessive undecidability within the impossible arrival. There is furthermore a double demand at work in the act of writing London. One the one hand, one has to allow events of urban revenance to manifest themselves on their own terms through a kind of textual conjuring (most immediately recognized in the writing of the peripatetic act). On the other hand, one has to respond in the shaping of narrative, as a minimal and provisional intervention dictated by the specificity of place through multiple temporal resonances. And this must take place through what might be termed the work of mourning the city, in gestures describable as textual *Nachträglichkeit*: posthumous or belated awakening as the response to the lightning flash of involuntary memory and the constellated image it carries.[25] Here, in the words of Nicola King, 'the provisionality of such construction suggests that it will remain open to later *re*construction, not in the sense of rebuilding of a ruined city, or of restoring the past "as it really was", but as a continuous process of revision and retranslation' (*MNI* 16).

That productive tension between randomness and singularity, where the singularity, the multiple singularities of the submerged traces of forgotten events within a place, informs further random motions. The narratives are both of and from the past, while never being assignable to any single past, to any one temporal location. Indeed, as we have seen throughout this volume repeatedly, what comes back never comes back as itself but does so in spectral traces to produce an image that is disruptive of all ontologies of temporal or spatial category. Loosely assembled through chance, doxa, anecdote, and so on, through the impossible conjunction of intimacy and distance, through the simultaneity of heterogeneous elements in narrative processes of montage and disruption, writing London is the projection of ensemble memory-making. With the ironic, if not paradoxical juxtaposition of traces and ruins in the manifestation of constellated images now, and now and now, as so many instances of the city's becoming, the materiality of the city's phantoms and phantasms enforces a recognition of the city through modalities of assemblage whereby the city itself figures itself and is refigured in its becoming-disfigured. Every text, every ruin touches by analogy and yet without comparable exemplification on every other, the singularity of trace acknowledging without resemblance the excess of iterable marks. And these are given visible articulation through an apprehension of the city text as always the experience of urban textuality and as the experience of both mourning *and* awakening. Through this experience, London *becomes*, but becomes undone constantly, its traces and ruins resonating before and beyond any determinable whole in the vertiginous echolalia of its visionary anamnesis. And the reader, sensitive to the ineffability of the city's true condition, comprehends the condition of the city's past and present selves, that which Michael Moorcock calls 'the deep fabric of the city . . . the deep life-stuff of London',[26] without the possibility of apprehending, attempting to keep hold of, or seeking to move towards any desired homogeneity of either representation or experience. For, if London is a ghost town, its apparitions remain to affect us materially – to live on beyond individual memory, and to return in every instance, at every passage, where now exceeds the present, where dreamwork exceeds mimetic or ontological stability, and where representation gives up the ghost to the spectral machinery, the machinic assemblage that is signed in the name of the city, as a fluctuating, serial translation, transport, and oscillation of itself. Receiving London in this fashion, we perceive it, if at all, indirectly, and as what Kant might name a finality without end. The ghost of an identity that never was, and all the more ineffable for all its spectral amateriality, in its ineluctable becoming London exceeds any sense of a fin de siècle, articulating instead a *fin de sens*. Or, to express the ineffable and illimitable more simply by recalling the inimitable: London, Londres, London . . .

SWEET THAMES
RUN SOFTLY
TILL I END MY SONG

REFRAIN FROM PROTHALAMION

EDMUND SPENCER

Notes

Introduction: London Disfigured

1. Geoff Nicholson, *Bleeding London* (Woodstock: The Overlook Press, 1998), 12.
2. Julian Wolfreys, *Writing London: the Trace of the Urban Text from Blake to Dickens* (Basingstoke: Macmillan, 1998), 4.
3. Aidan Andrew Dun, *Vale Royal* (Uppingham: Goldmark, 1995), 9.
4. Friedrich Engels, *The Condition of the Working Class in England* (1845), trans. Florence Kelly-Wischnewetsky, revised Engels (1887), ed. and int. David McLellan (Oxford: Oxford University Press, 1993), 36.
5. Tom Cohen, *Anti-Mimesis: From Plato to Hitchcock* (Cambridge: Cambridge University Press, 1994), 6.
6. Tom Cohen, '(A)Material Criticism', in Julian Wolfreys, ed., *Introducing Criticism at the 21st Century* (Edinburgh: Edinburgh University Press, 2002), 279–96; 285. Hereafter 'A'.
7. Samuel Weber, ' "Streets, Squares, Theatres": a City on the Move – Walter Benjamin's Paris', in *boundary 2* (30:1, 2002): 17–30; 19. Hereafter 'SST'.
8. Manfredo Tafuri, *Architecture and Utopia: Design and Capitalist Development* (1973), trans. Barbara Luigia La Penta (Cambridge, MA: MIT Press, 1976), 166.
9. Ignasi de Solà-Morales, *Differences: Topographies of Contemporary Architecture* (1995), trans. Graham Thompson, ed. Sarah Whiting (Cambridge, MA: MIT Press, 2000), 86.
10. Jean-Luc Nancy, *Being Singular Plural* (1996), trans. Robert D. Richardson and Anne E. O'Byrne (Stanford: Stanford University Press, 2000), 7. Hereafter *BSP*.
11. Jacques Derrida, 'Typewriter Ribbon: Limited Ink (2) ("within such limits")', trans. Peggy Kamuf, in Tom Cohen, Barbara Cohen, J. Hillis Miller, and Andrzej Warminski, eds, *Material Events: Paul de Man and the Afterlife of Theory* (Minneapolis: University of Minnesota Press, 2001), 277–360; 359. An extended and altered version of this essay, retitled just 'Typewriter Ribbon: Limited Ink (2)', is to be found in Derrida's *Without Alibi*, trans., ed., and int. Peggy Kamuf (Stanford: Stanford University Press, 2002), 71–160. Hereafter 'TR'.
12. Martin Heidegger, '. . . Poetically Man Dwells . . .' (1951), in *Poetry, Language, Thought* (1971), trans Albert Hofstadter (New York: Harper and Row, 1975), 213–29; 225. More than simply paraphrasing Heidegger, I have drawn from his essay in framing the opening gambit of this section of the introduction.
13. Tom Cohen, 'Political Thrillers: Hitchcock, de Man, and Secret Agency in the "Aesthetic State" ', in Tom Cohen, Barbara Cohen, J. Hillis Miller, and Andrzej Warminski, eds, *Material Events: Paul de Man and the Afterlife of Theory* (Minneapolis: University of Minnesota Press, 2001), 114–52; 125. Hereafter 'PT'.

14. Walter Benjamin, 'Theses on the Philosophy of History', in *Illuminations* (1955), ed. and int. Hannah Arendt, trans. Harry Zohn (New York: Schocken Books, 1969), 253–64; 262. Hereafter 'TPH'.
15. Alan G. Hill, 'Introduction', in Ford (*SL* xix–xxix), xix.
16. Hill, 'Introduction', xix–xx.
17. Doubtless, this is an outrageous and unsupportable claim.
18. Paul de Man, *Aesthetic Ideology*, ed. and int. Andrzej Warminski (Minneapolis: University of Minnesota Press, 1996), 121, 122. Hereafter *AI*.
19. Arkady Plotnitsky, 'Algebra and Allegory: Nonclassical Epistemology, Quantum Theory, and the Work of Paul de Man', in Cohen et al., eds, *Material Events*, 49–89; 65.
20. Hill, 'Introduction', xx.
21. Derrida, *The Truth in Painting*, trans. Geoff Bennington and Ian McLeod (Chicago: University of Chicago Press, 1987), 194. I am indebted to Derrida's discussion of the paradigm and its deconstruction from which the phrase is drawn in the opening paragraph of this section of the introduction. Hereafter *TP*.
22. Claire Colebrook, *Ethics and Representation* (Edinburgh: Edinburgh University Press, 1999), 34. Hereafter *ER*.
23. Salman Rushdie, *The Satanic Verses* (1988) (New York: Picador, 1997), 476. Hereafter *SV*.
24. On Walter Benjamin's conception of allegorization produced through the dialectic of modern and premodern, whether medieval, classical, or primal, see Chapter 1, 'Staging the City'.
25. On the image without or outside image, see Chapter 4, 'Peter Ackroyd and the "endless variety" of the "eternal city"'.
26. Sara Danius, *The Senses of Modernism: Technology, Perception, and Aesthetics* (Ithaca: Cornell University Press, 2002), 53.
27. The phrase – 'the impossible as that which arrives' – is taken from an interview between Antoine Spire and Jacques Derrida, in which Derrida has the occasion to use this phrase as a provisional definition of what he terms the 'diversification essential to deconstruction, which is neither a philosophy, nor a science, nor a method, nor a doctrine' (translation mine). Jacques Derrida and Antoine Spire, *Au-delà des appearances* (Latresne: Le bord de l'eau, 2002), 20.
28. Hélène Cixous, 'Savoir', in Hélène Cixous and Jacques Derrida, *Veils* (1998), trans. Geoffrey Bennington (Stanford: Stanford University Press, 2001), 1–16; 8.
29. Bernard Kops, 'Hackney! Sunday! Rain!' (1962), in *Barricades in West Hampstead* (London: Hearing Eye, 1988/89), 11–12; 11.
30. Neil Gaiman, *Neverwhere* (New York: Avon, 1997).
31. Bernard Steigler, *Technics and Time, 1: the Fault of Epimetheus* (1994), trans. Richard Beardsworth and George Collins (Stanford: Stanford University Press, 1998), 167. Hereafter *TT*.
32. Jacques Derrida, *Monolingualism of the Other, Or, the Prosthesis of Origin*, trans. Patrick Mensah (Stanford: Stanford University Press, 1998), 60.
33. John Brannigan, 'Nation', in Julian Wolfreys, ed., *Glossalalia* (Edinburgh: Edinburgh University Press, 2003), 209.

1. Staging the city

1. Marie Belloc Lowndes, *The Lodger* (1913), int. Laura Marcus (Oxford: Oxford University Press, 1996), 94.
2. J. Hillis Miller, *On Literature* (London: Routledge, 2002), 21.
3. Interestingly, one reviewer of the book, Isobel Armstrong, in the *Times Literary Supplement*, wondered, in passing, whether there was any pleasure in the city where all was so apparently ineffable. This is to assume that the ineffable is, in being literally inexpressible, close to the sense of awe or terror produced by the sublime. While I have no disagreement with the assumption of such a relationship, I do not believe that this rules out the possibility either that there is more than one aspect to the ineffable (or, to put it more radically, more than one ineffability), or that one's sense of the ineffable is not pleasurable in some manner. After all, there are those moments – perhaps 'events' might be the more accurate word properly speaking – when, through sheer joy one is left speechless. The question is one, I feel, of whether one takes ineffability to be a condition of an empirical object or material location, or whether it is a matter of phenomenological response. That the city can produce both joy and fear as components of the ineffable is attested to in a number of texts, not least De Quincey's *Confessions of an English Opium Eater*.
4. T. S. Eliot, *The Waste Land* (1922), in *Collected Poems 1909–1962* (1963) (London: Faber and Faber, 1974), 61–86; 65. Hereafter *WL*. Martin Rowson's comic book version (London: HarperCollins, 1990) admirably brings out Eliot's indebtedness to crime fiction, and to the urban mystery genre in general, in his employment of a hardboiled narrator-detective, Marlowe, a hybrid of high and popular culture, being both Conrad and Raymond Chandler's Marlowe.
5. Alan Moore and Eddie Campbell, *From Hell* (1999) (Paddington: Eddie Campbell Comics, 2001).
6. Richard Maxwell, *The Mysteries of Paris and London* (Charlottesville: University Press of Virginia, 1992), 292. Hereafter *MPL*.
7. David L. Pike, *Passage Through Hell: Modernist Descents, Medieval Underworlds* (Ithaca: Cornell University Press, 1997), 203. Hereafter *PH*.
8. Colin MacCabe, *James Joyce and the Revolution of the Word* (London: Macmillan, 1979), 21. Hereafter *JJ*.
9. Wilkie Collins, '*I Say No*' (1885) (Stroud: Alan Sutton, 1995), 51. Hereafter *I*.
10. Stephen Arata, *Fictions of Loss in the Fin de Siècle* (Cambridge: Cambridge University Press, 1996), 182.
11. Jean Baudrillard and Jean Nouvel, *The Singular Object of Architecture*, trans. Robert Bononno, foreword K. Michael Hays (Minneapolis: University of Minnesota Press, 2002), 3.
12. Carol L. Bernstein, *The Celebration of Scandal: Toward the Sublime in Victorian Urban Fiction* (University Park: Pennsylvania State University Press, 1991), 29. Hereafter *CS*.
13. Jean-Luc Nancy, *L'«il y a» du rapport sexuel* (Paris: Galilée, 2001), 14.
14. The murders were committed in December 1811. Seven people in two families were butchered in their homes.

15. Jonathan Crary, *Suspensions of Perception: Attention, Spectacle, and Modern Culture* (1999) (Cambridge, MA: MIT Press, 2001), 1. Hereafter *SP*.
16. Iain Sinclair, 'Introduction', in Arthur Conan Doyle, *A Study in Scarlet* (1887), int. Iain Sinclair (London: Penguin, 2001), vii–xxi; xii.
17. Rainer Nägele, *Echoes of Translation: Reading between Texts* (Baltimore: Johns Hopkins University Press, 1997), 17. Hereafter *ET*.

2. The uncanny example of Elizabeth Bowen

1. Maud Ellmann, *Elizabeth Bowen: the Shadow Across the Page* (Edinburgh: Edinburgh University Press, 2003), 146. Hereafter *EB*.
2. Without wishing to sound glib or facile, we might posit in passing the notion that the sofa is an ontic figure in the narrative economy, its lack of grounding the sign not only of the uncanniness of dwelling, but also of the fact that both mother and son are like Heideggerian animals, inasmuch as they have become poor-in-world.
3. Sigmund Freud, 'The "Uncanny"' (1919), trans. Alix Strachey, in Freud, *Writings on Art and Literature*, foreword Neil Hertz (Stanford: Stanford University Press, 1997), 193–233; 201.
4. As should be clear, I am invoking Benjamin's yoking of imagination and memory in their psychic and allegorical relationship and similarity (*AP* 346).
5. Elizabeth Grosz, *Architecture from the Outside: Essays on Virtual and Real Space*, foreword Peter Eisenman (Cambridge, MA: MIT Press, 2001), 49, 50. Hereafter *AO*.
6. Hubert Damisch, *Skyline: the Narcissistic City* (1996), trans. John Goodman (Stanford: Stanford University Press, 2001), 139. Hereafter *SNC*.
7. Avital Ronell, *Stupidity* (Chicago: University of Chicago Press, 2002), 93.
8. Guy Debord, 'Theory of the *Dérive*' (1956), trans. Libero Andreotti and Xavier Costa, in Andreotti and Costa, eds, *Theory of the Dérive and Other Situationist Writings on the City* (Barcelona: Museum d'Art Contemporani de Barcelona, 1996), 22.
9. Peter Schwenger, *Fantasm and Fiction: On Textual Envisioning* (Stanford: Stanford University Press, 1999), 4.
10. Maurice Merleau-Ponty, *Phenomenology of Perception* (1945), trans. Colin Smith, rev. trans. Forrest Williams and David Guerrière (London: Routledge, 1995), 207. Hereafter *PP*.
11. Ernst Bloch, *Essays on the Philosophy of Music*, trans. Peter Palmer (Cambridge: Cambridge University Press, 1985), 1.
12. Maurice Merleau-Ponty, *The Visible and the Invisible* (1964), ed. Claude Lefort, trans. Alphonso Lingis (Evanston: Northwestern University Press, 1968), 133.
13. Interestingly, to point to the motifs of indirection, phantasm, and marginality beyond the immediate concerns of this chapter, it should be noted that, of Ann Lee's hats, it is stated: 'These were the hats one dreamed about – no, even in a dream one had never directly beheld them; they glimmered rather on the margins of one's dreams' (*CS* 105).
14. The poetic work of colour therefore effects an other oscillation between 'places', the inhuman (colour is, strictly speaking, inhuman), and the human, wherefrom which latter location significance is inscribed.

15. T. J. Clark, 'Phenomenality and Materiality in Cézanne', in Cohen et al., *Material Events*, 93–113; 107.
16. Louis Marin, *On Representation* (1994), trans. Catherine Porter (Stanford: Stanford University Press, 2001), 312.
17. Jacques Derrida, 'Foreword', trans. Eric Prenowitz, in Susan Sellers, ed., *The Hélène Cixous Reader*, preface Hélène Cixous (London: Routledge, 1994), vii–xiii; x.
18. Gilles Deleuze, *Cinema 2: the Time-Image* (1985), trans. Hugh Tomlinson and Robert Galeta (Minneapolis: University of Minnesota Press, 1997), 79. Hereafter *C2*.
19. Henri Lefebvre, *Writings on Cities*, trans. and ed. Eleonore Kofman and Elizabeth Lebas (Oxford: Blackwell, 1996), 230.
20. Elizabeth Bowen, 'Out of a Book', in Bowen, *Collected Impressions* (London: Longman, 1950), 269.
21. I am drawing the terms 'actual image' and 'virtual image' from Deleuze, *Cinema 2*.
22. Alan Liu, *Wordsworth: the Sense of History* (Stanford: Stanford University Press, 1989), 63. Although Liu is addressing a passage from Wordsworth's *An Evening Walk* in the context of the Romantic concern with the picturesque, the phrase is apposite for certain sudden moments of suspension in Bowen's narratives. There is a relationship between experience and form in Bowen's writing that would appear to justify a consideration of particular urban images in Bowen in terms of the picturesque (hence my use of the word in the chapter in relation to particular phantom effects), given Liu's definition of the picturesque as 'a highly specialized experience of *form* . . . picturesque experience . . . made the very idea of form, or "picturicity," cognate with experience' (65). However, this needs immediate qualification: I am not suggesting that there is any simple correlation between Bowen's work and a particular aesthetic-phenomenal concern of the late eighteenth century, even were it to be argued that Bowen's depiction of war-time London records the ruins of bombed buildings and therefore includes in its representations images of ruins irregular in form appropriate in principle to the Romantic conception of the picturesque. Indeed, if there is discernible a form of urban picturesque it is very much a counter- or anti-picturesque, one which departs from, and leaves in disarray, the conventions of determinable limit and boundary, of finite and knowable form, by which the picturesque is understood to be distinguished from the sublime (hence my choice of phrase 'phantom-picturesque'). As is implied in other ways throughout this chapter, the very premise of formation and limit to be found in the picturesque is constantly exceeded and placed under erasure.
23. Theodor Adorno, *Minima Moralia: Reflections from Damaged Life* (1951), trans. E. F. N. Jephcott (London: Verso, 1978), 142.

3. Maureen Duffy's *Capital*

1. The other novels making up the trilogy are *Wounds* (1969) and *Londoners: an Elegy* (1983). The third epigraph to this chapter is taken from *Londoners* (85).
2. For a brief, informative discussion of the significance and practice of chorog-

raphy in Early Modern England, see Bruce McLeod, *The Geography of Empire in English Literature 1580–1745* (Cambridge: Cambridge University Press, 1999), 95–9.

3. On this myth, and the persistent association of London with Troy, see Ackroyd (*L:B* 16–18).

4. While I am privileging the radio as a spectral technology appropriate to apprehending the condition of London, there is also a reading to be produced that sees the city as telephone exchange and system, after Avital Ronell's invaluable work in *The Telephone Book: Technology–Schizophrenia–Electric Speech* (Lincoln: University of Nebraska Press, 1989).

5. On the crisis of historicism in relation to the work of Nietzsche, Heidegger, Foucault, and Derrida, see Allan Megill, *Prophets of Extremity: Nietzsche, Heidegger, Foucault, Derrida* (Berkeley: University of California Press, 1985).

6. Hélène Cixous, 'Savoir', in Hélène Cixous and Jacques Derrida, *Veils* (1998), trans. Geoffrey Bennington, drawings Ernest Pignon-Ernest (Stanford: Stanford University Press, 2001), 1–16; 9.

7. Jacques Derrida, 'Artifactualities', in Jacques Derrida and Bernard Steigler, *Echographies of Television* (1996), trans. Jennifer Bajorek (Oxford: Polity, 2002), 1–28; 23. Hereafter 'Ar'.

8. Charles Dickens, *Bleak House* (1853), ed. Nicola Bradbury (London: Penguin, 1996), 13.

9. Edmund Spenser, *Prothalamion* (1596), in *The Shorter Poems*, ed. Richard A. McCabe (London: Penguin, 1999), 491–7. See M. Wine, 'Spenser's "Sweete Themmes": Of Time and the River', *SEL* 2 (1962): 111–17.

10. Marc Augé, *Non-Places: Introduction to an Anthropology of Supermodernity* (1992), trans. John Howe (London: Verso, 1995), 77. Hereafter *N-P*.

11. Jean-Luc Marion, *Being Given: Toward a Phenomenology of Givenness* (1997), trans. Jeffrey L. Kosky (Stanford: Stanford University Press, 2002), 69.

12 Bernard Cache, *Earth Moves: the Furnishing of Territories*, trans. Anne Boyman, ed. Michael Sparks (Cambridge: MIT Press, 1995), 144.

13. Jacques Derrida, *The Gift of Death* (1992), trans. David Wills (Chicago: University of Chicago Press, 1995), 68.

14. Maureen Duffy, *The Microcosm* (1966) (London: Penguin, 1999), 163.

15. Luis Fernández-Galliano, *Fire and Memory: On Architecture and Energy*, trans. Gina Cariño (Cambridge: MIT Press, 2000), 5. Hereafter *FM*.

16. Henri Lefebvre, *The Urban Revolution* (1970), trans. Robert Bononno, foreword Neil Smith (Minneapolis: University of Minnesota Press, 2003), 144.

17. Edmund Husserl, *Cartesian Meditations: an Introduction to Phenomenology* (1950), trans. Dorion Cairns (Dordrecht: Kluwer Academic Publishers, 1995), 108–11. Hereafter *CMIP*.

18. Mieke Bal, *Travelling Concepts in the Humanities: a Rough Guide* (Toronto: University of Toronto Press, 2002), 182. Hereafter *TCH*.

19. Henri Bergson, *Matter and Memory* (1908), trans. N. M. Paul and W. S. Palmer (New York: Zone Books, 1991), 71. Hereafter *MM*.

20. Gaston Bachelard, *The Dialectic of Duration* (1950), trans. Mary McAllester Jones, int. Cristina Chimisso (Manchester: Clinamen Press, 2000), 64. Hereafter *DD*.

21. David Jones, 'Preface', in *The Anathemata: Fragments of an Attempted Writing* (1952) (London: Faber and Faber, 1972), 9–43; 21.

22. Bernhard Siegert, *Relays: Literature as an Epoch of the Postal System* (Stanford: Stanford University Press, 1999), 10.

23. Didier Maleuvre, *Museum Memories: History, Technology, Art* (Stanford: Stanford University Press, 1999), 272.

24. On the idea of now-time as opposed to the present, see the discussion of Walter Benjamin in Chapter 6, below.

25. See Aristotle, *Aristotle's On the Soul and On Memory and Recollection*, trans. Joe Sachs (London: Green Lion Press, 2001).

26. David Farrell Krell, *Of Memory, Reminiscence, and Writing: On the Verge* (Bloomington: Indiana University Press, 1990), 13.

27. For a brief, informative account of the political effectiveness of Herbert Morrison, Labour leader of the London County Council for six years, and on Labour's thirty-one years of control of the LCC, see Stephen Inwood, *A History of London* (New York: Carroll & Graf Publishers, Inc., 1998), 757–61.

28. Roy Porter, *London: a Social History* (London: Hamish Hamilton, 1994), 333.

29. Peter Ackroyd offers an uncanny reading of place in *London: a Biography*, when he looks as the association of Fetter Lane with generation after generation of radical and dissenting figures who had lived in or near that street, beginning with the 'radical and sectarian Moravian Brethren' and Charles Wesley, and culminating in that of Keir Hardie (234–5). For Ackroyd topographically marginal sites are closely connected to those Londoners belonging to political and religious margins.

30. The allusion to Kafka illustrates with great economy the multiplicity of traces to be unravelled in any glimpse of London; for, in the same passage, Duffy's narrator pursues the image of London, from the Kafkaesque, through the surreal (see the third of the epigraphs to this chapter), from there to a quotation from Shelley, which in turn is imagined as translated into Afro-Caribbean dialect.

4. Peter Ackroyd and the 'eternal city'

1. Ackroyd, caption to *Near Spitalfields Market*, photograph Don McCullin, in *London*, n.p.

2. In *London*, Ackroyd remarks apropos continuity that '[n]either vagrants nor children are on the same journey as those whom they pass on the crowded thoroughfares' (665). Those Londoners who are most vulnerable because most invisible are also those who, through the iterability of suffering, offer the most powerfully affecting figures of timelessness.

3. Michael Moorcock, 'Introduction', in Iain Sinclair, *Lud Heat and Suicide Bridge* (London: Vintage, 1995), 3–6; 5.

4. Peter Ackroyd, 'Interview between Peter Ackroyd and Julian Wolfreys, 21 December 1997', in Jeremy Gibson and Julian Wolfreys, *Peter Ackroyd: the Ludic and Labyrinthine Text*, foreword Peter Nicholls (Basingstoke: Macmillan, 2000), 249–63; 251.

5. Frédéric Neyrat, *L'Image hors-l'image* (Paris: Léo Scheer, 2003). In the discussion of silence following this citation, I am borrowing from Neyrat's initial chapters. Hereafter *L'I*.

6. I am borrowing again from Neyrat (*L'I* 17–18), his arguments haunting what might best be described here as a somewhat reckless translation.

7. See also Andrew Motion's fictionalized, confessional pseudo-autobiography, *Wainewright the Poisoner* (London: Faber and Faber, 2000).

8. J. Hillis Miller, *Topographies* (Stanford: Stanford University Press, 1995), 109. Hereafter *Top*.

9. Avital Ronell, *Dictations: On Haunted Writing* (1986) (Lincoln: University of Nebraska Press, 1993), xiv.

10. Clerkenwell is the principal location of Ackroyd's most recent novel, *The Clerkenwell Tales*, a novel of clerical terrorism, secret sects, and a nun with visionary powers, set in 1399. Peter Ackroyd, *The Clerkenwell Tales* (London: Chatto & Windus, 2003).

11. The argument of the paragraph in which this note is found is clearly indebted to Benjamin's discussion of the dialectical image and its legibility, particularly in *The Arcades Project*'s 'Convolute N [On the Theory of Knowledge, Theory of Progress]', 456–88.

12. The notion of dwelling expressed in this paragraph is indebted in its formulation to Heidegger's thinking of the concept in his essay, 'Building Dwelling Thinking', in *Poetry, Language, Thought*, trans. Albert Hofstadter (New York: Harper and Row, 1971), 145–61.

13. Jacques Derrida, 'Demeure: Fiction and Testimony' (1998), in Maurice Blanchot / Jacques Derrida, *The Instant of My Death / Demeure: Fiction and Testimony*, trans. Elizabeth Rottenberg (Stanford: Stanford University Press, 2000), 15–103; 28.

14. Jennifer Bloomer, *Architecture and the Text: the (S)crypts of Joyce and Piranesi* (New Haven: Yale University Press, 1993), 72. Hereafter *ATJP*.

15. Eric Korn, 'Evil in EC1', *Times Literary Supplement* (10 September 1993).

16. Donald Preziosi, 'Between Power and Desire: the Margins of the City', *Glyph Textual Studies, 1* (1986): 237–52; 237.

17. The article 'Romanticism and Crime', attributed to Gissing by Ackroyd, appears to be invented. Attempts to locate it in any of the existing published bibliographies, either in print or on website, have failed.

18. Arguably, there are violent aspects of the 'rush and immediacy' of both the city and language (to borrow a phrase of Ackroyd's describing a letter concerning the Gordon Riots of 1780), to be found everywhere throughout *London: the Biography*. In this, the text performs the violence of London in its broadest sense, and thus becoming part of the city, the latest relay in the materiality, historicity, and iterability of London's fury.

19. Elie Wiesel, *The Golem: the Story of a Legend*, illustrated by Mark Podwal, trans. Anne Borchardt (New York: Summit Books, 1983), 47.

5. Iain Sinclair's 'delirious fictions'

1. Jonathan Crary, 'Spectacle, Attention, Counter-Memory', in Tom McDonough, ed., *Guy Debord and the Situationist International: Texts and Documents* (Cambridge, MA: MIT Press, 2003), 455–66; 460.

2. Libero Andreotti, 'Architecture and Play', in McDonaugh, ed., *Guy Debord*, 213–40; 222.

3. Andreas Huyssen, *Present Pasts: Urban Palimpsests and the Politics of Memory* (Stanford: Stanford University Press, 2003), 13. Hereafter *PPUP*.

4. Giorgio Agamben, 'Difference and Repetition: On Guy Debord's Films', in McDonaugh, ed., *Guy Debord*, 313–19; 316. Hereafter DR.
5. Walter Benjamin, *Reflections*, ed. Peter Demetz, trans. Edmund Jephcott (New York: Schocken, 1978), 28.
6. Pierre Nora, 'General Indroduction: Between Memory and History', in *Realms of Memory: Rethinking the French Past*, 2 vols, under the direction of Pierre Nora; English language edition ed. and foreword Lawrence D. Kritzman, trans. Arthur Goldhammer (New York: 1996), I: 1–20; 1. Hereafter GI.
7. Iain Sinclair, 'All Change: This Train is Cancelled', *London Review of Books*, 21: 10 (13 May 1999): 211. Hereafter AC.
8. Eduardo Cadava, *Words of Light: Theses on the Photography of History* (Princeton: Princeton University Press, 1997), 64. Hereafter *WL*.
9. On this concept, see Chapter 6, below.
10. Joseph Conrad, *Heart of Darkness*, ed. and int. Robert Hampson (London: Penguin, 1995), 18.
11. There are twenty-nine prose pieces, all of which are 'occasions', being occasional pieces in response to invitations, demands, or contexts. In being occasional, the prose pieces each figure an irreducible singular instance of urban 'now-time', and refigure each other abyssally, rather than figuring or representing London as such. They are thus not constative truth-claims or observations, so much as they are performative tropes, figures for the drift and mutability in and of urban identities.
12. Gilles Deleuze, *Foucault*, trans. and ed. Séan Hand (Minneapolis: University of Minnesota Press, 1988), 67.
13. Jodey Castricano, *Cryptomimesis: the Gothic and Jacques Derrida's Ghost Writing* (Montreal: McGill-Queen's University Press, 2001), 101.
14. Jacques Derrida, 'Spectrographies', in Jacques Derrida and Bernard Steigler, *Échographies: de la télévision. Entretiens filmés* (Paris: Galilée-INA, 1996),131. Hereafter Sp.
15. Jacques Derrida, 'The Art of *Mémoires*'. In Jacques Derrida, *Mémoires for Paul de Man*, rev. ed., trans. Cecile Lindsay, Jonathan Culler, Eduardo Cadava, and Peggy Kamuf (New York: Columbia University Press, 1989), 45–88; 64. Hereafter AM.
16. Geoffrey Bennington, *Legislations: the Politics of Deconstruction* (London: Verso, 1994), 202.
17. Tamsin Lorraine, 'Schizoanalysis', in Julian Wolfreys, ed., *Glossalalia: an Alphabet of Critical Keywords* (Edinburgh: Edinburgh University Press, 2003), 269–76; 269. Hereafter Sch.
18. Chris Jenks, 'Watching Your Step: the History and Practice of the *Flâneur*', in *Visual Culture* (London: n.p., 1995), n.p; cit. Sinclair, *Lights Out*, 145.
19. Andrzej Warminski, ' "As the Poets Do It": On the Material Sublime', in Tom Cohen, Barbara Cohen, J. Hillis Miller, and Andrzej Warminski, eds, *Material Events: Paul de Man and the Afterlife of Theory* (Minneapolis: University of Minnesota Press, 2001), 3–31; 14.
20. 'La logique spectrale est *de facto* une logique déconstructrice' [*spectral logic is de facto a deconstructive logic*] (Derrida, 'Sp' 131).
21. This remark comes from an improvised speech by Derrida in Ken McMullen's film *Ghosts*, where Derrida comments on the possibility

that film and other forms of telecommunication serve to proliferate ghosts.
22. Matt K. Matsuda, *The Memory of the Modern* (New York: Oxford University Press, 1996), 15.

6. London undone

1. Gilles Deleuze and Félix Guattari, *A Thousand Plateaus: Capitalism and Schizophrenia* (1980), trans. Brian Massumi (Minneapolis: University of Minnesota Press, 1987), 12. Hereafter *TPCS*.
2. Martin McQuillan, 'Tele-Techno-Theology', in Julian Wolfreys, ed., *Glossalalia: an Alphabet of Critical Keywords* (Edinburgh: Edinburgh University Press, 2003), 279–95; 286.
3. The discussion I am pursuing here might usefully be compared with Gaston Bachelard's consideration of the dialectics of outside and inside in the chapter of the same name, in *The Poetics of Space* (1958), trans. Maria Jolas, foreword John R. Stilgoe (Boston: Beacon, 1994), 211–31.
4. Immanuel Kant, *Critique of Judgement* (1790), trans. Werner S. Pluhar (Indianapolis: Hackett Publishing Company, 1987), 130. Hereafter *CJ*.
5. F. W. J. Schelling, *The Ages of the World (Fragment) from the handwritten remains. Third Version (c. 1815)*, trans, and int. Jason M. Wirth (Albany: State University of New York Press, 2000), 76.
6. Nicola King, *Memory, Narrative, Identity: Remembering the Self* (Edinburgh: Edinburgh University Press, 2000), 35. Hereafter *MNI*.
7. Eduardo Cadava, *Words of Light: Theses on the Photography of History* (Princeton: Princeton University Press, 1997), 84.
8. Peter Ackroyd, 'Introduction', in Alan Palmer, *The East End: Four Centuries of London Life* (1989) (New Brunswick: Rutgers University Press, 2000), xi–xvi; xiv.
9. Paul Virilio, *A Landscape of Events* (1996), trans. Julie Rose, foreword Bernard Tschumi (Cambridge, MIT: MIT Press, 2000), 15. Hereafter *LE*.
10. Lavinia Greenlaw, 'Love from a Foreign City', *Night Photograph* (London: Faber and Faber, 1993), 44. Hereafter *L*.
11. Ken Smith, 'Encounter at St Martin's', *The London Poems*, in *Terra* (Newcastle: Bloodaxe Books).
12. Hans-Jost Frey, *Studies in Poetic Discourse: Mallarmé, Baudelaire, Rimbaud, Hölderlin* (1986), trans. William Whobery (Stanford: Stanford University Press, 1996), 48. Hereafter *SPD*.
13. All further quotations are taken from and all allusions refer to the second stanza (102).
14. Bernard Cache, *Earth Moves: the Furnishing of Territories* (1983), trans. Anne Boyman, ed. Michael Speaks (Cambridge, MA: MIT Press, 1995), 82. Hereafter *EMFT*.
15. Veronique Fóti, *Vision's Invisibles: Philosophical Explorations* (Albany: State University of New York Press, 2003), 18.
16. Stephen Barber, *Fragments of the European City* (London: Reaktion Books, 1995), 29. Hereafter *FEC*.
17. Kojin Karatani, *Architecture as Metaphor: Language, Number, Money*, trans. Sabu Kohso, ed. Michael Speaks (Cambridge, MA: MIT Press, 1995), 85.

18. 'The crossing of borders always announces itself according to the movement of a certain step [*pas*] – and of the step that crosses a line. An indivisible line . . . where the identity or indivisibility of a line (*finis* or *peras*) is compromised, the identity to oneself and therefore the possible identification of an intangible edge – the crossing of the line – becomes a *problem* . . . There is a *problem* as soon as this intrinsic division [traced in the drawing of a line] divides the relation to itself of the border and therefore divides the being-one-self of anything.' Jacques Derrida, *Aporias* (1993), trans. Thomas Dutoit (Stanford: Stanford University Press, 1993), 11. Hence, no pure presence, no present, which is not always already problematized, either spatially or temporally, by this movement, by the movement of the hauntological in excess of the ontological that is implied in the very idea of a border as the limit of identity, and as the dividing line between identity and non-identity, self and other.

19. Anthony Vidler, *Warped Space: Art, Architecture, and Anxiety in Modern Culture* (Cambridge, MA: MIT Press, 2000), 145; emphasis in original. Hereafter *WS*.

20. See the photograph in Vidler (*WS* 144).

21. Peter Nicholls, 'The Belated Postmodern: History, Phantoms, and Toni Morrison', in Sue Vice, ed., *Psychoanalytic Criticism: a Reader* (London: Polity Press, 1996), 50–67; 52.

22. Iain Chambers, *Migrancy, Culture, Identity* (London: Routledge, 1994), 92. Hereafter *MCI*.

23. Henri Lefebvre, *The Urban Revolution* (1970), trans. Robert Bononno, foreword Neil Smith (Minneapolis: University of Minnesota Press, 2003), 119.

24. 'L.A. n'est pas *anywhere*, mais c'est une singulière organisation de l'expérience du "*anywhere*".' Catherine Malabou and Jacques Derrida, *Jacques Derrida: La Contre-Allée* (Paris: La Quinzaine littéraire. Louis Vitton, 1999), 115.

25. In the work of mourning one runs the risk of nostalgia, of misrecognizing by attempted acts of willed memory, rather than being open to the possibility of involuntary memory's arrivals and returns.

26. Michael Moorcock, *London Bone* (1997) (London: Simon and Schuster, 2001), 125.

Index of names